SOMME

SOMME

141 Days, 141 Lives

Alexandra Churchill
with Andrew Holmes

The History Press

This book is dedicated with great appreciation (and affection)
to Jonathan Dyer and Diane Holmes, without whom it wouldn't
exist. Their months of hard work and dedication are a tribute
to the men whose stories they have helped to tell.

And in memory of Brian Holmes (1940–2016)

First published 2016
Reprinted 2017

The History Press
The Mill, Brimscombe Port
Stroud, Gloucestershire, GL5 2QG
www.thehistorypress.co.uk

British Library Cataloguing in Publication Data.
A catalogue record for this book is available from the British Library.

ISBN 978 0 7509 6532 3

Typesetting and origination by
The History Press
Printed in India.

CONTENTS

ACKNOWLEDGEMENTS

At The History Press: Sophie Bradshaw and editors; Victoria Wallace, Andrew Fetherston and Liz Woodfield at the Commonwealth War Graves Commission; Rugby School; Cheryl Sadana; Sarah Warren-MacMillan in School Library, along with the other library ladies: Shirley, Emily and Simo and also Lucy Gwynn in College Library, all at Eton College. Thanks is also due to College Library for use of the Macnaghten Library and Peter Devitt at the Royal Air Force Museum, Hendon.

The families of those included in the book: Stuart Disbrey, Jack Cowdy, William Hallidie-Smith, Miranda Pender, Vivian Sheffield, Jan Stephens, Edgar Lloyd, Robert Matthewson, Hazel Effie Morris and Kirk Butt, Muriel Chislett, Natasha Legge and the kind people of Robinson's Newfoundland for helping us to find her, Reverend William Hepper and the late Mr. F. Nigel Hepper, Lindsay Harford and Sarah Rhodes.

Kim Downie at the Unviersity of Aberdeen; Chris Edwards at St Edward's School, Oxford; Dee Murphy at Rugby School; Sally Todd at St John's School Leatherhead; Upper Canada College, Toronto. Ryno Human of Remember Us South Africa (@rememberussa) and Lieutenant Klehnhans of the South African Defence Force Documentation Centre.

The entry for William Dexter would not have been possible without the 'World War Zoo' blog produced by Mark Norris at Exeter Zoo and information provided to them for their William Dexter biography by ZSL London Zoo.

Both the Australian National War memorial and the Long Long Trail have been valuable online resources, as has Len Ashworth at the *Lithgow Mercury*, NSW; David Tulip at The Channel Heritage Centre, Margate, Tasmania; Lord Astor of Hever, Tom Donovan; and Rutland Remembers.

For help in India and Pakistan: Kamal Hyder and the staff at the Islamabad Bureau of Al Jazeera English and Ali Abbas Zafar.

Joshua Levine, Paul Reed and Peter Hart variously for their yoda-like presence and support, advice, assistance with maps and loan of their material, Alice and Tim Holmes, The La Boisselle Study Group, Simon Jones for his patience and generosity in helping with our tunnellers and Roger Stillman Photography for helping to digitally enhance some of our aged photographs.

Every effort has been made to trace copyright holders and to obtain their permission for the use of copyright material. We apologise for any errors or omissions and would be grateful if notified of any corrections that should be incorporated in future reprints or editions of this book.

AC: My sister, Karen Halls for multitasking as PA, personal motivator and human shredder, not to mention helping to save the manuscript for October from rattling round Newcastle on an empty football train. Work Husband Naz, for spreadsheet services and various other members of House Lannister: Paulbot Fernandes, Nathan, Nathan's Beard, Biggles and Mike for picking up the slack on occasion so I could get this done! Stamford Bridge's answer to Scott Tracy, you know who you are!

AH: Diane and Adam, not only for their contributions to the research, but for months of patience and support whilst we got this done and for making the battlefield trips all the more enjoyable.

JD: Jules and Lana, all I ever wanted; my father, David Dyer for passing on his love of history; Alex and Andrew, for having me along and not sparing the unicorns and Paul Kempton; you must come on a battlefield trip one day!

Poppy tributes placed beneath thousands of names carved into the Thiepval Memorial to the Missing on the Somme. (Alexandra Churchill)

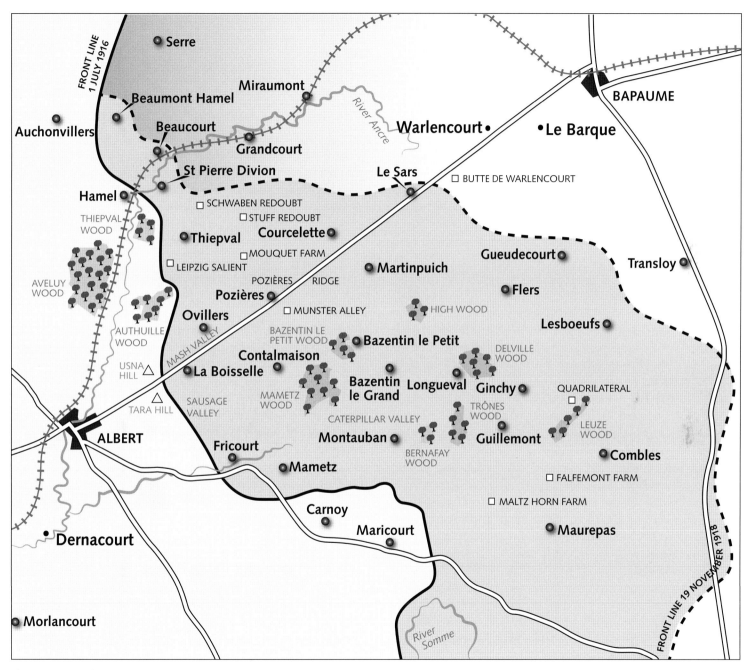

The Somme battlefield, 1916.

INTRODUCTION

A hundred years ago on the Western Front. On 30th June 1916, professional soldiers were lining up to go into battle alongside miners, farmers, labourers, clerks, accountants; men drawn from every walk of life. They assembled in lines with boys who had only just walked from their schools into the army. Gathered from the length and breadth of Britain, and her dominions, tens of thousands were assembled in Picardy to embark upon the most ambitious offensive the British Army had ever undertaken.

The year 1915 had not been a good one. British attacks in France and Belgium had been, for the most part, bloody failures. At the end of the year the BEF underwent a change of command and Douglas Haig was placed in charge. It was not only on his front that things looked bleak. In the East the Central Powers had shoved back the Russians in force. Italy was struggling against the Austro-Hungarian army in alpine terrain. Bulgaria had entered the war on the side of Germany and Serbia was in utter turmoil. Evacuation was about to prove the humiliating culmination to the campaign in the Dardanelles, Kut was under siege in Mesopotamia after any initial success had come to nothing and British East Africa was also under threat.

It was clear that the Allies, in their many different theatres of war, needed to organise and mount a coherent, joint attack against Germany and her allies. By mid-February it had been agreed that a combined offensive would proceed round about the beginning of July and would be the main attempt at defeating the enemy on the Western Front in 1916. Before this, the British would extend their line south, taking over more territory from the French.

But all Allied planning was thrown into disarray at the end of February when the Germans began their own brutal offensive against the French at Verdun. By the 26th the situation had been acknowledged as potentially catastrophic. They begged their allies on all fronts to keep the enemy busy to prevent as many German troops as possible from being fed into the battle and asked the British to make diversionary attacks elsewhere along the lines to take German focus away from Verdun. Casualties grew towards a quarter of a million. Justifiably, although they still planned to co-operate, the summer offensive had taken a step backwards in terms of where the French would be able to deploy their resources in the summer of 1916.

Thus the British Army, by circumstance, had now assumed the greater part of the responsibility for the offensive campaign on the Western Front. It was feared that the most that could be expected of the French, was that if a breakthrough was made they would try and help exploit it. At the end of May there was even a concern that the British Army might have to attack without any contribution from France at all, so badly had Verdun consumed their ally's resources. The summer battle was now ostensibly going to be fought to take pressure off the French.

The official history postured that the reason the French, who were ever-convinced that the British were not contributing their fair share, suggested the Somme right next to Haig's front was that it meant his force would be bound to take part in it. Until 1916 it had been a quiet sector. In terms of fighting, nothing of great significance had taken place since the French and Germans began digging in in 1914. Joffre could argue that the terrain was advantageous, but unlike, say, Neuve Chapelle, which ultimately had the strategic prize of Lille behind it; there was nothing of consequence by comparison on the Somme, no gain beyond the German line that would cause the enemy to collapse.

The enemy had also, by now, had plenty of time to fortify their positions in the area. They had an extensive front-line system of trenches. Anywhere between 1–3 miles behind that, the Kaiser's men had also constructed a second system. In what was to prove a significant move during the summer, villages along their defensive lines had been extensively fortified. The nature of the chalky soil underfoot had enabled the Germans to dig strong, safe dugouts deep underground to protect them from attack, which would never be possible further north, where the wet, low lying terrain of Flanders sometimes meant that the opposing armies had to build defences upwards in some spots to keep from sinking into the mud.

An immense amount of preparation was necessary to ready the area for battle. The Somme itself flows in a westerly direction between Peronne and Amiens and carves a valley into the rolling plains of Northern France. Bordered by marshy ground and meadows, on the northern banks, where the French lines came to an end, the terrain was punctuated by smaller valleys. In the more northerly part of what would become the 1916 battlefield, the River Ancre bisected the British part of the line and flowed through Albert, a hub of military activity. Although the French sector to the south was flat, the ground undulated on the British side, rising up to a 300ft high ridge that ran from Guillemont, through Longueval, Bazentin-le-Petit, Pozières and on to Thiepval. A number of large woods in the area were about to become haunting to those thrown into them and, although there were but a few isolated farms there were, however, a number of large villages, the occupation of which the enemy had turned to their full advantage.

At the beginning of 1916 the British Expeditionary Force had in the region of a million men on the Western Front. Many had been freed up by the end of the Gallipoli campaign, more of Kitchener's New Army men were to arrive in the months leading up to the battle along with volunteers from Britain's various dominions. The Fourth Army officially came into being under the command of General Henry Rawlinson in March 1916 when he took over more than 20 miles of front and absorbed the troops already in place. The bulk of responsibility for the summer campaign on the Somme would rest on his shoulders.

Many of his troops had never seen offensive action and any experience that men had was of holding trenches, if they had spent any time in France and Flanders at all. Additionally, although Haig's troops outnumbered the Germans, for the amount of divisions that were present, they were actually about 75,000 men short of what those should have comprised. A lot of the men had had less than the six months' training they should have ideally had. One division's artillery only had three days' practice before leaving for France.

Generals Rawlinson (*right*) and Haig (*left*) on the Somme in 1916. (Authors' collection)

Shell bursts during artillery efforts at wire cutting. (Authors' collection)

The Somme was rural. A main road ran through Amiens and Albert, up towards what would be the front lines, but other thoroughfares, if they yet existed, were thoroughly unsuitable for the amount of traffic that they would need to sustain. Railway lines were sparse and there were no causeways or bridges over the rivers. Roads and railways needed to be built, water supplies created, ammunition and equipment brought in, accommodation constructed and trenches dug. All the while, while this exhausting programme was carried out, as much concealment as possible needed to be sought, so that the attack would retain at least an element of surprise. One division alone in the build-up to July dug both assembly and communication trenches, emplacements for mortars and also helped to construct a water supply. It dug trenches for communication cables, laid the cables, helped to build twenty-eight bridges for the artillery and seventy-two emplacements for gas cylinders, and then carried up 671 of said heavy cylinders. All this labour was carried out before the division even began to factor in its rotating duty to man the lines or train for the upcoming offensive.

Britain's artillerymen were no less busy either. By the end of June 1916, some 3,000 field guns and heavier pieces had deployed along the intended battlefront on the Somme, along with nearly 1,500 trench mortars. The preliminary bombardment began on the 24th. More than a million rounds were fired, attempting to destroy German resistance and flatten all that may lay in the path of the artillery when zero hour came.

By 30th June the scene had been set for the British Army to attempt to make a decisive breakthrough in the German line in three enthusiastically planned stages, with the hope that during one of them the enemy's line would cave and Haig could have the cavalry sent through the breach to wreak decisive havoc upon the Kaiser's men. There would even be a diversionary attack to the north at Gommecourt made by another force. After a flurry of panic in mid-June over the French situation at Verdun, they had confirmed that they would fight on either side of the river, 'with [their] eye firmly on supporting the British offensive'.

Preparations had not been ideal; it seemed that even Haig himself was wavering in confidence with regard to the overall plan, but after delays caused by rain that waterlogged trenches and guns, it finally fell that the Battle of the Somme was to begin on 1st July 1916. The casualties accumulating on both sides of the lines would be devastating. By the end of the year hundreds of thousands of men would have been wounded, would have vanished on the field of battle or would have paid for this ambitious enterprise with their lives. Drawn not only from the length and breadth of Britain and France, combatants fought and died on the Somme from all corners of the globe, whether due to imperial allegiance or chance. In this book, we have tried to introduce a cross section of them, telling the story of the battle through the eyes of one individual who died on each day. For the next 141 days, the peace of Picardy was to be shattered as the Allies attempted to win the war by the year's end.

SOMME

141 Days, 141 Lives

1ST JULY
#15812 Private Herbert William Disbrey

11TH SUFFOLK REGIMENT

Private 'Billy' Disbrey. (Private collection)

THE BATTLE OF THE SOMME was to be the sternest of tests thus far, especially for the men of Britain who had answered Kitchener's call to arms. Up and down the line, on a scale like never before, the British Army was shaped by communities who had volunteered to fight in a time of national crisis. In the midst of the recruitment boom following the outbreak of war in 1914, the flood of men enlisting in Cambridge created a problem in East Anglia. Such were the numbers of locals volunteering to fight that an application was made with the War Office to form a unit specifically for these Cambridgeshire men. By the beginning of 1915 this had been approved and, with a number of the city's university men contributing towards their officers, with no room in their own county regiment the group had been designated the 11th Battalion of the Suffolk Regiment.

Among its number was a cheerful young man in his early twenties named Billy Disbrey. The third son of a telegraph engineer working for the Post Office, Billy and his brothers were farm labourers living in Barton, a small village just to the south-west of Cambridge with a population of some 250 souls. Leaving Cambridgeshire behind, for Billy and friends from Barton and the surrounding villages, after drills on Parker's Piece and Jesus Green, training began in earnest in May 1915 when the battalion was seen off by a large crowd at Cambridge Station and sent north to Yorkshire. By the end of August it had concentrated on Salisbury Plain and its division, the 34th, finally left for France in the New Year.

Once on the Western Front, the 11th Suffolks' first weeks on the Continent were surreal and hardly resembled war. Billy spent weeks at Renescure on the Franco-Belgian border, which reminded him and his friends so much of the Fens that it was uncanny. The men spent their leisure hours helping the locals to drive pigs, fill dung carts, and 'inspecting and passing professional judgements on cattle, poultry and the like'. Inevitably, the war soon intervened on their peaceful existence. For the Cambridgeshire volunteers, the nature of their role on the Somme had been decided and in May they arrived in Amiens in drizzling rain. Training had intensified before their move and Billy now spent several suspense-filled weeks waiting to learn when and how he would be used in the summer's campaign. 'Rumour and speculative fancy ran wild; supplying the spice of adventure to what was in fact a stern and ugly business.'

All was revealed in the run up to 1st July. Roughly in the middle of the British line, Billy's battalion would be attacking the southern part of a salient that bulged out of the German lines. At its apex was La Boiselle, a little village of about thirty-five houses that sat on their left; one of those that had been fortified by the Germans. It was a fiercely strong position for the enemy and, in front of the Suffolks, no-man's-land was intimidating and wide; half a mile across open ground towards the Kaiser's men.

The 10th Lincolnshire Regiment would lead the attack, with the 11th Suffolks advancing behind. Both were completely untried in battle and faced a formidable task. At 5am on 1st July, Billy and the rest of his battalion commenced their march. They were in position two hours later, despite confusion caused by neighbouring troops straying into their path. 'Though only a thousand yards from the German trenches, this spot seemed far away from the war.' They were near a chateau and the undergrowth was a riot of wild and garden flowers: 'Dogs barked at the guns, the vagrant cuckoo called to its mate, and nightingales sang through the hours of darkness.'

The men fell silent in anticipation. Then, at 7:28am, 60,000 tons of ammonal was detonated to their left. But, despite the savage explosion and the casualties caused to the enemy, it did not have the completely devastating effect that was hoped for. There were German troops still poised and waiting for the Lincolns and the Cambridgeshire men of the Suffolk Regiment to come at them to the right of the crater.

At 7:30am on 1st July 1916 the British Army launched its largest ever endeavour when the much anticipated infantry attack began on the Somme with eleven divisions attacking on the main British front. For the 11th Suffolks, staying out of the way of the mine explosion meant they had to advance from further back than the other 34th Division troops. Both the layout of the terrain and the enemy positions meant it was possible for the Germans to sweep any attackers relentlessly with hostile fire from multiple directions and, following the Lincolns, as soon as Billy and the 11th Suffolks left their trenches they became the targets of everything that the enemy could throw at them. Troops on their left failed to get forward and the enemy within La Boisselle was free to pour machine-gun fire into their ranks. 'Before the leading wave had advanced a hundred yards, before the men had time to shake out to their correct intervals and gain their proper formation, casualties began.'

Wave after wave of Cambridgeshire men were mown down before they could get anywhere near their objectives. Those that remained standing put their heads down and pushed on as if they were heading into a storm. Reports going back to commanding officers were erroneous, telling tall tales of a successful advance. In reality the few men that managed to make it to the German lines were not a coherent battalion. They were little groups of three and four who had somehow managed to dodge the relentless hostile fire. They began to link up with anybody that happened to be nearby, Suffolks or not, so that a helpless jumble of men populated parts of the German trenches, surrounded by the enemy.

Those carrying up supplies of ammunition and water were obliterated too, laden down with too much equipment. A Royal Engineer field company ordered to go forward and consolidate meagre gains could not even get out of the British lines. No-man's-land was utterly impassable owing to the enemy's machine-gun fire. Some of those that got near the German systems were rewarded for their efforts by being attacked by a flame-thrower. A dozen or so men dashing for an enemy trench were

engulfed by spouts of fire as they reached the parapet. 'The sight of their crumpled figures, staggering back from the tongues of flame and smoke, tearing hopelessly at their burning clothes, and then falling one by one was terrible to behold.' The impetus had gone out of the grand attack up and down the front; the fighting died down. Occasionally a Cambridgeshire man was seen running for safety, trying to get back to the British lines alone until he was picked off by an enemy bullet.

The 11th Suffolks, the men who were left, were in utter disarray. Their 34th Division was the worst hit on 1st July, with 6,380 casualties, roughly half their number and a huge percentage of their fighting men. Evidence suggests that Billy survived well into the day, but he was 22 years old when he was consumed by an attack that never stood a chance. The objectives of his battalion were far too lofty and the German position far too strong. At home in Barton it was heartbreaking to know that Billy had fallen on foreign soil, so far from his family and his fiancée Ethel. The family dedicated a small piece of poetry to his memory:

The blow was bitter, the shock severe.
  To part with one we loved so dear;
  It was God's will; it must be so,
  At his command we all must go.
  But his far-away grave is the bitter blow.
  Peace, perfect peace.

Though tiny, the village of Barton contributed painfully to the Great War with the blood of its young men. Ten were commemorated on the village memorial, including two that died as a result of the opening day of the Somme with the 11th Suffolks. In the aftermath of the war something had to be done to remember the thousands such as Billy who had simply vanished on the field of battle on a mortifying scale. The Thiepval Memorial was unveiled in 1932 and is inscribed with some 72,000 names; men who would be killed in action on the Somme before spring 1918 and denied the dignity of a proper grave by the circumstances of war. Herbert William Disbrey is among them and his name can be seen on Pier & Face 1c/2a.

2ND JULY
#659 Sergeant Frank Vallois

1ST LANCASHIRE FUSILIERS

AS THE SUN SET ON 1st July, the Somme battlefield was in chaos. The fighting may have settled down after the ferocity of the opening advance, but confusion reigned and units tried desperately to take stock and reorganise themselves. North of Billy Disbrey and the 11th Suffolks, the failure of the advance had been even more resolute, but among the men who had somehow come through the savagery unscathed was a 29-year-old reservist from Jersey.

Frank Vallois had served in the army for eleven years, eight of them in the heat of India, before leaving the service. Having returned home, he departed Jersey again immediately on the outbreak of war and rejoined the army. Forced along on the Great Retreat of 1914 he had fallen foul of that trying experience and was the first wounded man to arrive back on the island for sick leave. He made the most of his recovery time for the war effort, tirelessly promoting recruitment at home as the Jersey Company, all that could be expected of an island with such a small population, was being raised.

Frank was one of four brothers who had answered the call to arms. His brother Ernest, with the Jersey Company in an Irish Battalion, had already died at a casualty clearing station in April 1916 as a result of fatal wounds in both arms and his left leg and lay buried at Bethune town cemetery. The other two Vallois were hard at work in the artillery and the Royal Navy respectively. At the onset of July, Frank was serving with a new battalion of the Lancashire Fusiliers, his original regiment, because of the need to spread out the experience of valuable NCOs such as him. Part of the 29th Division, the battalion had served first at Gallipoli until being evacuated at the beginning of 1916. From Egypt it was sent to Marseilles and then found its way to the Somme.

On 1st July Frank's battalion had attacked towards Beaumont Hamel, another of the villages fortified by the Germans at the northern edge of the main battlefield. As on Billy Disbrey's front, a mine was detonated to attempt to smooth the way for the infantry by taking out a portion of the

The Thiepval Memorial to the Missing of the Somme. (Andrew Holmes)

enemy's front line, but with little effect as it was blown at a ridiculous time. After much argument about whether it should be blown hours in advance, or just as the infantry went over, a bizarre compromise was reached and it was detonated at 7:20am. In the ensuing ten minutes before the attack commenced, the enemy regrouped following the shock and in some places in the sector were even on top of the parapet aiming their weaponry and waiting to greet the British troops when they came forward.

Frank's battalion made a valiant effort to try to reach the German lines. As on Billy Disbrey's front, the chances of escaping savage machine-gun fire were slim. 'The enemy was ready for us and had plenty of machine guns ... against them no troops with the strength of 1½ men per yard can hope for success.' In all, half the battalion was killed or put out of action. Having somehow survived, the night of the 1st was an anxious one for Frank and the remnants of the battalion. The Lancashire Fusiliers found itself massively disorganised as it tried to take stock and form a coherent unit again. It was the same all over the Fourth Army front. Communications were shot, battalions were decimated. Some had almost ceased to exist as fighting formations.

On 2nd July Frank's battalion consolidated and wired their front. Men were still isolated up in front, having got forward, or were out in the open due to a lack of space in the trenches. In bright sunshine with a cool wind, they continued to take stock, attempting to get supplies of rifles, equipment and stores from the battle out of their way in order to take adequate cover. Throughout the day they were subjected to heavy artillery fire, amassing yet more casualties. Having come through unmitigated carnage the day before, Frank fell foul of the enemy's barrage and was not to survive the day.

In all, 6,292 men from Jersey served in the Great War, of whom 862 would not return home. Frank Vallois' body, if recovered, was never identified and he is commemorated on the Thiepval Memorial, Pier & Face 3c/3d.

3RD JULY
Captain Oswald Brooke Webb

11TH ROYAL IRISH RIFLES

Captain Oswald Webb. (Private collection)

ALSO TOWARD THE NORTHERN END of battlefield at the beginning of July was the 36th (Ulster) Division. The Derrys, the Donegals, Fermanaghs and the like were organised on community lines to the extreme: colleagues, friends and neighbours ready to fight side by side. The Ulster Volunteer Force (UVF) had some 80,000 members aged 17–65 when the war broke out and many, if eligible, enlisted to go to war. Among their number was a 36 year old who brought his experience as a company commander with the UVF when he joined the 11th Royal Irish Rifles. From Randalstown, County Antrim, Oswald Webb came from a family prominent in the local community. The Webbs owned the highly renowned Old Bleach Linen Co. which provided cloth for royal palaces and luxury liners, as well as other prominent clients.

Married with one son, Oswald had been a director of the company since leaving Rossall School. As the local minister wrote:

He was an outstanding member of our community, and he took a leading part in all the activities of this place. He gave his wholehearted assistance to everything he thought would promote the happiness and welfare of our people. Whether it was sports – and he himself excelled … Boy Scouts, Catch-my-Pal, Ulster Volunteers, he threw himself into everything he took up with the greatest ardour and thoroughness.

Oswald took his duties with the UVF particularly seriously, giving up every evening in the week to address or attend various meetings both at home and further afield, or helping to drill the companies.

When war commenced, it was thought the Webb family should lead by example and that one of the family should go. Oswald's elder sibling, Hubert, had a number of children and was the managing director at Old Bleach, so it was decided Oswald would be the one to fight.

He told his relatives that the men of the town and surrounding countryside could not be expected to volunteer unless a member of the firm led the way and he said he felt he was the one to go, and there can be no doubt at all that it was his example which induced so many of our men to follow his inspiring lead. He was able to inspire his men with the most entire confidence in himself and trust in his judgment, so that they would gladly follow him anywhere. As a partner in the firm, he was greatly beloved and thoroughly trusted by all the workers.

The opening throes of the Battle of the Somme had been the costliest effort ever made by the British Army. Some 57,000 men had become casualties, 19,000 were dead. A large proportion of the other 38,000 were wounded, and at the close of the initial advance lay scattered all over the battlefield and to the rear requiring medical attention.

The Ulster Division had been another of Kitchener's formations allotted a formidable task on the opening day of the battle. Thiepval was one of the bigger communities that lay along the front line and comprised precious high ground overlooking the battlefield and the River Ancre. Yet another village fortress, it was surrounded by marshy ground and the Ulstermen had had to build causeways out of sandbags filled with chalk to get around. Alongside no-man's-land was Thiepval Wood. It had been dubbed Porcupine Wood by the men. 'The trees were so stripped of foliage and lopped into distorted shapes by enemy gunfire that their bare limbs stood up like quills of the fretful porcupine.' On 1st July the 11th Royal Irish Rifles were ordered to emerge from it and attack near the Schwaben Redoubt, a German strong point to the north of Thiepval.

Captain Webb had thrown himself into recruiting for his battalion and nearly two companies, one of which he had been given command of, had been recruited from Oswald's family's own workforce at Old Bleach. At 7:15am they left their assembly trenches together to take up attack positions. There was heavy shelling all the way and entire platoons were 'practically annihilated on the way up'. The 11th Royal Irish Rifles burst forth with shouts of 'No Surrender!' As a division, the Ulstermen penetrated part of the front line near Thiepval, but their objectives were far too ambitious and, as the day progressed, German machine-gun and shellfire increased on both flanks. Only 322 men and half the officers were left to be inspected when they got out of the battle. This left several hundred unaccounted for.

Shortly before the 11th Royal Irish Rifles prepared to go 'over the top', a shell burst over the assembly trenches, wounding Oswald Webb. He never advanced towards the Germans and, with a stomach injury, began a painful journey towards medical assistance. The scene behind the battle on 1st July was horrific. On all the routes back and in all the trenches the wounded lay in their hundreds alongside the broken bodies of those who had fallen. The road to Martinsart was packed solid with men struggling away from Thiepval seeking help and with ambulances trying to get back with those such as Oswald, who were in a more severe condition. One sunken road on the way to Hamel became known as Bloody Road on account of the corpses piled up along it on 1st July.

Patrick Webb. (Private collection)

One artilleryman with the Ulster Division was horrified by the suffering that he saw:

> It was a terrible sight to see the wounded coming down in hundreds ... in ... wagons, motor lorries, or anything they could get. Those that could possibly crawl at all had to get from the trenches to the dressing station, which was about three miles, as best they could. Each time we were coming back from the guns with empty ammunition wagons, we packed as many wounded on as we could, as we passed the dressing station on our way back, but a lot of them were too badly wounded to stand the jolting of the wagon, and preferred to go on their own.

Oswald Webb's route took him via an aid post, most likely either one in Thiepval Wood or at Authuille, then on to Martinsart, where his stretcher could be put into a motor ambulance to travel to the dressing station at Forceville. Shortly after 8:30am a runner had arrived there to say there were 300–400 men lying on the battlefield requiring assistance. The staff at Forceville were so disbelieving of these numbers that they telephoned a command post to confirm them. Frantically, they braced themselves and sent a motorcycle rider off to secure additional morphia to help treat their patients. Six stretcher parties left to bring in as many men as they could.

As the men arrived, the doctor tried to look over each one, setting the dead to one side and checking the others. Those deemed to be hopeless cases were sent to a tent where the only prescriptions were morphia and cigarettes to make them comfortable. Men were assigned to see to them on that basis. 'It was a terrible thing to light a cigarette for a soldier and see him die before he finished it. All we did was re-dress a wound if he needed it and if somebody needed a bit of tidying up we did that as well.'

For those such as Oswald with a better prognosis, the only operations generally done at Forceville were the removal of a leg or an arm or the stitching up of wounds. He would require more delicate attention and so his journey ended further to the rear at a casualty clearing station, south-west of the battle raging on at Warloy where they specialised in head and abdominal wounds.

An officer there who knew him wrote to his brother:

I saw him when he was brought into hospital, and thought he looked pretty bad, but he was quite conscious, and not suffering any pain. I was talking to him for a few minutes and he told me he got hit before he got past our wire. He was very pleased with the way his men went forward, and seemed quite cheerful.

Nonetheless, Oswald's wounds were severe. The battlefield was cleared away; identity tags removed from the dead and the bodies sorted, stacked in dugouts and then buried. He passed away on 3rd July at Warloy, as exhausted doctors and nurses continued to try to treat the never-ending procession of wounded without falling asleep where they stood.

Ulster was in mourning after the division's initial exploits on the Somme. At Randalstown there was a memorial service two weeks after the attack on Thiepval for Oswald and the men who had gone to fight with him; seventeen of those who had died side by side were from the same district. Oswald had kept a pocketbook on him at the front listing each of his men and keeping a note of their progress in the war. Now dozens of them were lost alongside him in Northern France. In his last letter to his wife, Kathleen, he had made sure she would look in on them, 'if anything befell him ... and so far as she could to minister to their needs'.

Patrick Webb was 12 when his father died. Oswald had written him a letter from Martinsart as he waited to go into battle on 30th June. 'My Dear Patrick,' he began, 'Just a line to let you know I am alright ... I hope you are getting on well at school – I will have some good souvenirs with me next time I go home.' His last words were simple: 'Write good long letters to your mother, your ever loving father.' Captain Webb was laid to rest at Warloy-Baillon Communal Cemetery Extension, plot III.B.2.

4TH JULY
#10531 Company Sergeant Major John Addison

11TH ROYAL SCOTS

THERE WAS ONLY SOME SEMBLANCE of success to weigh up against the disastrous attempts of 1st July and that was at the opposite end of the battlefield, where the British Army met the French just north of the River Somme. The 11th Royal Scots, formed of Edinburgh recruits, had been in reserve on 1st July when troops in this sector attacked up a slope towards the Germans above them. Montauban fell by lunchtime, the enemy ran and the British soldiers found themselves with a view over Caterpillar Valley. Montauban was the first German-held village to fall on the Somme and was a significant gain on what was otherwise a truly miserable day for Sir Douglas Haig and his forces. Here the preliminary barrage had successfully smashed the enemy wire entanglements to pave the way for the infantry and actually, had they not been reluctantly (in some cases) reined in, the men could have gone on further that day. Instead, though, they were told to consolidate their gains and get ready to move on in conjunction with more troops at some point later on.

In the aftermath of the seizure of 'Monty-Bong', as it was known by the men, the 11th Royal Scots were ordered up to relieve the victorious attackers. Among them was a 24-year-old company sergeant major named John Addison. Born on Easter Road, he had worked as an apprentice plumber in Edinburgh under his father until joining the army as a teenager in 1909. Aside from once being written up for not getting his men out of bed promptly enough and instead enjoying an unauthorised lie-in, John's service, all of which had taken place at home until he left for the Western Front in 1915, was impeccable. On the outbreak of war he was routed as an experienced NCO to one of Kitchener's New Army units, who were in dire need of such men. 'This man is thoroughly steady and reliable,' wrote one officer. 'He has a good education and ... is a total abstainer.' As John was promoted steadily prior to the war, another report noted that he was 'an exceptionally smart and intelligent man'.

John's battalion entered Montauban before dawn on 3rd July and took up a position along the east side of the village. There were practically no trenches, and those that had been made had been destroyed by shellfire. The task of the 11th Royal Scots was to consolidate these meagre lines and establish strong points while under heavy German artillery fire. Montauban was a mass of rubble. Underneath them were the enemy's deep dugouts, and they now proved a respite for the Scots every now and again as the men withdrew from the shells that plagued them as they worked. It had begun to rain heavily and John and his men worked soaked to the skin, their shallow trenches filling up with water and mud clinging to them. The only escape from this back-breaking, miserable work was a foray into Bernafay Wood for reconnaissance, which the German gunners responded to by attempting to wipe it off the face of the earth with their shells. Casualties mounted.

In the early hours of 4th July the position of the 11th Royal Scots was hit by 'extremely intense' shellfire, making work almost impossible. John's consolidation work continued, though in many cases the trenches being dug were destroyed by enemy shells almost as soon as they were fashioned. Steady shelling continued throughout the day, with the British retaliation adding to the din as fierce as the barrage falling on John and his men. Before the end of the day, his life was claimed by one of the shells that fell among the brick dust and ruins. Although the troops at the southern end of the battlefield had smashed into the German front-line trench system, they had not managed to force through the other side. Continuing the battle would not be easy, for there were two more systems of defence in the way and the prospects for the grand offensive of 1916 looked bleak. John Addison left behind a widow, Lily Elizabeth. His body, if recovered, was never identified and he is commemorated on the Thiepval Memorial, Pier & Face 6d/7d.

5TH JULY
#37298 Private Frederick Emery
15TH ROYAL WELSH FUSILIERS

Private Frederick Emery.
(Authors' collection)

DESPITE THE DISAPPOINTMENT OF THE opening endeavours on the Somme, the battle could not be abandoned. It was the defining action of 1916, supposed to bring about a crushing end to the German Army on the Western Front. The situation regarding how to carry on was complicated. The advance had progressed to the south, but had got absolutely nowhere in the north.

At noon on 4th July Haig called on General Rawlinson. It was not feasible, in terms of ammunition to say the least, to continue attempts to smash the entire German line at once. The British Army needed to make a stand at one point while progressing at another. The choice was whether or not to press in the north to bring the advance into line with the success achieved around Montauban, or to take advantage of that success and continue pressing on there. Eventually Haig decided on the latter.

For the troops on the battlefield, this meant that the next week or so would be about establishing positions for the next major advance, taking German strong points and local objectives in order to give them an advantageous start line when the main advance resumed. Then Haig's plan would be enforced, pushing forwards to try to seize the original German second system of defences that stretched along the ridge running between Bazentin and Longueval.

One of the localised objectives that would be beneficial to the main advance was Mametz Wood, the seizure of which would prevent a salient protruding from the British line and secure the left flank of the force that would make the next large-scale attack in the south. The wood consisted of 'hornbeams, limes, oaks and a few beech trees'. The undergrowth was a thick, unruly mess of hazel and bramble. Artillery had already gone to work on it all, shells ripping down trees, and some guns had even been rolled inside. German machine gunners had crept among the foliage too. Their equipment was painted green and they lurked within, positioned over clearings and ready to repel British troops that may venture inside. In some areas barbed wire had been strung from tree to tree to keep out invaders. Nonetheless, preparations now gained pace to try and snatch it from them.

On 10th June, while holding the line near Neuve Chapelle the 38th (Welsh) Division received orders to proceed south to take part in the Somme fighting of 1916. Mametz Wood was to become synonymous with Wales. Welshmen enlisted in droves at the onset of the war, including recruits who volunteered to serve in a London Welsh contingent. The men lived at home until the organisation of the battalion could be set up at the Inns of Court Hotel, Holborn, and the Benchers of Gray's Inn lent their garden squares as drill grounds. This unit had since been designated the 15th Battalion of the Royal Welsh Fusiliers and among their number was 28-year-old Frederick Emery, who worked as a barman. The son of a butcher and originally from East London, Fred had since relocated to Birkenhead, Merseyside. He had enlisted late, in November 1915, when the battalion had long since left London behind. He joined as the finished unit was already being inspected by the King in slight drizzle on Crawley Down. Two days after his future comrades had formed up for George V's inspection, Fred married his sweetheart Maggie before going off to train.

He joined his battalion in France, where the division was undergoing its induction into trench warfare. The 15th Royal Welsh Fusiliers proved themselves to be brave trench raiders and were mentioned in despatches. Having travelled south, on 1st July Fred and his comrades were in reserve, tentatively told to stand ready to follow the cavalry in the event of a breach being punched into the German lines. When this failed to transpire, their orders changed and they were ordered up to relieve some of the initial attackers in the line.

Fred marched up through the old front line to Mametz Village, which had already been taken, and then entered the former German communication trench that ran along the front of the wood, struggling through the damp lines which were not fitted with wooden boards to pave the way.

The Royal Welsh Fusiliers relieved a battalion of Warwickshire men and took up residence in easy range of the German guns. Here they began accumulating casualties immediately, and on 5th July Frederick Emery was struck down before he ever had a chance to advance on the wood. His wife, Maggie, was heavily pregnant when he died and his only child, a boy named after him, was born just two weeks after he became one of the first Welsh casualties at Mametz Wood. There were to be thousands more. Fred's body, if recovered, was never identified and he is commemorated on the Thiepval Memorial, Pier & Face 4a.

6TH JULY
Captain William James Henderson

9TH THE LOYAL NORTH LANCASHIRE REGIMENT

AUGUST AND SEPTEMBER 1914 SAW a huge rush of university men desperate to go to war. One such boy was William James Henderson, who was due to begin a classical scholarship at Corpus Christi College, Oxford, having just left his public school, Dulwich College. With several years of service in his school's Officer Training Corps, his extreme youth, however, was evident when he offered his services still suffering from teenage acne.

Originally from Forest Hill, William was a gentle boy, and devout with a 'simplicity and naturalness of faith'. An earnest Christian, 'who offered up his free time to help with his local mission school. There he was 'a most capable leader and immensely popular' with the children. One fellow officer said that he was 'very reserved, yet frank and open ... and though never weak could be as sweet and tender as any woman. He was indeed his mother's boy.'

Kitchener's New Army officers were liberally dispersed, not necessarily to a battalion with which they would have any affiliation, and William was granted a commission in the 9th Loyal North Lancashire Regiment being raised in Preston. With his men, he was in final training

at Aldershot by June 1915 and, once in France, he was awarded the Military Cross for a battalion exploit on 15th May when four mines and a camouflet were detonated under the German trenches and the 9th Loyal North Lancashire helped seize the crater nearest to them.

On 30th June the battalion marched into Warloy to begin its endeavours on the Somme. Close to where Billy Disbrey had attacked on 1st July, the village of La Boisselle was not seized until the 4th, largely by bombing and fierce scrapping at close quarters. This one village had caused almost 7,000 casualties as the British Army attempted to seize it. When William Henderson arrived in the area and looked out on no-man's-land, he saw 'a confused and tumbled mass of white chalk craters, debris, a mass of brick and mortar, strewn here and there with the beams and rafters of tumbled roofs'. La Boisselle itself was barely recognisable as a site of recent habitation.

Having taken it, it was now planned to push the Germans further away from the village, and as such William and his battalion were to attack trenches immediately to the east. On 6th July they moved off. 'About a mile along the road we halted, dished out rations and handed out [ammunition] ... then picked up bombs and tools...' In single file they continued, slowed down by the machine gunners, who were so weighed down with their equipment and extra ammunition that they needed to make continuous stops before, finally, they reached their assembly position. 'There we sat among a heap of dead German and English, the faint sweet and sickly odour rising as the day grew warmer.'

The Loyal North Lancashire attack commenced at 8:30am, targeting two lines of German trenches in an attempt to continue chipping away at further objectives. These were duly captured along with some 200 German prisoners and when enemy troops were seen massing for a counter-attack the Lancashires promptly dispersed them and sent bombers out to keep them at bay. Consolidation began, but the battalion's success came at a cost. Its officers had been decimated by the assault. Six of them were dead, including 20-year-old William Henderson. Once the wounded were evacuated just two remained to oversee the improvement of their position under heavy shellfire until the North Lancashire men were finally relieved on 10th July, having lost nearly half their number as casualties for a tiny gain.

Captain William Henderson. (Private collection)

William's Colonel wrote that 'he was the most promising Officer of [the] battalion, full of resource and energy and ready to undertake any task'. He claimed William's loss as one of the worst the battalion had suffered. Those associated with Dulwich College grieved no less. One of his schoolmates wrote:

I knew no one who stood so unfailingly for all that is the very best in the life of a public school, no one who did so much unnoticed ... work, or set so consistently high an example. There are many who mourn for him and can never forget his unfailing cheerfulness, his joyousness and gladness in living, the ideals and earnestness which were the keynote of his actions and often an unconscious inspiration to his friends.

William Henderson's family paid a heavy price during the war for its willingness to serve. Four of his cousins fell too, one exactly a month after William and three more over the course of one terrible month in 1918. If anything good can be said to have come from the conflict, it would be for his sister, Maud. In the aftermath of the Battle of the Somme, she began to visit a wounded fellow officer of William's to find out about her brother's death. Over time their relationship blossomed and they were married shortly after the war. Captain Henderson's body, if recovered, was never identified and he is commemorated on the Thiepval Memorial, Pier & Face 11a.

7TH JULY
#G/16741 Private Harold Lamb

9TH ROYAL FUSILIERS

IT WAS PERHAPS NATURAL FOR 18-year-old Harold Lamb to enlist in a cavalry regiment. Born in the village of Hasfield, an idyllic, rural part of Gloucestershire, he worked as a groom. However, having spent several months in the 3rd Hussars, in the middle of 1915 an appeal was made for men to join the 9th Royal Fusiliers, a London infantry regiment. In what must have been a severe culture shock for this country boy, Harold joined a battalion built around worldly young men from the capital that had been established in Hounslow.

On 2nd July Harold went into trenches to relieve shattered troops from the 8th Division who had been largely wiped out by machine-gun fire while attacking the village of Ovillers on the previous day. Signs of the attack's failure were everywhere. Hundreds of bodies lay strewn about, and there were men on stretchers awaiting treatment. One Fusilier ascended a small hill on his way up to the battlefield and saw lumps strewn across the landscape. He thought that they were bombs but, as the Royal Fusiliers approached, they transpired to be severed heads. He made a quick exit.

Harold helped to hold the front and collected the wounded and, apart from the British bombardment, it was quiet for several days until they were relieved again. Respite was to be unexpectedly short-lived. Sent back into the line, Harold discovered that the battalion was to attack Ovillers in one of several smaller assaults due to take place on 7th July, aimed at securing advantageous positions before the main offensive was resumed.

The first attempt on Ovillers was to be made at 8am, approaching from the south. Less than twenty-four hours after his death, William Henderson's battalion was among those that made it to the German front line but were stopped by machine-gun fire. Slightly later, Harold Lamb attacked from the west. Hundreds of men were never to make it out of the assembly trenches. The Germans laid down a fierce barrage on the battalions waiting to attack. The 9th Royal Fusiliers suffered more than 200 casualties because for several hours they had to sit and stomach every shell the Germans could throw at them without abandoning their position.

At 8:30am, though, their attack commenced as planned, each man laden with ammunition and carrying twenty grenades in a sandbag – about 40lb in weight. This was nothing like their training, months of bayoneting harmless objects and scouring mock battlefields that contained neither bursting shells nor barbed wire. Heavy rain had commenced along with a stiff breeze and Harold battled through deep, sticky mud laden down with his ammunition and equipment, bombs and extra small arms ammunition. Every other man was also lugging a shovel or a pick.

The battalion walked into a storm of machine-gun fire. One company was decimated by it along with more men sent after them. The remaining two platoons behind were ordered to remain in the trench as it was seen to be useless to send them to the same fate. Two more groups on the left

of the attack were greatly weakened but managed to fight their way into the German trenches. Communications were problematic. One poor officer dragged wireless equipment all the way into the German lines only to find out it was broken. All the messenger pigeons had been shot, or else the men carrying them. And not until the evening did supporting troops manage to get across with a large supply of bombs. Machine guns played on them as they advanced, 'like spraying us with a hose'. Two machine guns were put out of action and fifty prisoners were captured despite the fact that the Royal Fusiliers could not get reinforcements or ammunition to those in front past the German barrage that pinned them back. Continual bombing attacks were then beaten off.

That night Harold Lamb's battalion was relieved and marched back to Albert in tatters. His body had to be left on the battlefield. When names were called only some 180 men answered. Ovillers would not fall for a few more days. The only consolation for all of those lives lost was that the attack on the village on 7th July had brought the British line forward to a better starting point for a further advance. The 12th (Eastern) Division, to which Harold's battalion of Fusiliers belonged, despite not taking part on the opening day, had suffered 189 officer casualties and the loss of more than 5,000 men by the time it was relieved. One man who had been sent back with the transport watched the stragglers emerge: 'Blimey I could have cried, when I seen the few that were there; it had rained, they was wet and tired ... so and so, where's so and so?'

In the aftermath of the battle, Harold's mother received a somewhat vague letter from a captain after he failed to reappear and it was assumed that he had been killed on 7th July. 'I am told that your son was always a credit to his platoon and company and he will be missed.' Somewhat distant, this young man was writing dozens of these letters to grieving relatives about men he didn't necessarily know at all. Just 20 when he died, Harold lay where he fell to the west of Ovillers. He was later recovered from the battlefield and he was laid to rest at Ovillers Military Cemetery, plot IX.K.4.

8TH JULY

#17583 Sergeant Albert Klemp

6TH WILTSHIRE REGIMENT

THE VILLAGE OF CONTALMAISON WAS another of the objectives deemed necessary in order to secure the left flank of the troops set to assault in the upcoming large-scale advance on the Bazentin Ridge, which had been set for mid-July.

Among the men who would have to try to help capture it was 20-year-old Albert Klemp, the son of a P&O harbour master. Raised in Southend-on-Sea and educated at the local high school, by 1914 Albert was working as a clerk at the customs office in the City of London.

At the height of the rush to the colours in the first week of September, Albert enlisted at the busy recruiting station at St Paul's in the City and was allocated to a battalion of the Wiltshire Regiment. Albert had seen much in the opening week of the Battle of the Somme. On 2nd July his battalion had been ordered in at La Boisselle prior to its capture, but their endeavours had proved unsuccessful at a cost of almost 300 casualties.

Given approximately forty-eight hours to reorganise, on 7th July Albert and his battalion moved off again to take part in an attack near Contalmaison. The 6th Wiltshires went forward, making steady progress on the right flank of the attack. In the centre, 'so eager were the troops to get on' that they even ran into the divisional artillery barrage and were held up. Three times during the day they were left with their right flank in the air and suffered the nerve-wracking effects of German snipers throughout the afternoon until their bombers took care of them that evening. The night was a very wet and trying one, but the enemy did not attempt to counter-attack.

Men of the Wiltshire Regiment advance. (Authors' collection)

On 8th July it was dry and warm, but the weather had taken its toll on the ground and the mud underfoot was awful. Albert continued helping to consolidate the Wiltshire's position. The battalion adjutant recorded 'little activity' in terms of fighting but Albert and his comrades were subjected to heavy artillery fire during the day, leading the Wiltshires to suspect that a counter-attack may be about to come towards them. In the end, this was not to be the case, but the constant stream of enemy fire had taken its toll, claiming the life of Albert Klemp. Five weeks later his family would suffer further loss when his brother was accidentally killed off Harwich when Submarine E41 collided with another vessel during exercises. Albert's body, if recovered, was never identified and he is commemorated on the Thiepval Memorial, Pier & Face 13a.

9TH JULY
#7624 Lance Corporal Eric Measham

16TH MANCHESTER REGIMENT

ERIC MEASHAM WAS A 21-YEAR-OLD gardener who worked at Cranage Hall in his home county of Cheshire. Born in Marple in 1894, he was the youngest of numerous sons now serving in the army, but did not rush to the colours. He waited until March 1915 to enlist, travelling some 25 miles into the nearest major city to join the 16th Manchester Regiment. Formed as the first city battalion out of the influx of New Army recruits late in 1914, the 16th Manchesters were drawn from clerks, warehousemen; a Pals battalion 'in stark contrast to that of the nearby Salford Pals, whose battalions were drawn from the working-class terraces, slums, docklands, mills and mines west of the city centre'.

The population of Manchester was immensely proud of its battalions, and the first arrived in the Somme area in December 1915 to receive its introduction to trench warfare from men of the Gloucesters and Worcesters. Eric found himself in the thick of it on 1st July when the battalion went over the top towards Montauban in that successful advance. Despite heavy machine-gun fire, they pressed on, wiping out the offending weapons and entering the village in the middle of the morning to find it deserted. Less than an hour later, Eric and his fellow Manchesters had moved on to their second objective. The Germans turned and ran. It had been a costly day, with more than 350 casualties, but Eric had survived it and helped to consolidate the village.

On 3rd July the battalion came out of the line, to a valley behind the British defences, where four days of training and reorganisation were rendered miserable by wet weather. Tired, soaked and hungry, the brisk message of congratulation that they received was slightly callous following their exploits at Montauban. 'Well done 90th Brigade. You will attack again soon.' New drafts came up to replenish the hundreds of friends lost, but they were not Manchester men. Some of them were southerners and already the battalion was not the same. There was to be hardly any respite after their success either, for by the evening of 8th July, Eric was on his way back into battle.

Trônes Wood was another of the objectives marked as essential to prepare for the future attack on the Longueval/Bazentin ridge. Pear shaped, with a railway line leading to Guillemont through the middle, it had not been cut for two years and was very dense with thick undergrowth. Frustratingly, after the rout of the Germans in the area on the 1st, it had lain open, but this was not followed up and now, semi-destroyed by shellfire, the wood was being defended fiercely by the enemy.

Nonetheless, claiming this prize now would help to secure the right flank of the upcoming British advance. As a result, fighting for it in the early days of July would become desperate and Eric and the 16th Manchesters would again be in the thick of the action. Their attack on Trônes Wood was scheduled for the morning of 9th July and was delayed by both the density of the foliage and gas shelling. Other Manchester men eventually went forward in their respirators with the rain obstructing the view through their masks. Nonetheless, the wood was taken in two hours. But not for long. As was all too common throughout the Battle of the Somme, taking a wood was not necessarily the problem, it was holding on to it once the enemy decided that they wanted it back.

The Germans began a systematic barrage and by mid-afternoon the troops inside had been compelled to retire to the shelter of Bernafay Wood, just to the west. Waiting near Montauban, Eric and the

16th Manchesters received orders to move up under heavy artillery fire and occupy the southern part of Trônes Wood. They were not to push on from there until they received further instructions.

In the meantime, the enemy delivered a counter-attack along the edge of the wood that was largely driven off, but the north-west section was penetrated. At 6:40pm Eric and his battalion advanced to try and drive the Germans back out of Trônes Wood again. Approaching from a sunken road, they were subjected to heavy machine-gun fire and shrapnel shelling, but the speed at which the Manchesters moved minimised their casualties somewhat. They reached a spot 60 yards from the south-west edge of the tree line, running into some men from another of the city's battalions, and began digging in. By 8pm most of Eric's battalion were occupying the corner of Trônes Wood, surrounded by enemy bombers. Here they were again showered with German artillery fire and picked off by snipers in trees, as well as a machine gun. 'Repeated attempts were made by patrols to clear up the situation in the wood but the undergrowth and fallen trees ... made progress by night almost impossible.'

Possession of Trônes Wood had still not been assured when the 16th Manchesters were finally relieved on 11th July. Eric Measham was not among them, and nobody could explain what had happened to him. It was believed he may have been part of a bombing party after they reached the wood. It was not until May 1917 that the army added 'presumed killed' to his record. His mother still did not give up on him. She was still writing to the war office for information in the middle of 1919, still hoping to find out what had happened to her boy. 'The address

Trônes Wood in 1916. (Authors' collection)

is still the same. But I have had no new farther news of my son, 7624, Eric Measham. I should be grateful for any tidings of the fate of my boy.' She was never to receive any definitive information. Twenty-one-year-old Eric's body, if recovered, was never identified and he is commemorated on the Thiepval Memorial, Pier & Face 13a/14c.

10TH JULY

2nd Lieutenant Donald Simpson Bell VC

9TH YORKSHIRE REGIMENT

'DONNY' BELL, OF HARROGATE, WAS 25 years old, a school teacher and sometime professional footballer, having turned out for both Crystal Palace and Bradford Park Avenue. In November 1914 he walked away from his job and enlisted as a private soldier in the West Yorkshire Regiment. Within six months, he had been recognised as officer material and was granted a commission in the 9th Yorkshire Regiment, the Green Howards.

By 10th July, Donald had seen much dramatic action on the Somme. Five days earlier the 9th Yorkshires had attacked Horseshoe Trench, between La Boisselle and Mametz Wood. The lines that they found themselves in were unfamiliar, broken and the weather was damp. Yorkshiremen struggled through mud in the face of shell and machine-gun fire. In the midst of the attack, heavy enfilade fire was opened on one of the attacking companies by a German machine gunner. Seeing what was transpiring, Donald, who had observed the gun on his left, took the initiative and crept up a communication trench, trailed by two men.

Donald's sporting prowess did not stop at football. He was a talented cricketer and rugby player too, 14st and over 6ft tall. A friend of his said that 'he was … able to hurl himself at the German trench at such speed that the enemy would hardly believe what their eyes saw'. He burst forth, running out into the open under heavy fire in the direction of the machine gun. Brandishing his revolver, his first shot hit the gun from about 20 yards away and knocked it down. Then his little team began slinging bombs 'and did in about 50 Boches'. For this act Donny Bell

would be awarded the Victoria Cross. 'I must confess,' he wrote, 'it was the biggest fluke alive and I did nothing. I only chucked one bomb, but it did the trick … I am glad to have been so fortunate, for Pa's sake, for I know he likes his lads to be at the top of the tree.'

By nightfall Horseshoe Trench was in British hands, searched and the enemy cleared out. Their brigadier was impressed with what he saw. 'The losses in all battalions was considerable, but their energy in hunting out and destroying the enemy at the end of the long and confused operations in spite of their own physical exhaustions was worthy of the highest traditions of the Yorkshire Regiments which they represented.'

'I believe that God is watching over me and it rests with him whether I pull through or not,' Bell wrote home in the aftermath of the incident. His faith would be tested again five days later. On 9th July the 9th Yorkshires received orders to attack in the direction of Contalmaison the following day to seize what was left of the village. From across no-man's-land it appeared as a mass of rubble, but this disguised the fact that underneath the village the enemy had fashioned a warren of dugouts, cellars and tunnels. Like moles, the Germans had thus far lived underground and had beaten off their British attackers, including Albert Klemp, as a result.

The main attack was to be delivered in part by the 9th Battalion of the Green Howards, but for the day Donald Bell and his bombing party were attached to the 8th Yorkshires on their right. At 4:50pm they left from Horseshoe Trench, the scene of his previous exploits, and immediately came under shrapnel fire. When they closed to within 500 yards of the village, machine guns were opened on them from both their left flank and in front. They were forced to struggle through enemy wire and hedges to get to Contalmaison, picking up heavy casualties. Pressing on regardless, as the battalion approached the village, the Green Howards found the enemy retreating. But suddenly machine-gun fire erupted behind the Yorkshiremen. 'Not more than four officers and 150 men reached the village,' where they began pulling German prisoners out of dugouts along with valuable equipment: six machine guns and thousands of rounds of ammunition. With so few men, the two battalions of Yorkshires began to put themselves in a state of defence, ready to hold off inevitable German counter-attacks. The first came at 7:30pm, but they were dispersed by fire from their own usurped machine guns. The second was far more costly. An hour and a half later about forty Germans made a second attempt coming from the south of

Above: The ruins of Contalmaison. (Authors' collection)

Right: Commemorative cigarette card for Donald Simpson Bell. (Authors' collection)

the village. A barricade was swiftly put up but, with his customary zeal, Donald went beyond it with his bombers, attempting to force the enemy back. For his bravery he was cut down by enemy fire.

Five weeks before his death, Donny had married at the Wesleyan Chapel in Kirkby Stephen. Evidently still under the impression that he was a bachelor, the War Office notified his father of his death and it fell to him to inform his son's new wife, Rhoda. She was sent his belongings by his batman, who was heartbroken at his death when he wrote to her several months later, after she had collected her late husband's VC from the King at Buckingham Palace. 'I sit down and write these lines in deepest regret,' he began. 'I would to God that my late master and friend had still been here with us, or better still, been at home with you … [The company] worshipped him in their simple, wholehearted way and so they ought, he save the lot of us from being wiped out, by his heroic act.' Donald Bell was originally laid to rest to the south of Contalmaison, where he fell. He was later exhumed and is now buried at Gordon Dump Cemetery, plot IV.A.8.

Temp. 2nd-Lieut. D. S. BELL, V.C.

11TH JULY

#20649 Lance Corporal Henry Hardwidge

15TH WELSH REGIMENT

BACK AT MAMETZ WOOD, WHERE Fred Emery had been killed on his arrival, the spot was becoming a nightmare for the Welsh Division. In the days following Emery's death, the men had tested the enemy's resistance and grown somewhat accustomed to the area. Like Trônes Wood, Mametz was a daunting prospect. There were rides within, but such was the tangle of hawthorn and briar, and the mess of oak, beech and birch ripped down by vicious bombardments that any path was near impossible to spot.

The Welshmen had begun their task with small, haphazard attacks on 7th July. Two separate attempts made by Cardiff and Gwent men failed owing to heavy machine-gun fire and they could not even reach the wood. Troops fared no better on the 8th. Unimpressed by the lack of progress, Haig swept aside the division's commanding officer and replaced him on 9th July as it was decided to attack again the following day. This time there were to be no small efforts to hack away at this objective. On 10th July the full force of the Welsh Division would be applied to the task.

Included among them were two brothers from the town of Ferndale, near Pontypridd, where the first mine had been sunk in 1857. Serving in the 15th Welsh Regiment, 24-year-old Henry Hardwidge and his brother Tom, 34, were miners, living just a few hundred feet apart in the middle of town when they enlisted together in 1914. The two waited as the big thrust on Mametz Wood began at 4:15am on 10th July. Two battalions swept inside, clearing the middle of the wood quickly; but a third was held up and so the 15th Welsh was called upon to go and support the attack.

The Welshmen had a foothold in the wood, but the situation was far from secure and far from clear. Henry and Tom were able to get inside without much opposition, aside from the occasional sniper, and the battalion even managed to round up a few prisoners as they went searching for the 13th Welsh. Eventually, with three battalions together in the confusion, including theirs, the brothers helped to form a line in the southern part of the wood. Indecisive fighting took place until 2:30pm. At one point it looked as though the enemy was massing for a counter-attack. At another, a German machine gun got in the rear of one of the companies and began cutting men down, wiping out almost two platoons. Snipers were everywhere, gradually eroding the numbers of those attempting to navigate the confusion or consolidate their positions throughout numerous advances and retirements.

The confused troops were ordered forward again to make their way through the chaos via one of the rides to consolidate a position gained. There was so much traffic on it that it was impossible for the Hardwidge brothers to negotiate the path. As men tripped over each other, machine-gun fire opened up on the tangle of wrecked trees. For ten minutes all was mayhem. The 15th Welsh were scattered across Mametz Wood, unsure of their exact positions as night set in.

The 11th July began with redeployment of the Welsh resources that remained available after the previous day's fighting. Henry and Tom's battalion was sent forward to make a further advance on the north-west end of the wood in mid-afternoon. 'Owing to own artillery barrage falling short and very thick undergrowth,' progress was incredibly slow and the starting point was not reached until 4pm. After another delay waiting for the neighbouring battalion to get into position, the attack finally went forward hours late. Tom Hardwidge was hit by a sniper's bullet. Henry ran to him and was giving him water when he too was shot. The brothers died in each other's arms.

Henry left behind a wife, Jennie, and daughter, Edna aged 3. Tom's widow, Annie, was left to raise their three children alone; Mary Ann, Lilian and Phoebe. On the anniversary of their deaths a touching poem was posted in the local newspaper for Henry and reflected the pain of their ends having occurred so far from home:

Your last faint whispers I should like to have heard
And to breathe in your ear just one loving word
Only those who have suffered are able to tell
The pain of the heart in not saying farewell

The brothers' headstones, side by side at Flatiron Copse Cemetery. (Andrew Holmes)

Henry (*left*) and Tom (*right*) Hardwidge with their wives and some of their children at home in Wales. (Private collection)

One of their officers wrote to the two widows:

> I had known them for nearly twelve months, for they were in my platoon. More cheerful, willing and capable soldiers I do not think it is possible to find, and their presence is greatly missed by everyone in the platoon and by myself.

Henry and Thomas Hardwidge were originally interred in the south-east section of Mametz Wood. They were later exhumed as the wood was cleared in 1919 and are now buried side by side at Flatiron Copse Cemetery, plots VIII.F.5 & VIII. F.6. Their brother, David, was killed on Christmas Day 1916 while serving with the 2nd Battalion of the regiment. His body, if recovered, was never identified and he is commemorated on the Thiepval Memorial, Pier & Face 7a/10a.

12TH JULY
#25526 Lance Corporal Henry Bellis

17TH ROYAL WELSH FUSILIERS

FOR THE WELSH, THE TORMENT of Mametz Wood was still not over. Henry Bellis was an ironworker from Mold, Flintshire, who enlisted at Llandudno comparatively late for a New Army man on the Somme. Apart from suffering from scabies as a somewhat inevitable result of the squalor of the Western Front and once being admonished for losing his rifle, Henry had had an uneventful war in terms of personal injury since arriving on the Continent in December 1915.

Like the Hardwidge brothers, Henry had already been fully embroiled in the desperate fighting at Mametz Wood. On 7th July he moved up to attack. Going forward at 8am, the 17th Royal Welsh Fusiliers suffered slight casualties that day when compared with some of their countrymen's battalions. Throughout the 8th, Henry remained in the line, entrenched in thick mud, tortured by the miserable weather engulfing the battlefield and waiting for others to come and relieve him. They never arrived. Henry did not get back to the camp until late afternoon on the 9th when exhausted, he and his comrades were at last ordered to rest until early morning.

Henry's respite was curtailed. By 3am on 10th July the 17th Royal Welsh Fusiliers had been ordered back into action and were ready to march off. Frustratingly, no orders came for a further five hours when they moved up to support another attack in the wood. By the end of the day they had been sent in to assist their fellow Welshmen and by 6:30pm, Henry and his battalion had got to within 30 yards of the edge of the far side of the wood, where they began to dig in. It had been a costly day, despite their supporting role. The battalion's commanding officer was wounded, the adjutant left with shell shock, and 200 men were lost.

The inside of the wood was traumatic, to say the least:

Detail from the Welsh Division Memorial at Mametz Wood. (Alexandra Churchill)

Heavy shelling of the southern end had beaten down some of the young growth, but it had also thrown trees and large branches into a barricade. Equipment, ammunition, rolls of barbed wire, tins of food, gas helmets and rifles were lying about everywhere. There were more corpses than men, but there were worse sights than corpses. Limbs and mutilated trunks, here and there a detached head, forming splashes of red against the green leaves, and, as in advertisement of the horror of our way of life and death, and of our crucifixion of youth, one tree held in its branches a leg, with its torn flesh hanging down over a spray of leaf.

Early on 11th July, as the various Welsh battalions scattered throughout Mametz Wood reorganised and took up a coherent line, orders were received for the advance to be pushed forward again. Already exhausted, Henry's battalion went forward at 3:30pm. By the time that they were relieved on the 12th, another 200 men were casualties and more officers had been lost. Such was the chaos that nobody knew precisely when Henry Bellis had died. Sometime later, a battalion of the Northumberland Fusiliers reported they had come across his body and buried him. His date of death was marked down as 12th July.

The Rhondda Valley, Swansea, Cardiff, Carmarthen, Gwent, Glamorgan; the whole of Wales mourned their dead in the aftermath of their battle for Mametz Wood. It would take more than a year to rebuild the Welsh Division and for it to be capable of fighting again. Some 4,000 Welshmen lay dead in and around the wood after just a few days' fighting. The exact location of Henry Bellis' grave was subsequently lost and he is commemorated on the Thiepval Memorial, Pier & Face 4a. His brother Samuel, 35, died with the 10th Battalion of the regiment a month later elsewhere on the Somme and his name was also inscribed on the memorial on the same panel as Henry's.

13TH JULY
#G/2387 Private Arthur Randall
7TH QUEEN'S OWN (ROYAL WEST KENT REGIMENT)

ON 8TH JULY GENERAL RAWLINSON had begun giving orders to prepare for the much-anticipated big offensive on the original German second-line position running along the Bazentin Ridge. Minor attacks leading up to it were ill thought out and costly in both men and materials, but time spent getting ready for 14th July had been well used. One of the most significant successes would be the preliminary bombardment laid down on the enemy. It was targeted effectively on barbed wire, German trenches, strong points, enemy batteries, and on a much smaller front than had been demanded of the artillery at the onset of the battle on 1st July. Sixty-six per cent of the number of guns employed on the opening day of the Somme campaign were now registering on just 5 per cent of the

original targets. Additionally, roads were cleared, tracks laid, useless trenches backfilled and guns rolled up with plenty of ammunition. At 5pm on the 12th final orders were issued. Zero hour was to be at 3:20am on 14th July. A night attack.

One young man, though, was part of a battalion that would go into action several hours earlier. Arthur Randall was a farm labourer from Cliffe-at-Hoo in Kent. Eighteen years old when he travelled to Chatham to enlist in 1914, he subsequently joined the 7th Battalion of the Royal West Kents, arriving in France the following June. With his unit, Arthur had taken part in the opening throes of the offensive at the beginning of July, when his battalion suffered almost 200 casualties.

As zero hour on 14th July approached, Trônes Wood was still not in British hands. Arthur and the 7th Royal West Kents were to be summoned to attack it before the main assault began, so that the newly won position could be used to help secure the right flank at 3:20am when everyone else went forward.

Since Eric Measham had been killed assaulting the wood on 9th July, higher command had continued to order unsuccessful attacks on the difficult objective. By the night of the 10th there were no British troops inside the wood at all. The spot then appeared to change hands several times before, on 11th July, it was reported that Trônes Wood had fallen and that, despite exhaustion, the British conquerors were managing to hold on inside. Unfortunately, the following day, the whole place would fall back into German hands. Later on the 12th, the fight again swung slightly in the direction of the British, but Trônes Wood was far from secure.

Arthur Randall's task on the 13th was to prove a nightmare. The Royal West Kents were to attack from the south and capture the bottom half of the wood. It was to be taken 'at all costs' by midnight on the night of the 13th/14th, three and a half hours before the main offensive on the Somme began again. The situation was confusing. A number of German strong points had been marked among the remains of the trees and one pointed right at Arthur as he advanced. If he and his comrades did not find themselves being showered with machine-gun fire in the dark, they 'wandered about in a dense jungle of fallen trees and thick brushwood, and lost all notion of their whereabouts'. It was as if units went inside and simply disappeared. All telephone wires were cut and the battalion's commanders knew nothing of what was going on inside Trônes Wood.

The spot in Trônes Wood where Arthur Randall was discovered in 1929. (Andrew Holmes)

Battling on, Arthur and his battalion reached the railway line that ran horizontally through the wood, at a significant cost in men. The trees were in full leaf, the fallen foliage concealing enemy snipers and dead bodies. One soldier lifted a tangle of branches and found a German soldier shot away to his hip, the poor man's entrails hanging out and covered in flies. If that wasn't disturbing enough, he was left vomiting when a severed leg fell out of the remains of a tree on to his head.

As with previous attacks, the battalion's formation was quickly shattered and the men roamed in small groups, cut off from their leaders in the dark. At midnight it began to rain. Indiscriminate heavy shelling continued to decimate the Royal West Kents. British shells killed British soldiers, sniping went on all night. One group suddenly realised that the enemy had got behind them. It was a terrifying experience. 'We reversed every other man, and put in rapid fire ... but creeping up under cover of the fallen trees the Germans got to within ten yards of us ... Then they organised attacks in relay and came at us every quarter of an hour.'

Zero hour for the large-scale advance on Bazentin Ridge approached and still Trônes Wood had not been secured. It was not until mid-morning that it was reported that this stubborn objective had finally fallen.

The troops went forward bravely, many even managed to enter the bounds of the wood, but once inside they were lost, isolated in a tangled jungle of smashed trees, heavy undergrowth and the unmentionable mangled debris of men and equipment.

During the course of the fight, Arthur's company commander was wounded. Seeing his plight, the 20 year old ran to him and pulled him up, attempting to drag him to safety. As they struggled along, Arthur was struck and killed. His final resting place remained a mystery for more than a decade until Arthur was recovered from just inside the south-east treeline at Trônes Wood. He was identified by his uniform and by a wristwatch inscribed 'Miss G. Langham to Arthur'. His father had been dead for five years when his boy was finally given a grave and laid to rest at Serre Road Cemetery No. 2, XXIX.J.15 on 19th June 1929.

14TH JULY

#12374 Private Luther Cordin

7TH LEICESTERSHIRE REGIMENT

WHILE ARTHUR RANDALL FOUGHT FOR Trônes Wood throughout the night of the 13th, troops marked to take part in the offensive proper were preparing to deploy ready for zero hour. Among them were four battalions belonging to the Leicestershire Regiment, forming a brigade known as the Leicester Tigers. Rawlinson's men were to be attacking on a front of 3½ miles and the battle was to be innovative. The Leicestershire battalions crept forward under cover of darkness for their night attack, a point that Rawlinson had fought hard for with Haig. Creeping out of the cover of Mametz Wood, the men formed up on lines of tape, having already quietly conquered some of the ground that would inevitably be showered with machine-gun fire when the battle began.

Waiting to begin the rush towards the enemy was a tall 23 year old named Luther Cordin. A miner from the village of Annesley Woodhouse, near Nottingham, he enlisted at Hucknall at the beginning of the war and was immediately routed into the Leicestershire Regiment, embarking for France at the end of July 1915. Facing roughly north-east towards Bazentin-le-Petit, Luther watched as shells continued to fall on the remains of the trees that masked the battered village. His battalion, the 7th, were on the left of the Leicester attack, committed to bursting uphill and taking the left side of Bazentin-le-Petit Wood.

'At 3:20am the whole sky behind the waiting infantry ... seemed to open with a great roar of flame.' In order to maintain an element of surprise, British artillery and machine gunners had waited until five minutes before zero hour before unleashing an intense hurricane bombardment on the enemy positions ahead. Luther Cordin rushed forward with his battalion in the dark. In front of him the artillery laid down an elementary creeping barrage to protect the advancing troops. The British infantry was instructed to stay as close to its own moving curtain of shells as possible, which meant that projectiles were screaming down literally a few feet above their heads. The concept was incredibly dangerous and frightening but a most effective tactic. Firing a creeping barrage required excellent communication between guns and batteries, and detailed planning between artillery, infantry and aircraft to make sure they followed it at the right speed.

On either flank, the 7th Leicesters began to drop into the German front line but, in the centre, Luther and his company found themselves pinned down for nearly half an hour by vicious machine-gun fire. Troops on their right helped work down their flank and then they too were able to engulf the enemy. Men swept over the enemy trenches and began to surge for the German support line as planned. After initial resistance in the front trenches, and taken by surprise, the enemy retreated into Bazentin-le-Petit Wood and put up little resistance. In little over half an hour, the first two objectives of the 7th Leicesters had been seized.

Success had come at a cost. The Leicester Tigers had become confused and their leaders had taken heavy casualties. Only one officer of Luther Cordin's company was still in action; the same was true of another and in a third every officer was dead, missing somewhere on the battlefield or in no shape to continue the fight. Nevertheless, at 4:25am survivors set out to capture the third objective. On one side this was straightforward enough but on the other the Leicesters came under fire from both a machine gun and snipers. Confusion reigned and in some cases the men pressed forward too far and came under the British barrage.

As the day continued, the 7th Leicesters were bombarded with shells from German howitzers, but up and down the line, the continuation of the main offensive on the Bazentin Ridge had been almost universally successful. With a combination of a night attack and a meticulous, relentless bombardment in the lead up to zero hour that had paved the way for the infantry, Trônes Wood had fallen along with almost the entire original German second system from Longueval to Bazentin-le-Petit. The 14th July was a well-planned triumph on a limited front, but in the grand scheme of things, these were objectives still outstanding from 1st July and had only come after nearly two weeks of resource-consuming minor attacks made up and down the line in less than ideal circumstances. There did now, however, appear to be hope for the Somme offensive.

The cost of progress along Bazentin Ridge was nearly 10,000 men. That night, back on the Leicester front, the various county battalions were attempting to sort themselves out after the confusion of the day's fighting. It would be a lengthy process and keeping tabs on what had happened to a single individual could be impossible. Luther Cordin

Men of the Leicester Tigers Brigade relax in the aftermath of the Battle of Bazentin Ridge. (Authors' collection)

was reported wounded by 22nd July, probably because one or more witnesses furnished such information. In August the army decided to classify him as 'missing' because he had not been located at any casualty clearing station or hospital. Finally, at the end of September, the authorities decided that too much time had elapsed for him to emerge as a prisoner of war and the War Office vaguely determined that Luther Cordin had been killed in action at some point during the Battle of Bazentin Ridge and, for neatness, applied 14th July as his date of death. Luther's body, if recovered, was never identified and he is commemorated on the Thiepval Memorial, Pier & Face 2c/3a.

15TH JULY

#330159 Corporal Lorimer Headley

1/9TH (GLASGOW) HIGHLAND LIGHT INFANTRY

BORN IN AYR, LORIMER HEADLEY had been raised in Glasgow and was one of five brothers serving; four in the army and one in the Royal Navy. Educated at Whitehill Higher Grade School, he was bright, with an aptitude for modern languages and maths. After leaving, he had gone to work as an apprentice for the Royal Bank of Scotland at its St Rollox branch near Springburn. Lorimer had joined a Glasgow territorial battalion of the Highland Light Infantry in 1912 and was at the front by November 1914, shortly after his 19th birthday. The chaplain was especially fond of him, telling his parents that he was 'a splendid soldier', who 'kept the men in his charge and many of his comrades bright by his own happy disposition'.

Although Lorimer was now becoming an experienced soldier, unfortunately the precision planning that had served so well on 14th July appeared to be disregarded and the 9th Highland Light Infantry was about to fall victim to what was to be one of the first of many costly attempts to conquer smaller-scale objectives on the Somme throughout the rest of the summer.

Stone of Remembrance amongst a sea of headstones at Delville Wood Cemetery. (Andrew Holmes)

Continuing in a north-easterly direction from Bazentin-le-Petit, where Luther Cordin had disappeared the day before, was High Wood. This isolated piece of woodland was to bleed the British Army of valuable manpower for weeks. At the onset of the battle it had been behind the German second-line system, on slightly raised ground; in such flat country it was precious. 'From this vantage point the Germans could see any attempt by the Allies to approach.' The enemy had taken full advantage by readying themselves for a siege. Thick with undergrowth, it was also full of young saplings, which were to be a hindrance to troops on the move.

While battle raged on 14th July, Lorimer's battalion was ordered to move to Flatiron Copse to the right side of Mametz Wood. Led by pipes through sweltering heat, they passed motor ambulances waiting in Mametz. 'Wild and exciting' rumours abounded that the enemy line had been broken and that the cavalry was chasing the Kaiser's men away. Wounded and captured Germans passed in the opposite direction, helped by their friends or carried on stretchers. The air shook with the concussion of shells and the men fell quiet as they filed by piles of corpses and dead horses. Wounded Indian cavalry passed them too, 'slumped over their mounts', having been sent up speculatively in the direction of the wood. One of them was in tears as he led his wounded animal and travelled on foot towards the rear. The situation was already confused. The Glasgow Highlanders had orders to support troops in the area, but do not appear to have ever received them. That night, the skyline was lit up by gun flashes and high-explosive shells continued to rain down.

At dawn on 15th July a thick ground mist completely obscured both High Wood and the village of Martinpuich to the left of it. At 5:30am orders were received that the Highlanders were to attack Switch Trench, an advance pushing almost due north. Lorimer Headley and his battalion readied themselves for their battle. The mist was clearing, there was no cover as the Glasgow Highlanders formed up to the west of High Wood. Machine-gun fire streamed out of it. It seemed that any attempt on their objective would be suicide unless neighbouring troops managed to secure the wood first, but protestations fell on deaf ears.

At 9am the Highland Light Infantry attacked and men began to drop before they had even advanced a few yards. Heavy shrapnel fire from High Wood and the trench that formed their objective cascaded on to them. The advancing line was annihilated and the few survivors attempted to rush forward in isolated groups. They became confused as to what direction they were supposed to be going in and veered towards High Wood itself. Men crawled along the ground trying to avoid enemy fire or hid in shell holes. The attack was quickly rendered void of all coherence, all leadership as officers fell and machine guns and artillery continued to play on them. The direction in which the Glaswegians were attacking even made it possible for a German battery to fire almost at the backs of them from near Martinpuich.

At most, Lorimer Headley and his fellow Highlanders only advanced about 150 yards before they were scythed down. A battalion was sent up to support them but suffered a similar fate.

Reinforcements strayed into High Wood too. Any movement on the gently sloping hill was hammered by enemy fire. Stragglers tried to get back to safety, or attempted frantically to dig in in the confusion, while British artillery was directed erroneously to shell British troops running across the battlefield. By early evening the surviving troops taking part in the attack had collected right back where they had started. The 9th Highland Light Infantry suffered the loss of twenty-one officers, almost every one, and some 400 men.

In the confusion of the day, to the west of High Wood the slope had become covered in dead Glaswegian volunteers and writhing, wounded men torn down by the enemy's relentless fire. Lorimer Headley was reported missing in the aftermath and when he failed to appear in the ensuing weeks he was confirmed to have been killed 'on or about' 15th July. His body was later recovered from the battlefield and Lorimer was ultimately laid to rest at Delville Wood Cemetery, plot XXVIII.G.2.

16TH JULY
Captain Ernst Albert Linsingen Hahn

1ST REGIMENT, SOUTH AFRICAN INFANTRY

INSTEAD OF SEIZING THE INITIATIVE after the success of the attack on the Bazentin Ridge, the British offensive on the Somme began to drift. One place would come to define the tireless attempts to press the enemy further back from his second-line positions at the bottom end of the British front. Consisting of about 156 acres of sturdy trees and dense thickets of hazel, Delville Wood was split by grass thoroughfares that had now been named familiarly Buchanan Street, Campbell Street and Haymarket by the troops in the area. The village of Longueval, another of those reinforced by the enemy, ran right up to the edge of it and made the two combined objectives an incredibly difficult prospect, populated by machine-gun nests and even German artillery pieces that had been wheeled inside.

If Mametz Wood was to be synonymous with Wales, then Delville, or 'the Devil's Wood' as it became known, would haunt South Africa. For the dominion troops who had made the long journey from the southern tip of their continent, the opening months of the war had been spent on closer fronts, such as German South West Africa, or concerned with internal friction, but in the summer of 1915 the Union Government decided to furnish a force to fight in Europe. Raised largely from those of British extraction, the numbers of the white population and the inevitable need to replenish those killed meant that recruitment was limited to a brigade. Four battalions of infantry were duly produced. Loosely speaking, the 1st came from the Cape, the 2nd from Natal and the Orange Free State, the 3rd Transvaal and Rhodesia and the 4th was the South African Scottish.

Ernst Hahn, seated centre of the front row, with his family in Paarl, 1912. (Courtesy of @rememberussa)

Twenty-eight years old and the son of a church minister, Ernst Hahn was a bank clerk from Paarl, about 40 miles from Cape Town, the third oldest European settlement in South Africa. With strong German ancestry, Ernst's grandfather had been instrumental in the founding of the Lutheran congregation in their town. Born near Riga, Carl Hahn had moved to Germany before travelling to South Africa to spread his religion in the 1840s. Ernst's father had served as the leader of the congregation since 1883. Paarl retained very Germanic sensibilities, although Ernst's father was liberal in his outlook. Though he tried hard to remain faithful to the local population's roots in keeping the town's German school open, he also drew criticism for teaching confirmation classes in English for children not fluent in the Kaiser's tongue. The war caused severe divisions in the community and tensions obviously ran even higher when some of their minister's five sons began joining the Allied cause early in the war; Ernst's father was eventually compelled to take a pay cut.

In the meantime, his boys left for war. The South African contingent began embarking in August 1915 and by the beginning of November everyone was on English soil and in training. After a somewhat unconventional introduction to fighting in North Africa, Ernst and the rest of the South Africans embarked again at Alexandria in mid-April and sailed for Marseilles. Once on the Western Front they became part of the 9th Scottish Division, men of Kitchener's first 100,000, and in June they moved towards the Somme.

The fighting of 14th July took a portion of Longueval and up to where the village met Delville Wood. The Scottish Division battled fiercely to take the hardest of objectives allotted by Rawlinson that day. Given the necessity of conquering both village and wood at the same time though, plainly not enough weight was being thrown at such a difficult obstacle. That evening, Rawlinson ordered his army across the board to continue the offensive the following day. They were to exploit anything gained so far and take care of any outstanding objectives, which included Longueval and Delville Wood. By the morning of the 15th, though, the Germans had reinforcements on the way and were poised, expecting further attacks.

The South African Brigade was ordered to take Delville Wood 'at all costs' and for the most part moved up before dawn on the 15th. The southern half of the wood was seized in fewer than two hours 'although progress was very difficult among the shell holes and the tangle formed [by] the trunks and branches'. Having arrived back from being loaned to another brigade, most of Ernst's battalion was thrown in too, past snipers, a mass of ruins, wire entanglements, garden fences, half-fallen trees 'together with every description of debris and shattered building material'. A fresh advance on the wood took more ground, but the enemy ensconced in the north-west corner held out. At the end of 15th July the task of seizing Longueval and Delville Wood was incomplete and the South African battalions had suffered serious losses. As the sun went down, the activity of the enemy guns increased and the sky was lit up by liquid fire. All night long, Ernst and his men were trying desperately to dig in.

There was no possibility of any rest for the sleep-deprived men fighting for Delville Wood. By dawn orders had been received to continue trying to conquer this stubborn objective. They would go again at 10am. The 16th July was overcast, but muggy. Attempting to direct any kind of accurate artillery barrage on a spot that was so hopelessly full of confused troops was impossible for either side's gunners to attempt without causing significant casualties to their own, and so a preparation would be made by mortars instead.

The attack went forward as planned. After a heavy mortar bombardment of Longueval, the 11th Royal Scots advanced parallel to the Western edge of Delville Wood while the South African troops went the opposite way, entering the western part of the wood at Princes Street, which ran eastward through the remains of the trees. Both advances failed under heavy machine-gun fire and the troops were largely annihilated.

Elsewhere in the wood, Ernst and his men had been sent to defend another tenuous spot and were clinging on for dear life. During the course of the day the South Africans' commanding officer arrived to take stock of the situation and came to the conclusion that the German position was so strong that the wood could only be taken after proper artillery preparation. The man commanding Ernst's battalion was beside himself. He asked for his exhausted men, who had now been fighting for days, to be relieved. But their brigadier could only repeat his divisional instructions 'that at all costs the wood must be held'. Relief would not be forthcoming.

Shaking off sleep to stand in their shallow trenches, the South Africans wavered in the heat. No further progress was possible at all on 16th July and, although the British mortars continued to fire on the German positions at intervals throughout the day, they could not silence the enemy's machine guns. The sun set again on Delville Wood and the 9th Scottish Division, South Africans included, remained inside.

The six days and five nights that the South African contingent were to spend inside the Devil's Wood exacted a miserable toll on their ranks. Some 121 officers and a little over 3,000 volunteers had marched into 'a corner of death on which the enemy fire was concentrated at all hours from three sides'. It was still untaken when they departed a few days later, a haggard remnant of a brigade. The men who had sailed all the way from the southern tip of Africa to fight for the Allies ultimately assembled to be counted and could muster no more than 750 men. When they paraded before their commander he was distraught. He 'took the salute with uncovered head and eyes not free from tears'.

Ernst Hahn fell on 16th July. His younger brother Benno also died during the war when he was killed in an accident training to fly at Upavon. Despite social pressures at home, their father was in no way ashamed of his sons' choice to fight for Britain. He later named the family home Delville. The name remains deeply associated with South Africa. Captain Hahn's body, if recovered, was never identified and he is commemorated on the Thiepval Memorial, Pier & Face 4C.

17TH JULY
#25610 Private Samuel Brough

15TH SHERWOOD FORESTERS
(NOTTS & DERBY REGIMENT)

AT THE BEGINNING OF THE war, the army was so inundated with volunteers that recruiting stations could afford to be somewhat selective. One group that found themselves continually turned away were those that failed to meet the minimum height requirement of 5ft 3in. Naturally, these men were indignant, for why should their lack of stature make them surplus to the requirements in this time of national emergency? An MP in charge of his local recruiting committee wrote to Kitchener suggesting some battalions devoted to these enthusiastic men and was told that if he wanted to put one together, the War Office gave its blessing. In the end he underwrote the cost himself and advertised for 'small but pugnacious' men between 5ft and 5ft 3in with a chest measurement of at least 34in. The first Bantam battalion was born. Other counties began to follow the Cheshire Regiment's lead and by mid-February, Nottingham had begun recruiting diminutive volunteers for what was to become the 15th Sherwood Foresters. The first eighteen men enlisted on 16th February and calls went out for more in Nottinghamshire, Derbyshire, Staffordshire, Leicestershire, Rutland and Lincolnshire. Poaching vertically challenged but willing men from even further afield was also not unheard of.

One of those answering the call at the Mechanic's Institute in Nottingham was 22-year-old Samuel Brough, who stood 5ft 1in and weighed in at just 8st. A labourer from Park Street in Derby, Sam was the sixth of seven children and had been orphaned at 13 when both his parents died in the space of a year. In April 1915 he left his sister's house and, although he may have been rejected previously for military service, he joined the army and began training.

The town of Nottingham was proud of its diminutive warriors. Articles and photographs were prevalent in the local press, and drummers marched around outlying villages looking for more volunteers. The Mayor of Nottingham made a public appeal to get the battalion its uniforms and one recruit from Oldham was so excited about finally being accepted into one of Kitchener's battalions after having been rejected elsewhere that he declared the recruiting sergeant could keep the King's Shilling. The battalion's send-off was topped by a matinee at the Hippodrome, where the recruits got to watch footage of themselves before listening to a 'spirited rendering' of Land of Hope and Glory, amongst other songs. Samuel left for Yorkshire to join his division, the 35th, which was to be formed primarily of Bantams. Then they waited it out on Salisbury Plain desperate to depart. The 15th Sherwood Foresters finally embarked for France on 1st February 1916 and moved south to the Somme in the first few days of July.

On the 16th they relieved a group of Northampton men in trenches south-east of Trônes Wood near Maltz Horn Farm, in heavy rain and in darkness, mud sucking at their boots. The men fought their way through it and were exhausted before they even began settling in to their new surroundings. The spot Samuel found himself in was prone to counter-attacks and day-to-day attrition caused by snipers and shellfire accounted for the lives of those sent in to man the line. Bodies hung in the Bantams' way, one dead Tommy in particular leaning over the parapet. His shoulder badges revealed he belonged to the The Buffs, the East Kent Regiment. 'It was a rough journey. The smell was awful, and every now and then we trod on a dead "Buff".'

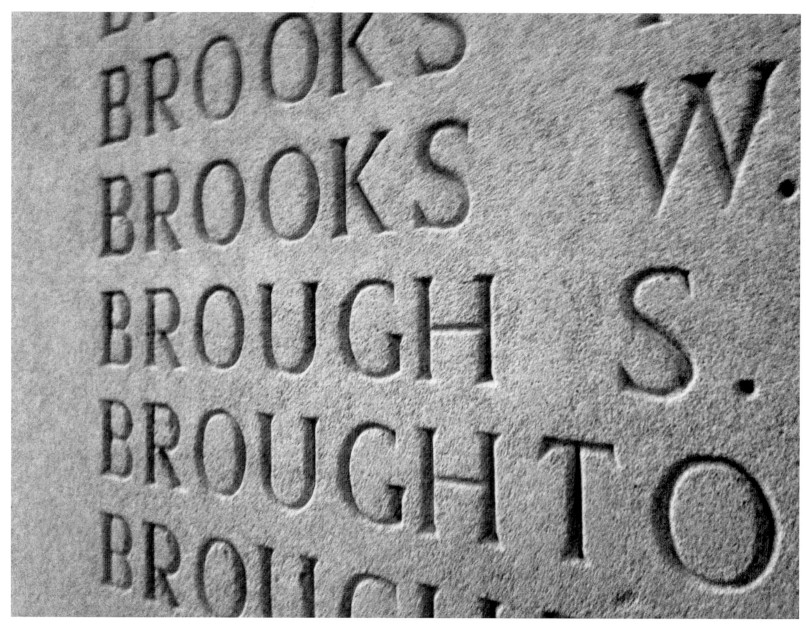

Panel inscribed with Samuel Brough's name on the Thiepval Memorial. (Alexandra Churchill)

On the following day, the Sherwood Foresters took over the far right of the British line, next to the French, from the much put upon Buffs. The French had been pushing eastwards too, and shelling in the area had been continuous, though not accurate all day as the French artillery attempted to level Maltz Horn Farm. Within a few hours Sam Brough had become a quiet casualty of war, not associated with any grand offensive. On the Somme just standing in the wrong place at the wrong time could place a man on the casualty lists. His body, if recovered, was never identified and Samuel is commemorated on the Thiepval Memorial, Pier & Face 10c/10d & 11.

Howitzers on the Somme. (Authors' collection)

18TH JULY
Lieutenant Leslie Robert Schrader Gunson

31ST HEAVY BATTERY, ROYAL GARRISON ARTILLERY

THE BATTLE OF THE SOMME was ruled by one aspect of warfare that dominated the experience of almost every man who set foot on it: the artillery. The modern industrialised outlook of the Great War was overwhelmed by the destructive power of the guns and those who fought in it had to adapt to living with shellfire on a constant basis. Up to 800,000 men served in the artillery during the Great War, with the loss of some 50,000 of them, a testament to just how much of Britain's available manpower was marked to keep the guns firing on all fronts. But it was not just in size that the branches of the artillery had developed rapidly since 1914.

The creeping barrage that Luther Cordin followed on 14th July at Bazentin Ridge was just one of dozens of innovations that would be introduced. To find their targets the gunners now relied on the co-operation of the Royal Flying Corps and the Royal Naval Air Service, as well as observation balloons. Identifying targets by the flash of the guns firing back at them and by sound ranging was also introduced. Meteorological assessments of factors such as wind speed and air pressure were used to help fire accurately once such targets had been identified. The design of the shells themselves had been revolutionised, whether it be by more sensitive fuses designed to blow away obstructions like barbed wire without the shell having to impact the ground, or by adapting them to deliver such modern nightmares as poisonous gas.

One 21 year old experiencing this advancement and dominance over the battlefield was Leslie Gunson, from Whitehaven in Cumberland. Having been educated at St Bees School, in a bitter twist of irony for someone who was now expected to maim and destroy on a daily basis, Leslie was a medical student at Edinburgh University when war was declared. Having served in the University Officer Training Corps' artillery arm, his progression into the Royal Garrison Artillery once given a commission in August 1914 was a logical one.

The British artillery had undergone much reorganisation before the commencement of the campaign on the Somme. Numbers of heavy artillery units, guns like Leslie's, had grown rapidly since 1914: the number of batteries had more than quadrupled. In March 1916 they were redistributed at various levels to maximise their contribution to the Battle of the Somme. Their work had started early. There were approximately 400 heavy guns on the Somme and together they flung nearly 200,000 shells at the enemy's defences in the run up to 1st July, pounding the villages fortified by the Germans, as well as strong points and trenches.

Panorama of the eastern end of Caterpillar Valley, where many British guns saw action during the Battle of the Somme. (Andrew Holmes)

Prior to 1st July one of the important jobs allocated to the artillery was counter-battery fire, i.e. silencing rival guns. On Leslie's front they had paid more attention to this than most, and as a result the infantry attack on the opening day had been the most successful. But Leslie's battery had been allotted to a group that had come to rest in a particularly unhealthy spot. In fact, he had already been lightly wounded at the onset of the battle. Caterpillar Valley, to the north of Montauban, was packed from end to end with guns of all types: field guns, big howitzers, monstrous 60-pounders and anti-aircraft guns, 'which kept up an almost continuous roar' at all hours. Fully overlooked by the enemy, the Germans promptly shelled it unceasingly.

There was hardly any cover for detachments, which were kept as small as possible to avoid losses, only holes dug in the ground covered with corrugated iron and earth, which afforded little protection against the 'Caterpillar Valley Barrage' that swept relentlessly down the Valley at intervals during the day and night.

On 18th July, as the troops in front struggled to take Delville Wood, Caterpillar Valley was once again under heavy fire and Leslie had gone out into nearby trenches looking for two men who had disappeared towards Longueval. After having no luck he was killed returning to his battery. Leslie Gunson was laid to rest at Quarry Cemetery, plot VI.D.4.

19TH JULY

#12933 Private Cyril George Bunclark

8TH NORFOLK REGIMENT

BACK AT DELVILLE WOOD, TROOPS had arrived to augment those who had already endured days of torment in trying to force possession of the mangled foliage and Longueval beside it. The night following Ernst Hahn's death, the whole area was under terrific artillery fire; Longueval was ablaze. New troops attempted to seize the wood again in pouring rain in conjunction with the Scottish and South Africans still inside, but had to be withdrawn 'to save them from annihilation'.

Among those about to join the fight was a tall, slim 21 year old from East Finchley. Cyril Bunclark had enlisted at St Paul's Churchyard at the height of the recruitment boom in early September 1914. He found himself placed, as did Albert Klemp and many others flooding to that centre, in a somewhat random regiment, joining the new 8th Battalion of the Norfolk Regiment.

Cyril was sent to Shorncliffe, where the manifest problems of the New Army were epitomised. Where would they sleep? How would they be fed and clothed? The men pitched in and shared everything. Sixteen men slept to each tent, between them they had perhaps two plates and a handful of cutlery, and drank from tobacco tins. More volunteers kept arriving. 'A Company would start a route march 300 strong and return with 310, and no one knew or could find out who were the new men.' Without uniforms, they sported a whole array of costume; from sailors in rough sweaters to boys in straw hats bearing Cambridge colours.

The 8th Norfolks were already familiar with the southern end of the battlefield. In action on 1st July near Montauban, the battalion suffered almost 350 casualties. Having been withdrawn, they were expecting a good long rest when an urgent call came for troops to go to the aid of the Scottish Division in Delville Wood. Cyril Bunclark's battalion was one of those selected, having seen less action than their divisional counterparts, and now, having been lightly wounded on 14th July whilst the Norfolks sat behind the main battle, he passed haggard-looking Scotsmen and South Africans who had thus far escaped the clutches of the wood on his way up.

On the morning of 19th July, Cyril's battalion was instructed to clear the southern portion of Delville Wood, deploying at an orchard on the outskirts of Longueval and pushing east. Cyril's company was to lead the attack. Moving up in file, they reached the orchard at 6:30am and in four waves prepared to enter the chaos of the wood. Half an hour later they moved off and immediately met with stubborn resistance. All the officers leading the first two waves of the company were cut down and the men were raked with both machine-gun fire and the bullets of snipers concealed within the wreckage of brambles and trees.

Several Germans surrendered as soon as they saw the Norfolks coming, but so livid were the advancing troops at the enemy's sniping methods that they simply shot them. Pushing forward to Buchanan Street, they found a resolute band of tired South African troops. In some areas the advance went on without much opposition, but at Campbell Street Cyril's company found the enemy in force, hidden in dugouts, with machine-gun nests and with yet more snipers concealed among the debris. Along the southern edge of the wood the Norfolks had met with obstinate opposition, but having been reinforced by the companies behind, they prevailed. Thirty or so Germans surrendered. 'While the remainder threw down their arms and ran round to the north side of the wood, [losing] heavily from our fire.'

By 10:45am, the south-east corner of Delville Wood had been cleared and the survivors of the 8th Norfolks took up a position 100 yards away while the spot was bludgeoned by the British artillery. As soon as the barrage lifted, they surged back inside. More machine guns, however, hampered their progress. Bombers tried desperately to silence them, but without success, although patrols reported small groups of Germans retiring to high ground to the east.

With time to breathe, Cyril Bunclark's battalion could take stock of the devastating scene around them. They found a South African hiding in a haystack 'where he had been for two days; needless to say he was more than pleased to see this portion of the wood again pass into our hands'. Another of his countrymen was discovered where he too had been lying for several days 'with a broken leg, a smashed arm and a hole in his back'.

Men attempt to dig in at Delville Wood in the summer of 1916. (Authors' collection)

Finally he was carried off to safety. Germans, South Africans, Scots, Englishmen – Delville Wood was carpeted with hundreds of wounded and dying men, littered among the remains of those already carried off by the fighting. There was only one well within the confines of the wood and the men gasped with thirst. At least one battalion received no food at all the entire time they were within the mangled trees.

The 8th Norfolks had lost another 300 men. Some two-thirds of the battalion had now been wiped off its strength in a little over two weeks and still Delville Wood had not been conquered. Cyril Bunclark was one of those consumed among the ruined foliage and never seen or heard from again. In August his mother still hadn't given up. The War Office was being inundated with correspondence from worried relatives who read daily about the struggle on the Somme. 'I apologise if I am giving you trouble,' she wrote, 'but if you could kindly inform me where my son: 12933 Pte. Cyril Bunclark is, I should be so grateful.' At that point Elizabeth Bunclark's boy had lay dead on the battlefield for almost a month. Cyril's body, if recovered, was never identified and he is commemorated on the Thiepval Memorial, Pier & Face 1c/1d.

20TH JULY
Major William La Touche Congreve VC

BRIGADE MAJOR, 76TH BRIGADE

Major 'Billy' Congreve VC.
(Authors' collection)

IN COMMAND OF THE SOUTHERN end of the British front, directly subordinate to General Rawlinson, was a Victoria Cross recipient named General Sir Walter Norris Congreve. As more troops arrived to help with the struggle that encompassed Longueval and Delville Wood, his eldest son was to come under his command.

Billy was 6ft 5in and had been born in Cheshire in 1891. He spent his early childhood in India and in Surrey before, in 1904, he was sent to Eton College. Not slow, Billy was, however, quite lazy and prone to mood swings, although he was a good oar. Perhaps inevitably given his father's occupation, he joined Walter's regiment at Tipperary in 1911. Billy was not long with the Rifle Brigade on the Western Front at the outbreak of war though, instead taking up a post as a divisional aide. It was a job that ground him down and made him feel he was not contributing to the war effort sufficiently, although he had picked up a Military Cross in 1915 and was then awarded the Distinguished Service Order for single-handedly forcing the surrender of a substantial body of Germans. He was modest about how it came about. 'Imagine my surprise and horror,' he recalled, 'when I saw a whole crowd of armed Boches ... I stood there for a moment feeling a bit sort of shy, and then I levelled my revolver at the nearest Boche and shouted, "hands up, all the lot of you!" A few went up at once, then a few more and then the lot; and I felt the proudest fellow in the world as I cursed them!'

Tired of being an aide, in December 1915 Billy was appointed Brigade Major of the 76th Brigade. A fellow old Etonian had summed up what the role entailed rather succinctly the year before. 'Brigade Major is a plum job and they do not give it to fools. It is like being adjutant to a Brigadier, you do all his dirty work for him.' Billy worked long and strenuous hours but loved it. 'Of all the jobs ... this ... is the most dear to my heart,' he said. 'I am more or less my own master ... there is unending work to do [and] there is heaps that's definite to show for it.'

Billy and his brigade were not present when his father enjoyed his comparative success on 1st July. In fact, as summer began, Billy's thoughts could not have been further from the war. He had gone home on leave and married Pamela Maude, the daughter of two actors, on 1st June and they seized the opportunity for a brief honeymoon at Beaulieu. Within days though, Billy was on his way back to the front. By the time the Battle of the Somme had commenced, he was at Saint-Omer with the rest of the brigade when they were ordered to entrain for the south to join his father's troops. Having caught up with him on arrival, Billy made off to reconnoitre his new surroundings.

On 17th July 76th Brigade had received short-notice orders to assault the village of Longueval and the north-west corner of the Delville Wood the following morning. The attack moved off at 3:45am, but the north of the village was behind too much uncut barbed wire and it was too well shielded by enemy rifles and machine guns to make a proper advance. At 4:30pm the Germans launched a counter-attack. The northern half of the village was by now completely untenable and when the enemy came

Billy Congreve's widow with her baby daughter, born eight months after her husband's death. (Authors' collection)

on in four waves the British troops withdrew to the south. Together, the combined elements of Billy's brigade managed to strengthen their positions and began digging in.

The following day things did not go well at all. General Haldane, commanding the division to which they belonged, travelled through the ruins of Montauban into the very south of Longueval, where he found brigade headquarters ensconced in a quarry. They were under a heavy artillery barrage and Billy had just returned from a dangerous visit about the village to assess the situation. He looked tired, but Haldane said nothing. 'I knew that if I said he was overworking he would scorn the idea.' Billy had worked himself into a state of exhaustion. His batman was snapping at his heels, urging him to calm down, but Billy characteristically (for they loved to snipe at each other) told him to shut up. The brigade was shelled heavily until dawn on 19th July. Headquarters was hit repeatedly with gas shells and the occupants had to evacuate. Billy was pulling casualties out of harm's way with a medical officer despite having been exposed to the gas himself (not the only instance of him attempting to help treat wounded men under heavy shellfire).

That evening orders arrived for the 76th Brigade to attack again the following morning, 20th July. At 10:30pm Billy arrived at a Suffolk battalion's headquarters to describe their task. He spoke to all officers and platoon commanders and explained that they were to push off east, clear Longueval and sweep north-east along a road running through the splintered remains of Delville Wood to gain touch with the 10th Royal Welsh Fusiliers, another of 76th Brigade's battalions. They were then to consolidate the entire area together.

Having explained the plan, Billy then went out to superintend arrangements for the attack. The Suffolks were in place by 3am but the Royal Welsh Fusiliers had a much harder time getting to their jumping off point thanks to lost guides and shoddy intelligence, and had already had to repulse two German attacks while they were trying to get ready. It was mayhem and a testament to their resolve that they managed to form up at all. To make matters worse, the leading company of Welshmen was being shot at by their own comrades because the commander of the nearby 11th Essex had not been told that friendly troops would be moving about on his front, or even that there was to be an advance.

The Suffolks went off at 3:35am and the Welshmen, despite all that they had thus far endured, ten minutes later. The Royal Welsh Fusiliers were hit hard and, because they were unable to co-operate with each other, the attack folded and the men had to be withdrawn. They fell back and dug in, changing tack from offensive to defensive. Reports coming back to the brigade from wounded men and prisoners had initially seemed to indicate that everything was going well. Then silence fell and worry began to seep in. Patrols were sent out but could not make any contact with the two companies that had gone out. It was feared that the men of 76th Brigade had been wiped out entirely.

Billy had been on the move all day trying to establish just what was actually going on. Standing on a road leading to Longueval from the west, he was attempting to get the 2nd Suffolks to secure their position. He had just about decided that he had gathered all the information he could and was looking to the higher ground in front when, from inside the cornfield he was observing, a German sniper fired a single bullet. It struck just below the breastbone and 25-year-old Billy Congreve was dead soon after he hit the ground.

His father Walter was still attempting to command the battle. Word reached a member of his staff early in the afternoon via telephone. Events at Delville Wood had reached a critical juncture and Walter was about to send his men forward again in 'a very important and very daring operation'. General Congreve had to be informed, but his keeping his head was absolutely essential for the tens of thousands of men under his command. A staff officer entered the room and gently informed the general that his eldest son had fallen:

> He was absolutely calm to all outward appearance, and after a few seconds of silence said quite calmly, 'He was a good soldier.' That is all he allowed to appear; and he continued dealing with everything as it came along in the same imperturbable and quietly decisive way as usual.

But the staff man was not at all fooled. 'You know perhaps better than I,' he wrote to a friend, 'what the loss of that son meant to him.'

Billy's servant was utterly heartbroken but fiercely determined to go up under fire and bring his body back. As he was carried away from Longueval, brigade men of the Gordon Highlanders followed with wild poppies and cornflowers to lay upon him.

Billy Congreve had excelled himself on the Somme. In the build-up to the attack he had personally reconnoitred the enemy and taken out patrols more than half a mile in front of the British lines. He also escorted one of the brigade's battalions to its jumping off point to make sure they found their way and then remained in the line of fire to get an accurate assessment of how the fighting had played out. For his example he was posthumously awarded the Victoria Cross and at 25 became the first infantry officer in the Great War to be awarded all three gallantry medals available to him.

Unbeknownst to Billy, he had left his new wife pregnant and their daughter, Pamela, was born eight months after her father's death on the Somme. Major William La Touche Congreve was laid to rest at Corbie Communal Cemetery Extension plot I.F.35.

21ST JULY
Lance Corporal Robert Henry Boughton

1ST EAST SURREY REGIMENT

WHILE THE VICIOUS FIGHT FOR Longueval and Delville Wood continued, casualties mounted elsewhere along the British front. From Longueval the line ran north-west towards High Wood and it was along this sector there sat a pre-war soldier who already bore plenty of scars thanks to the Great War. Twenty-five-year-old Bob Boughton had been born in Islington and listed his occupation variously as a labourer or a toy maker before he enlisted as a teenager in 1908. He had spent much of his service before 1914 in Burma, serving in the same battalion as his elder brother. They were still abroad when war was declared and were recalled swiftly. The 2nd East Surreys disembarked at Devonport the day before Christmas Eve 1914 and left for France a month later.

Shot in the left forearm near Ypres after less than four weeks on the Western Front, Bob found himself back in England in mid-February. While he recovered, his brother William was killed during heavy shelling at Hill 60 near Ypres. Shortly afterwards, Bob had to return to duty, joining the 1st Battalion of the regiment. The war found new ways to have an adverse effect on his health. At the end of 1915 the misery of the trenches was compounded when he was compelled to spend more than two months in Rouen recovering from a severe case of trench foot.

Fit again in time for the campaign on the Somme, on 19th July Bob's battalion received orders to go up and reinforce men who were holding the line between Longueval and High Wood. They had seen the Somme before, 'But what a change had come over the scene!' The villages that they had once viewed were gone, 'now only heaps of debris, with a mound of white stones marking the ruins of the Church in each place'. The lines they had known were unrecognisable:

High Wood viewed from Bazentin Ridge. (Alexandra Churchill)

Instead of a clearly defined system of trenches, with grassland and trees in between, there was a vast expanse of shell-torn ground, covered with deep, wide gashes ... over all were scattered bombs, unexploded shells, arms, equipment, and all the other debris which marks the trail of modern battle.

That night the men listened to the chaos at Longueval and Delville Wood on their right. There was not enough room to accommodate the battalion and more trenches had to be dug to provide shelter for them all. Bob and his comrades went to work with their shovels. They had barely settled down when they were suddenly ordered off to relieve battered troops in Longueval.

The relief was complete at 2:30am on 20th July. An hour later nearby troops once again assaulted the remains of the village and Delville Wood. Bob spent all day under heavy shellfire frantically digging and helping to improve the battalion's surroundings by burying the dead lying in and about the trenches. Merely staying put had cost the 1st East Surreys nearly fifty casualties by lunchtime.

The following day, High Wood burned nearby, 'a mass of broken, blazing trees'. Enemy aeroplanes buzzed overhead at a great height, and it was no coincidence that when they left again the German artillery began to lay down an intense barrage on the valley. Bob Boughton was once again under heavy shellfire, which ripped into one company and even took out some of their cookers. While battle raged on both sides, Bob became yet another victim of the relentless artillery duel being played out on the battlefield. His widowed mother lost her last son and Robert Boughton's body, if recovered, was never identified. He is commemorated on the Thiepval Memorial, Pier & Face 6b/c.

22ND JULY
Major-General Edward Charles Ingouville-Williams

COMMANDING 34TH DIVISION

Major General Edward Ingouville-Williams. (Authors' collection)

FIFTY-FOUR-YEAR-OLD GENERAL INGOUVILLE-WILLIAMS HAD a long and distinguished army career behind him before the onset of the Great War. He had joined The Buffs in 1881 and later transferred to the Worcestershire Regiment, serving in the Nile Expedition and the Sudan. Assuming a notable staff role in South Africa throughout the Boer War, he took part in the relief of Ladysmith and was awarded the DSO during the campaign before being appointed Commander of the School of Mounted Infantry at Longmoor. By 1916 he had been given command of 34th Division, in which Billy Disbrey served when it became the worst hit division on 1st July. The general had lost a miserable 6,380 of his men as casualties during the attack in the vicinity of La Boisselle. He was greatly saddened by the losses his battalions sustained on their over-ambitious objectives. 'Never shall I cease singing the praises,' he wrote, 'of my old 34th division, and I shall never have the same grand men to deal with.'

An infantry officer in his division said that although the general was a regular martinet, 'he was loved by every man in his command'. He recalled one incident before 1st July. A train of wagons carrying ammonal was being taken up to the front line and the general found it halted by the side of the road. When he enquired why this was so, the men told him the road was under artillery fire. 'He took charge of the first vehicle and led it through the shelled area. He never asked men to do things he would not do himself.'

On 22nd July Ingouville-Williams had left his car at Montauban and walked off to reconnoitre the ground up by Contalmaison. He was walking back around the southern edge of Mametz Wood towards his vehicle with an aide when at about 7pm he was mortally wounded by shellfire. In eulogising him, his division's historian said that he was 'an absolutely fearless man; a stern disciplinarian, but with a tender heart; he worked his men hard, but he loved them, and looked after their well-being and comfort'.

As he lay mortally wounded, Ingouville-Williams had asked that the Royal Scots Fusiliers provide the firing party at his funeral. The service was held at Warloy the following afternoon, 'You know my antipathy to bagpipes,' wrote one witness, 'but there were few dry eyes amongst those present.' A large number of the division's officers and men turned out to pay their respects, including the fighting battalions that could get away from their work. Major-General Edward Charles Ingouville-Williams was the highest ranked of all the casualties on the Somme. He left behind a widow and was laid to rest at Warloy-Baillon Communal Cemetery Extension, plot III.D.13.

23RD JULY
#4154 Private Horace William James Callaghan

9TH BATTALION, AUSTRALIAN INFANTRY FORCE

HORACE CALLAGHAN'S FATHER JAMES WAS from Salop, but had emigrated to Australia looking for work in the 1880s. Horace was his fourth son and one of nine children, born in Lithgow, New South Wales. At the age of 18, having worked as a grocer's assistant and a driver, he had attempted to sign up to go and fight in Europe but had been rejected on account of his age. Still determined, Horace then went off to Longreach, in the middle of Queensland, and found a more lenient recruiting office.

All that the authorities near Brisbane required was that his parents telegraph their permission through to the camp, and this they duly did, so that Horace became the first of his family to join the army. In January 1916 he set sail on a lengthy journey to Alexandria. From there Horace went on to Marseilles before travelling through France to Étaples, joining the 9th Battalion of the Australian Infantry Force at the end of May. Acclimatising to the Western Front was not all that some of the Australians had hoped. Those who had seen Gallipoli 'had dreams of again sleeping between sheets and breakfasting with linen tablecloths' in the civilisation of Europe. When they reached the promised land what they got was 'fifty men in a batch, through a muddy farmyard containing a vast pit of manure, into an ancient barn with a leaky tiled roof and cracked walls of timber and daubed mud, left to sleep there on the ground, in the hay-loft, amid the crowded rat holes, the shock was a sharp one'. Some of the battalion's first experiences in their new theatre of war were of trench raids, the likes of which were unknown in the Dardanelles. They were learning quickly that the Germans appeared to be a meticulous and determined foe.

On 3rd July the troops at the northern end of the battlefield had been made independent of Rawlinson and designated the Reserve Army, under General Hubert Gough. By the 14th, several divisions of Australians and one of New Zealanders were concentrated on the

A composite photograph of privates Horace (*rear*) and Stanley (*right*) Callaghan with their brothers. (Private collection)

Thompsons Paddock Camp in Queensland. (Private collection)

Somme. Selected men immediately began visiting the front lines 25 miles to the east. It was all new to Horace, and to the men who had served at Gallipoli too, for they heard terrible tales of the 'barrage' – fierce artillery bombardments that as yet they could only imagine.

On 23rd July there was to be a concerted effort made at capturing key objectives at High Wood, Longueval, Delville Wood and the village of Guillemont to the east of Trônes Wood. Standing on a ridge in about the middle of the Somme battlefield, the village of Pozières comprised a fiercely defended outpost to the original German second system and another target. After the success of 14th July around Bazentin, higher command was keen to make progress further north and capturing Pozières would be vital to this plan. Pushing the enemy away from here and Ovillers, which had fallen on 16th July, would enable guns to be moved up to better ground and, if they could take the line just beyond Pozières, Gough could cut off German observation on the ridge and take it for themselves. Small attacks on the village had, as was becoming standard on the Somme, proved to be costly failures so far. They were repeated nonetheless, gradually reducing Pozières to rubble. Now it had been ordained that on 23rd July, Australian

troops, including Horace Callaghan, would launch themselves at this position in a forceful attack as part of the wider offensive.

The Australians had been creeping ever nearer to the battlefield in preparation for their first action on the Western Front, or in Horace's case, their first experience of battle at all. Now they were instructed that just after midnight on the 23rd they would first assault enemy trenches in front of the Pozières. The second phase of their night action would look to seize the village itself. Beyond that was a third objective, formidable trenches known as the 'OG Lines'.

The 9th Australian Infantry went into British lines in front of the village a few days before the battle, finding the area liable to sweeping shellfire and 'literally choked with dead bodies, British and German'. The preliminary bombardment started on the 19th, hurling tear gas and phosgene towards the enemy troops huddled in Pozières for three days. Then it was the turn of the infantry to attack.

After being shelled in his assembly position, Horace Callaghan crept into no-man's-land in the middle of the night and deployed alongside the rest of his Queensland Battalion on lines of tape. For the first time the Australians watched the full horror of a Western Front barrage increase in ferocity to pave the way for their advance. Deafened, when it lifted they rushed through the darkness into action towards the trenches blocking them from Pozières. Only on Horace's front did they meet determined resistance, but the Australians battled on.

Within half an hour, they began clambering into the village, through abandoned back gardens. The Germans were retreating to the other end of Pozières. Supporting battalions came up, prisoners were taken, but here the Australian advance was checked. The OG Lines proved a far harder prospect.

At 5:30am an enemy counter-attack was launched. Although it was repulsed, the Germans put up a stout resistance at OG1 and OG2, with troops hiding in dugouts and manning machine-gun nests. Here the darkness had hampered the advancing Australians. The artillery barrage had ruined the ground and made it difficult to ascertain where they were. The best that they could do for the time being was secure their position back in the village. When daylight came the only gain as part of the third objective had been in a part of OG1.

Horace Callaghan was declared missing on 23rd July. Back home in New South Wales, his father began writing frantic letters looking for news of his boy. On 28th August he penned one in anger to the authorities, frustrated at a lack of communication. 'Whatever has happened,' he argued, 'the boy in question, and his two brothers, also serving, are simply fulfilling their obligations to their country. But there are also obligations due to them, and their relatives ... It appears to me that the knowledge that somewhere, something is being done, and its nature is due to myself.' All Mr Callaghan wanted was a reassurance that someone in France was concerned with finding out what had happened to his son. 'Now Sir, we all have our cross to bear in connection with this disastrous, but necessary war and the information sought would considerably lighten my load. I remain yours, for Australia.'

James Callaghan's sad torment was being mirrored in tens of thousands of homes worldwide since the advent of the Somme campaign. No trace of 19-year-old Horace Callaghan was ever discovered. Rather than the Thiepval Memorial, a separate monument stands at Villers-Bretonneux near Amiens for Australian servicemen who fell on the Western Front and have no known grave. Horace's body, if recovered, was never identified and he is one of 10,738 of his countrymen commemorated on this memorial.

24TH JULY
#1309 Sapper Edwin Victor Hatch

1/1ST CHESHIRE FIELD COMPANY, ROYAL ENGINEERS

Sapper Edwin Hatch. (Authors' collection)

EDWIN HATCH WAS THE YOUNGEST son of four in his family, born in Bromborough Pool, Cheshire, in 1892. His occupation as a wood turner and machinist meant that when he enlisted in November 1915, he was an ideal candidate for a very particular type of role in the army. The Royal Engineers was always on the lookout for practically skilled young men and he found himself posted to a field company as a sapper. The Royal Engineer field companies could be asked to turn their hand, and their initiative, to almost anything in preparation for action, after it had subsided or as battle raged around them. He had only arrived on the Western Front in the middle of May and as the Somme offensive began, the 1/1st Cheshire Field Company arrived in the area on 6th July.

Since then their backbreaking work had epitomised the diversity of Edwin's role. Since 7th July this company had been engaged in making notice boards and other joinery work, working on communication trenches, deepening other lines, forming dumps of materials for future use, attempting to blow up captured German field guns in Caterpillar Valley, constructing strong points, making bridges for horses and wagons and others sturdy enough to support artillery, cutting wire in front of old enemy lines and making or repairing tracks for traffic to get across the valley. In that time, three weeks, they had had just one day of rest and two standing by to be ready for action during which they had not been called upon.

When the next staged advance on the Somme went forward on 23rd July, the infantry on Edwin's front made initial progress, but were eventually forced back, subjected to heavy counter-attacks. Whilst Horace Callaghan and the Australian contingent were clinging to their gains in Pozières, the Fourth Army to the south of them was flailing. Troops were attacking ground that they had never even seen before; this was doubly hard within a lot of units, where new drafts had arrived and the men lacked experience. Orders were received late, planning was ill conceived and start times varied randomly up and down the line, leaving the whole advance with a distinct lack of cohesion that meant it didn't resemble a large-scale attack at all but lots of small ones.

The brigade that Edwin Hatch's field company had been attached to had been told it would not be required during the assault of the 23rd, and so the sappers' plan was to go out and resume work repairing the road between Carnoy and Montauban. As the sections were about to move off though, orders were received to recall all working parties of engineers, so that they could proceed to work on a half-finished trench at the northern end of Trônes Wood. They marched off in the early evening and met 200 infantry of Billy Congreve's 76th Brigade, where they began work under shellfire. As darkness fell Edwin Hatch was mortally wounded. His fellow sappers managed to get him as far to the rear as Bernafay Wood, but he died of his wounds inside before they could find help. Edwin had survived just fifty-eight days at the front. A nearby chaplain oversaw his burial in the north-east corner of the wood, but Edwin Hatch's grave was subsequently lost and if he was recovered again, his body was never identified. He is commemorated on the Thiepval Memorial, Pier & Face 8a/8d.

25TH JULY

#7612 Sergeant Reginald James Minahan

1ST GLOUCESTERSHIRE REGIMENT

Sergeant Reginald Minahan.
(Authors' collection)

BORN IN GLOUCESTER IN 1887, Reginald Minahan was raised by his grandparents in Clarence Terrace and by an uncle, Jimmy, who was secretary of East Midlands Rugby, dapper in his bowler hat and destined to be a member of the RFU committee after the war. Reginald joined the Gloucestershire Regiment in 1904 and made the most of the affinity for rugby that he shared with his uncle during his time in the army. A flanker who was present in the first fifteen when the regiment won the Army Rugby Cup in 1910, he had even played in Toulouse and in France several times, including at the head of a Midlands Wanderers team. Even at the front he had continued playing, as the Gloucesters managed to take on scratch sides from other battalions, teams from the supply lines and even artillery brigades.

Having left the army, Reginald was working for Michelin in London when war was declared. His old battalion was ordered to mobilise on the afternoon of 4th August. As a reservist, he wasted no time at all in jumping on a train bound for the West Country and was the first to arrive at the depot in Bristol, reporting for duty before midnight. Reginald had been badly wounded on 9th May during the fighting at Aubers Ridge. After failed attempts the battalion was eventually ordered to retire to its original trenches, but he was fit again in time for when the Gloucesters were called to the Somme.

The Fourth Army was trying busily to deal with the consequences of failure up and down the line on 23rd July. Although it was not instructed to attack on the 23rd, Reginald's division was now ordered to make an assault on Munster Alley, which was proving to be a particularly problematic trench, one that ran into the difficult OG Lines, where the Australians were still in action and enduring savage fighting at close quarters.

The 1st Gloucesters had reached Contalmaison to the rear of this sector on 14th July. The attack carried out on the 23rd, like most of those up and down the line, had failed. At 7:30pm that night orders were received for Reginald Minahan and his battalion to assist in replacing the tired men who had made the assault and were now ensconced in the old German line. They set off at 5:30am and by 10am on the 24th they were in the trenches on the right of the brigade front, being shelled heavily. 'Life here was as exciting as the most ardent fire-eater could desire,' one officer commented.

In the meantime a conference was being held to plan another assault that night, in which the Gloucesters would support a battalion of South Wales Borderers advancing on a portion of Munster Alley at 2am on the 25th, while other troops continued to try to take the OG Lines beyond Pozières to their left. In spite of a heavy bombardment, a strategically placed machine gun halted the Welsh attack. Throughout the day yet more intense shelling by the enemy came down on the whole front. Two German counter-attacks came at the Australians, who were engaged in much heavier scrapping, and on one of them the Gloucesters were able to assist them by raking their attackers with a Lewis gun.

The Gloucesters were withdrawn that evening, having suffered nearly fifty casualties without even attacking. With two others, Reginald Minahan was killed as he prepared to depart the line. Thirty years old, he was about to receive a commission. He was laid to rest at Contalmaison Chateau Cemetery, plot II.D.3.

26TH JULY
#11274 Lance Corporal Percy Williams

2ND WELSH REGIMENT

PERCY WILLIAMS WAS A 20-YEAR-OLD colliery worker from South Wales, driving an engine at Gwaun-cae-Gurwen. Born in Cardiff and educated at the National School in Swansea, he enlisted particularly early, ten days after war broke out, and arrived on the Western Front in February 1915.

As the Gloucesters were withdrawn from the fight for Munster Alley and Reginald Minahan fell, it was the turn of another band of Welshmen to enter the fray when his battalion, the 2nd Welsh Regiment, relieved the South Wales Borderers in the line. That night they were to attack Munster Alley shortly after midnight, but their advance was postponed for two hours because of confusion in the trenches owing to the number of wounded lying in them. Two hours later they rushed forward with no preliminary bombardment in the hope that it would catch the German machine gunners by surprise and ease their path. They got nowhere.

During the morning, news of Australian progress on their left came in and Percy's battalion was ordered to commence bombing up Munster Alley to attempt to link up with them. At first they gained 250 yards of trench and appeared to have reached their objective, but the Germans counter-attacked with their own bombs and also over open ground. In spite of inflicting heavy losses on the enemy with their Lewis guns, the Welsh were exhausted and were driven back to their original position, where they set about consolidating a portion of Munster Alley that was now in British hands.

Percy Williams was reported wounded and missing after the day's fighting and was later assumed to have been killed on 26th July. His body, if recovered, was never identified and he is commemorated on the Thiepval Memorial, Pier & Face 7a/10a.

27TH JULY
#F/32 Private William Jonas

17TH MIDDLESEX REGIMENT

Private William Jonas. (Private collection)

BORN IN 1890 IN NORTHUMBERLAND, the son of a miner, William Jonas had followed his father and taken up work at Cambois Colliery before becoming a professional footballer. He signed a contract with Clapton Orient in 1912 and was so popular with the female fan base that he felt the need to have the club publish a statement in a match day programme to say that, while he appreciated their letters, he was a happily married man. After being harangued in the press, the footballing profession decided to take action against criticism that players, supposedly the most able-bodied men in the country, were not enlisting in high enough numbers. In November 1914, Chelsea, Millwall and Orient instigated meetings in West London to discuss what they could do together to encourage enlistment. More clubs joined them, along with officials from the FA, two West London MPs and the Mayor of Fulham. They formed a committee and decided they would approach the War Office officially with regard to forming a specific battalion for footballers to join. It was a variation on a theme already occurring up and down the country, that of the Pals battalion.

On 15th December some 500 men congregated at Fulham Town Hall, a few yards from Stamford Bridge, to discuss the formation of the 17th Middlesex Regiment. Good progress was made. Officials represented a whole spectrum of London football clubs, including Chelsea, Fulham, Orient, Tottenham, Arsenal, Millwall and Crystal Palace. Clubs would need to be sympathetic, both for the players wanting to go and in giving up their time and facilities to help recruit men. Players would have to have Saturdays off too, to fulfil their club commitments until the end of the season still in progress. Train fares would have to be covered to get men back to the appropriate grounds in time for kick-off at the weekend.

At the December meeting, Fred 'Spider' Parker, the Clapton Orient captain, a married man with three children, was the first to commit to joining the battalion. Frank Buckley of Bradford City followed, as did another player from Brighton. After gentle prodding and more stirring words more men stood up and as the meeting concluded thirty-five players had expressed their intention to serve, including William Jonas. In all more than forty men connected with Clapton Orient would volunteer to serve with the battalion, which arrived on the Western Front in November 1915.

The 24th July 1916 was a dull and cloudy day on the Somme, riddled again with heavy artillery fire on both sides. At 3:45pm Sir Douglas Haig arrived for a conference nearby and insisted on the importance of consolidating the positions already held and of clearing Longueval and Delville Wood of enemy troops. William Jonas and the Footballer's Battalion were about to be among the newest additions to the fighting in this poisonous spot.

On the 27th four British battalions attacked in two waves following a stiff bombardment of more than 100,000 shells. The first deluge rushed through the shaken Germans still occupying Delville Wood and an hour later the second passed through their compatriots on their way further into the bedlam. They began trying furiously to consolidate their position under less opposition than they might have expected and the wood was largely back in British hands when men of the Royal Fusiliers pushed on and cleared the Germans en masse out of its northern section, taking nearly 200 prisoners. The Allies alone had had nearly 400 guns trained on Delville Wood throughout the day in an attempt to clear it, but the enemy was not about to back down. The German artillery too had no qualms about smashing the remains of the trees and undergrowth to pieces with artillery.

The Footballer's Battalion, players and fans alike, had spent 26th July digging and resting near Bernafay Wood, subjected to gas alarms as the Germans were using these particularly monstrous shells further forward. Almost 900 men of the 17th Middlesex watched more than two dozen aeroplanes buzzing like wasps, criss-crossing, diving upon each other in the evening, under orders to move at short notice should they be needed to support the attack transpiring on Delville Wood.

As early as 11am on the 27th, William Jonas' battalion received orders to go forward to help drive the Germans out of the wood. Gathering up rifles and equipment, he and the rest of the men prepared for their most daunting task yet. Off they marched via Montauban and Trônes Wood, towards the hellish bombardment going on in front of them, the crashing of artillery shells becoming louder and louder as they approached the fierce fighting ahead.

As the men of the 17th Middlesex trudged towards the right hand side of the wood, weighed down with ammunition, bombs and petrol cans full of drinking water to share out with those already inside, the sheer volume of shellfire made it extremely difficult for the likes of the Footballer's Battalion to get to those dwindling troops trying to cling on to their tenuous position. Further back a pile of ammunition burned, struck by the German artillery; one gun team watched two men and two of their horses smashed to pulp. Finally, at 5:15pm, two companies of the 17th Middlesex and two of the 17th Royal Fusiliers managed to get through, though suffering heavily on the way up.

A fellow Clapton Orient man named Richard McFadden who was with Jonas later recalled that they found themselves pinned down in a trench. 'Willie turned to me and said "Goodbye Mac. Special love to my Sweetheart Mary Jane and best regards to the lads at Orient."' They were the last words that William spoke to him. 'Before I could [reply] he was up and over. No sooner had he jumped up out of the trench, my best friend of nearly twenty years was killed before my eyes. Words cannot express my feelings as this time.' Dick McFadden had just three months to live himself.

By smashing Delville Wood with an obscene amount of guns, the British Army had, although it turned out only to be temporarily, managed to subdue the Germans inside. Yet more men would need to be sent inside, though, if it was to be captured properly. Three players from Clapton Orient would fall during the war in total. William Jonas' body, if recovered, was never identified and he is commemorated on the Thiepval Memorial, Pier & Face 12d/13b.

The Footballer's Battalion Memorial, Longueval. (Andrew Holmes)

28TH JULY

#59 Lance Sergeant Nicholas Caesar 'Corsellis' Lawton

22ND ROYAL FUSILIERS

BY MIDNIGHT ALMOST THE ENTIRE Footballer's Battalion was occupying a position roughly in the centre of Delville Wood. Elsewhere in its environs there were several battalions of the Royal Fusiliers still battling on and among them was a unique recruit. Almost 40 years old when he enlisted at Shepherd's Bush, West London, Corsellis Lawton was an accountant who had been educated at Repton School. From Sorley, in Yorkshire, this wasn't the first time he'd volunteered to join the army, having served with the South African Constabulary for two years during the Boer War. A divorcee, Corsellis' wife, the mother of his two sons, had petitioned for divorce after fourteen years of marriage in 1910. Since then he had spent time living in France prior to the outbreak of war. Wounded at Souchez in March 1916 when fragments of a shell that landed nearby hit his back and shoulder, Corsellis rejoined his battalion in time to go to the Somme, before which he had found time to take a second wife, a Frenchwoman in Paris.

Corsellis was a machine gunner and his battalion did not attack as a unit during this period of fighting in Delville Wood. Scrapping was confused, with small bands being sent to troublesome spots. Other men found themselves split into companies and employed as carrying parties, although throughout the course of the 27th, Corsellis' entire battalion would be thrown into the fight. By the end of the day nearly 200 men were dead, wounded or unaccounted for and all the carrying parties had been scraped together to form a force of 250 men to help continue the fight within the wood.

On 28th July the situation in the north-east corner of Delville Wood remained confusing. At 7:40am a message from the Footballer's Battalion arrived at headquarters reporting German troops massing at the east end of Delville Wood for what might be a counter-attack. The response was to bludgeon that spot with yet more shells. By mid-morning officers within the wood were advising brigade commanders that the enemy had penetrated far inside the remains of the trees and that the men were coming under increasing pressure on their left from incessant artillery fire from the direction of Guillemont to the south-east.

'Every endeavour should be made to hold the wood' was the instruction being handed down to Corsellis Lawton and the men within, but this hardly accounted for any impetus coming from the German side. By midday his brigadier, who had now assumed control of the area completely, was dispatching news up the chain of command of a horrendous barrage coming from the German lines. Rapid rifle and machine-gun fire poured into the British ranks, but the artillery pitched in and came to their aid and the troops inside the wood dug in their heels and clung on. In the darkness the scene was one of utter confusion.

When the din of shell and machine-gun fire finally died down late in the evening, the strength of the 22nd Royal Fusiliers was given as just eighteen officers and 400 men, although a few more continued to drift in. Thanks to their efforts, the British flank was held up, 'and unless this had been accomplished the wood would have been lost almost before it was won'. A fellow machine gunner reported Corsellis Lawton as having been killed, but his body, if recovered, was never identified and he is commemorated on the Thiepval Memorial, Pier & Face 8c/9a & 16a.

29TH JULY
#61876 Sapper Thomas Blakeley
82ND FIELD COMPANY, ROYAL ENGINEERS

THOMAS BLAKELEY WAS A CARPENTER and joiner in his early thirties from Lancashire. Enlisting at home in Preston, he was quickly singled out for the Royal Engineers. Leaving his wife Harriet and two little boys, aged 6 and 2, Thomas sailed for France in July 1915 with the 82nd Field Company.

On 29th July, he and his section were hard at work at a junction on the road from Bazentin-le-Petit and Longueval, south of High Wood. The infantry of 19th Division, to which the field company belonged, had been sorely tried by enemy artillery throughout the previous week. Lacking cover, the sappers had gone out to help dig new trench lines, but under dangerous circumstances they could not make them deep enough for occupation. While infantry rotated in and out of the

The Nine Brave Men Memorial featuring Sapper Thomas Blakeley's name. (Andrew Holmes)

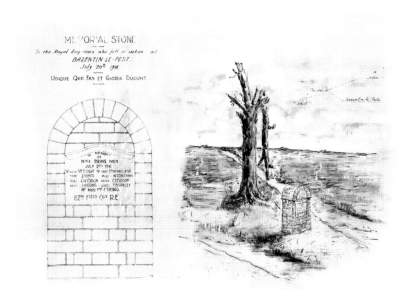

Plans for the Nine Brave Men Memorial. (Courtesy of the Commonwealth War Graves Commission)

lines on the 29th, after dark Thomas was out forming dumps of barbed wire for later use on their front before he moved to take up work at Crucifix Corner, a dangerously exposed spot to the rear. There was heavy fighting going on at High Wood to the north that night and shelling was prevalent. Finishing work, the men split up into small groups of three or four, a contingency designed to minimise casualties if stray ordnance came their way. No sooner had they separated for the walk home, than a shell plunged into the middle of Thomas' section, impacting a much wider area and causing two dozen casualties.

Several men were simply obliterated, including 34-year-old Thomas. Attempts were made to find them the following day, but all that was discovered was a loose, gruesome collection of indeterminable body parts where the men had been walking.

Before the company left the area, an officer marked the spot and vowed to return and put up something in memory of the men killed. He later had a stone engraved at the Divisional Workshop and in 1917, using bricks from nearby ruins, a memorial was built to the six killed on 29th July, Thomas among them, and three other members of the company.

Thomas' younger son, John, also died during the war, aged 5, during the influenza epidemic raging at the end of 1918. Harriet was with him as he passed away and spent 11th November 1918 not celebrating peace but registering the death of her little boy. With no remains to be buried, as well as on the Nine Brave Men memorial, her husband Thomas was commemorated on the Thiepval Memorial, Pier & Face 8a/8d.

30TH JULY
Captain Leslie Stafford Charles
60TH SQUADRON, ROYAL FLYING CORPS

Captain Leslie Charles. (Authors' collection)

AERIAL WARFARE ON A LARGE scale hadn't even existed at the beginning of the Great War, but by 1916 the role of the airman: directing artillery, constantly photographing enemy positions, bombing and monitoring infantry progress, had become vital. Innovations and tactics rapidly progressed as pilots and observers established their place in modern battle. The pendulum of aerial supremacy swung back and forth. Ostensibly, as the Great War progressed, the airmen's work was so critical that whoever ruled the skies could stake a claim to rule the battlefield below. Rival air services now deemed it essential to attack each other's machines to prevent them fulfilling their tasks and in turn they had begun to fly in packs, scouts protecting the working machines, destroying the enemy before he destroyed them, chasing each other out of the sky. The Great War was bringing about the advent of the fighter pilot.

In 1916 the Royal Flying Corps would enjoy a dominance on the Somme in the height of summer that caused the Germans to completely reorganise their air operations. Germany wrought misery on British airmen during 1915, led by men such as the since fallen ace Max Immelmann. In time for 1916, the British air services, the Royal Flying Corps for the army and the Royal Naval Air Service for the Navy, had learned valuable tactical lessons, improved their aircraft and steeled themselves to take the aerial initiative and support the offensive on the Somme. Since before 1st July, airmen had worked tirelessly to support the infantry attacks in every capacity that they could. Mounting hours spent aloft were exhausting. Nerves frayed quickly and life expectancy was pitifully short.

Based with Haig's headquarters was a group of squadrons that covered many aspects of aerial work: reconnaissance for GHQ, distant bombing raids and a meticulous offensive aimed at enemy machines. With one of these latter squadrons was a 20-year-old pilot who had only just arrived on the front at the end of July. From Stanmore, Middlesex, and educated at Harrow, where he went on a mathematics scholarship, Leslie Charles had been head of his house, a member of the school OTC and of the Philatelic Club. His was a typically glowing, physically active profile of a public school pilot in the Great War.

Having originally joined the Worcestershire Regiment straight from school in summer 1914, Leslie had served at Gallipoli during the third battle for Krithia, only arriving on the peninsula the week before. He was also in action during the attack on Chunuk Bair at the beginning of August, where his battalion suffered almost 800 casualties. He was invalided home later in the month with shellshock, having spent a prolonged stint under fire in the trenches. 'The battalion has been 27 days in the firing line straight off the reel,' wrote one of his fellow officers. 'Even Charles has gone back to the base with a touch of nerve shock.' It seemed hardly surprising when his recent stint in the Dardanelles was put into perspective:

Poor Charles, he did stick it magnificently, until it became too much for him. He had an extremely hot corner to hang on to throughout the Saturday and Sunday following the advance, and, although his platoon was under an incessant shell and rifle fire, he kept them well in hand. Eventually shells began dropping actually in the trench, after knocking down his parapets and machine gun emplacements; one shell killed four, wounded another and knocked off Charles' hat, leaving him for a moment practically speechless. He never gave way until relieved, and his line is still intact.

Leslie joined the Royal Flying Corps at the beginning of 1916 and took his pilot's licence in April before leaving for the Western Front. There, on 21st July, he joined 60 Squadron, piloting a Morane biplane. Not exactly a cutting edge machine, it didn't handle particularly well and was prone to stalling.

On his arrival air activity was building, with the Germans desperate to stop the destruction being exacted on their vital infrastructure by rampant Allied airmen. Leslie took his first trip over the lines on 26th July with several other members of his squadron and did well, helping two of his comrades to drive off an enemy machine. He spent the next few days twiddling his thumbs, as inclement weather prevented patrols. Then, on the evening of 30th July, he took off again.

Four machines, including Leslie's, battled twelve of the enemy over Saint-Quentin. Aeroplanes were highly temperamental and the 20 year old and his observer were last seen descending into the German lines with engine trouble; blue smoke pouring behind them: 'Which would mean,' his squadron leader explained to Leslie's family, 'not that the machine was on fire, but that a bullet had pierced one of the cylinders. The machine, as I say, was going down under perfect control.' He was not able to witness Leslie come to ground though, and finally, in October the Germans confirmed he had died of wounds in their hands on 30th July. In an example sadly too common on the Western Front, Captain Charles had survived just over a week at the front and taken part in precisely two flights. He was respectfully laid to rest by the enemy at Roisel Communal Cemetery Extension, plot II.L.3.

31ST JULY
Lieutenant Cecil Stanley Oliver
2ND AUSTRALIAN MACHINE GUN COMPANY

Lieutenant Cecil Oliver. (Australian National War Memorial)

CECIL OLIVER WAS A 23-YEAR-OLD builder from the Melbourne suburbs. A member of the Malvern Rifle Club, he had also spent two years with a territorial artillery unit before, waiting for his parents to take a trip to Queensland, he volunteered to go to war in 1915. Like Leslie Charles, Cecil had been invalided to England from Gallipoli. He suffered painful stomach problems owing to dysentery picked up in the squalor of the Dardanelles. It took weeks for him to be able to resume a normal diet and it was not until February 1916 that he managed to rejoin his unit, which had by then been evacuated to Egypt.

Cecil initially served in a machine-gun company within the 6th Australian Infantry Battalion, but it was becoming increasingly obvious that, as the industrialised nature of the war progressed and the dominance of the machine gun was established in the tight, static landscape of the trenches, their function called for expansion. At the end of 1915 it was approved that, rather than serving within a battalion, gunners with mounted machine guns, who by now were recognised as specialists, should be withdrawn and come under the newly instigated banner of the Machine Gun Corps. In infantry terms, one company would be attached to each brigade; one to every four infantry battalions.

Cecil joined the 2nd Australian Brigade's Machine Gun Company in March 1916. As he arrived on the Somme, he wrote home to say he had heard that his transfer had been approved to join the flying services, but he was awaiting news of his departure and so work carried on as normal. The Australians planned to expand upon their gains at Pozières, but as a result of being the only success story among numerous failures on 23rd July, the Germans focused their attentions fully on them in the aftermath. The enemy wanted the village back, with all of its defensive benefits, and made several attempts on the 23rd alone. Cecil and his machine-gun company left for the forward lines and came into the line at a strong point nearby on 25th July. The outgoing troops were exhausted, having been in action since zero hour more than forty-eight hours before.

Throughout the 26th, the village was showered with artillery shells. In the early evening, believing that the rate of fire could only mean that an attack was imminent, the Australians appealed for a counter-barrage. British and Australian gunners leapt into action. The Germans met their fire in kind and it was not until late in the night that it finally began to die down. Harrowed Australians had never experienced such savagery. Trenches dug in the morning had been smashed into oblivion by the evening.

It then remained to count the cost of the artillery bombardment and the enemy fire that the 2nd Machine Gun Company had been forced to endure. Cecil had been shot in the chest. As the rest of the company began to march back towards Albert, he was evacuated to a field ambulance.

Horace Callaghan and Cecil Oliver were just two casualties inflicted upon the 1st Australian Division. In the opening throes at Pozières the formation suffered more than 5,000 casualties in their first fully fledged action away from Gallipoli. Those that watched them march out were horrified. 'They looked like men who had been in Hell. Almost without exception each man looked drawn and haggard, and so dazed that they appeared to be walking in a dream.' It had been a harrowing introduction to the Western Front. When they reached the rear, they collapsed into a state of quiet exhaustion. 'They were like boys emerging from long illness. Many lay quietly apart from the others, rolled in their blankets under the trees, reading books, smoking, writing … letters.' Lieutenant Cecil Stanley Oliver died of his wounds on 31st July and was laid to rest at Warloy-Baillon Communal Cemetery Extension, plot I.D.13.

1ST AUGUST
#132430 Sapper Samuel Gomersall

183RD TUNNELLING COMPANY, ROYAL ENGINEERS

DIGGING UNDER ENEMY POSITIONS WAS a siege warfare tactic that had been employed over hundreds of years. In January 1915, the Germans detonated a series of mines south of the La Bassée Canal that prompted the War Office to sanction the creation of specialist tunnelling companies of the Royal Engineers; comprising of miners and other workers with suitable specialist skills, such as those involved with sewer or tunnel construction. The perceived urgency of the situation saw recruits almost bypass the usual military recruitment process. One of the early groups of tunnellers moved from working on civilian construction projects to working under the front in just four days in February 1915. In addition to civilian recruits, existing battalions from mining areas were scoured for soldiers with suitable experience and, by the end of 1915, thirteen tunnelling companies had been formed.

Samuel Gomersall was a 40-year-old miner from Darfield in Yorkshire who enlisted in Pontefract on 30th September 1915. Within a week he was at the Royal Engineers' headquarters at Chatham, Kent where he was appointed a tunneller's mate and was put on a salary of 2s 2d per day. By 30th October, just a month after enlisting, Samuel was in France and had been placed with the 183rd Tunnelling Company. The British engaged five such companies on the Somme and allocated each its own sector. The 183rd Tunnelling Company was responsible for the area between Carnoy and Maricourt on the southern part of the front.

With no mines to place on its frontage, before the offensive on 1st July the 183rd Tunnelling Company was responsible for the construction of a series of Russian saps in its sector; tunnels dug out into no-man's-land

A tunneller in action. (Simon Jones)

just beneath the surface. Once dug all the way across, the sap offered a covered tunnel suitable for moving troops or other equipment across no-man's-land into the enemy trenches after capture. Some of these saps constructed by the 183rd Tunnelling Company were also used to house forward machine-gun emplacements and even flame-throwers, which would be used by the British for the first time as the attack commenced.

On 1st July one officer and six men from the 183rd Tunnelling Company went over with the attacking troops in their sector. They entered all German mine shafts, cutting all leads and wiring, and disarmed forty to fifty Germans and sent them back to the British lines. The 183rd Tunnelling Company was able to spend the first week of July exploring and surveying the abandoned German tunnel galleries at Mametz and Carnoy and collecting German plant and equipment. Work was also undertaken to connect the German tunnel networks with those of the British.

In addition to the offensive works, tunnelling companies also worked on other engineering projects required by the army. For the remainder of July, Samuel Gomersall and the 183rd Tunnelling Company were responsible for sinking new wells at Carnoy, Montauban and Mametz; constructing new dugouts and road repairs between Mametz and Bernafay Wood.

Samuel was wounded some time at the end of July or on 1st August 1916. It is not clear how he was wounded, but he was treated and ultimately died of his injuries at the 36th Casualty Clearing Station at Heilly on 1st August 1916. In August 1917 his possessions, amounting to photos and cards, a watch, a small pocket case, a tobacco pouch and bag, were sent to his sister Annie in Castleford. Samuel Gomersall was laid to rest at Heilly Station Cemetery, plot II.E.24.

2ND AUGUST
#26712 Private John Arthur Facer

90TH MACHINE GUN COMPANY, MACHINE GUN CORPS

JOHN FACER WAS A 40-YEAR-OLD fishmonger from Yorkshire. Unmarried, he lived with a sister some fifteen years his senior in Bridlington. Having enlisted in May 1915 he was placed in the East Yorkshire Regiment and went off to Redcar for training. While there he began to specialise as a machine gunner and, in February 1916, John was transferred to the Machine Gun Corps and relocated to Grantham to complete his preparations for life at the front. By August 1916, he had been in France for nearly five months and, serving in a company alongside the likes of Eric Measham's battalion of Manchesters, in early July had come through numerous actions on the Somme and was unscathed by the month's end.

At noon on 26th July, Rawlinson met with the French to hash out details of the next joint offensive at the southern end of his line. The French were eager, planning to attack both north and south of the river in force, and Haig wanted Guillemont taken as soon as possible. It was decided that a combined effort would be launched on Maurepas in the French sector, after the British had taken Falfemont Farm and up to Guillemont. Once again John Facer would be in the thick of the action as he and his company of machine gunners would advance with the infantry through another division towards the village. As they moved up on the night of the 29th, the Germans lay down a heavy bombardment on Trônes Wood, from which they were to emerge.

Zero hour came at 4:45am. On 30th July, John was helping to man one of six guns ready for battle as they stared into a thick mist. Visibility was down to just 40 yards. Infantry and machine gunners alike ploughed through the fog and entered Guillemont from the south-west, emerging from Trônes Wood, although men were hampered severely by a crossfire of machine guns from both the quarry and the station, where uncut wire also delayed any attempts at advance. Still, the 90th Brigade forged on through the village, its machine-gun company included, repulsing a counter-attack. It was largely operating alone, for the artillery were reluctant to lay down a heavy barrage on the position because of the British troops inside the village. 'A withdrawal was followed by a fresh advance ... but the effort only resulted in fresh losses.'

It was an all too familiar tale for those trying to wrench Guillemont from enemy hands. Information as to the progress of the attack was not easy to transmit to the rear, and for some time headquarters received no news at all. With mist cloaking the battlefield and communication wires cut, units were reliant on pigeons to ferry back messages. In hot sunshine, and under a heavy barrage, the men within spent the rest of the day organising the line so far as it had been established, but Guillemont remained unconquered. It is little wonder that the attack made on 30th July should have taken almost the exact course of action as that on the 23rd, because the conditions under which it was delivered were practically the same.

British losses had been very heavy. The machine guns had had mixed success, but only one had got into the village. Others got close but, by then, Guillemont was being evacuated again. Three guns had to be buried in a sunken road so that men could go back up and recover them later. Mortally wounded on 30th July, John Facer died of his wounds on 2nd August at a casualty clearing station. He was laid to rest at Corbie Communal Cemetery Extension, plot II.A.12.

3RD AUGUST

#729 Private Wesley George Wade

17TH BATTALION, AUSTRALIAN INFANTRY FORCE

WESLEY WADE HAD LIED ABOUT his age to join up, travelling 30 miles from his home in Sydney to do so and listing his occupation as a carpenter. Wesley's father had run off and deserted the family in 1912, and Wesley's mother didn't know if he was dead or alive, so at the time of his enlistment she was raising her family alone. Her son reached Marseilles on 23rd March 1916 after a brief stop in Egypt after the Dardanelles had already been evacuated. When the Australians bedded in on the Western Front in more northerly areas of France, Wesley was wounded slightly in his left eye on 23rd April.

Without him, during the last week in July his outfit moved up to take over the front line to the east of Pozières from Horace Callaghan's battalion. Unlike the units they were replacing, Wesley's had no experience of a major offensive operation, the most complicated manoeuvre they had been involved in thus far being the evacuation of Gallipoli. Since arriving on the Somme front though, the 17th Battalion had already been engaged in localised fighting. Most notably, this included a fierce bomb-throwing contest that occurred as Reginald Minahan and Percy Williams were scrapping for Munster Alley on 25th and 26th July, where all modernity was cast out in favour of old-fashioned survival of the fittest, 'each side being as dependant as the Homeric Greeks and Trojans on their sheer strength and endurance'.

Having been sent back to a hospital at Étaples to recover, Wesley spent a suspiciously long time at the base after his recovery, possibly because someone had an inkling that he was extremely young. He rejoined the 17th Battalion on 1st August to find that the position was ostensibly the same as when the initial Australian attackers had left it. The Germans sat on the crest of the ridge in the OG Lines, the Australians faced them and were preparing to attack again.

Wesley's would not be an easy task; advancing out of a salient from cramped positions in the face of the German artillery. In fact, the brigade was already so exhausted by the constant shelling, bomb throwing, digging and carrying that a suggestion was put up to have at least part of it relieved. The commander simply explained that is was his 'desire, and, I am sure, the wish of all, that the whole of the battalions of my Brigade should remain and play the part allotted to them'.

And so on his arrival Wesley found the rest of the men exhausted, not through having done battle, but in the main through having to lie in the range of the German artillery for days on end. 'There they live and are slowly pounded to death,' surmised one of his countrymen. The bombardment for the next charge had begun the day before Wesley's return. The men were digging assembly trenches like mad and

Private Wesley Wade (*back row, centre*). (Australian National War Memorial)

reinforcing their communications through Pozières, trying to rectify the dual issues of maintaining contact with their headquarters and evacuating the wounded that had occurred during the last attack. The 17th Battalion was still preparing to help assault the OG Lines again when Wesley was injured on the morning of 3rd August. Medical personnel rushed him to the nearest field ambulance, but he would never now go 'over the top' to have a go at the Germans despite travelling half the world to do so. Wesley Wade was dead before he arrived. The 17 year old had survived forty-eight hours on the Somme. He was laid to rest at Contalmaison Chateau Cemetery, plot II.D.1.

4TH AUGUST

#30185 Private Thomas William Collingwood

1/6TH WEST YORKSHIRE REGIMENT

THE LINE AT THE NORTHERN end of the battlefield had barely progressed at all since 1st July. Since then it had been the scene of sporadic, vicious artillery bombardments or localised intense, but essentially unprofitable fighting aimed at holding fast or perhaps edging forward the line slightly. Other than that, as the artillery in the area helped occupy potential reinforcements that could move south on the enemy front by harassing them with their fire, roads were improved, trenches dug and communications secured.

Since Oswald Webb's Ulster Division had pulled out of the line, shattered, on the night of 3rd July, part of the sector by Thiepval had transferred from Irish hands to those of the 49th (West Riding) Division. Tall and fair, Thomas Collingwood was one of the youngest of nearly a dozen children from a large family in Tow Law, near Consett in County Durham. The son of a coal hewer in a family where all the men and boys worked in the mine, he was a labourer before the war. Enlisting into the Durham Light Infantry at Newcastle in December 1915, once Thomas got to France though, as was the case with thousands of reinforcements arriving at the front, he went where he was needed and, a specialist bomber, he was routed to the 1/6th West Yorkshire Regiment.

Throughout August, Rawlinson's Fourth Army was to take the lead role in the Somme Offensive, but scrapping continued on Gough's front. With it, casualties mounted in miserable circumstances brought about by attritional warfare. Haig wanted to wear down the enemy here before another large-scale advance in September. He believed that nothing more could be gained unless the conditions were just so before going forward, after meticulous preparation and not without his troops steeling themselves for any counter-attacks to prevent inevitable losses. Not to put too much strain on anyone, but he also wanted the enemy chipped away at like this while expending the least amount of

men and equipment possible. Such perfection in balance was a tall order and one that his generals could not, as it turned out, carry through.

Thomas Collingwood and his battalion were carrying out training at the northern end of the battlefield behind Thiepval and Beaumont Hamel until they were called up on 3rd August and moved into trenches facing the fearsome Leipzig Salient, formed by a bend in the German lines on the long slopes of a spur and to which the enemy appeared to attach much importance, to the south of Thiepval. No offensive was in the offing, but as usual there was endless backbreaking work to be done to maintain or better the lines and to be ready should the enemy attack. Preparations were made to start on a new dugout on the 4th, using the elaborate German model, as advancing past some of these during the battle so far had revealed all manner of luxuries, in both amenities and protection, that hitherto the British could only have dreamed of. As Thomas began work, the trenches were heavily shelled, others were blown in to the extent that they were completely uninhabitable. During the course of the day, Thomas Collingwood was killed. His would become an all too common story for thousands of men who were to be sent into battle for the remainder of the campaign. The 21 year old had survived less than a month after being sent to reinforce the numbers on the Somme. He was laid to rest at Authuile Military Cemetery, plot F.31.

5TH AUGUST

#6044 Private William Fenton

5TH (PRINCESS CHARLOTTE OF WALES'S) DRAGOON GUARDS

BORN AT CASTLEBLANEY IN COUNTY MONAGHAN, right on the border with County Armagh, 23-year-old William Fenton was a cabinetmaker. His family having relocated to Scotland, he had actually enlisted in the cavalry in Stirling almost immediately on the outbreak of war. Posted to an illustrious regiment of Dragoon Guards, he was sent to Aldershot for training before joining it at the front in October 1915.

Military attitudes to the cavalry were already changing prior to the Great War. There had been calls to disband it altogether and the

Swathes of cavalrymen wait to the rear on the Somme. (Authors' collection)

regiments were already trained to wield a rifle, unlike their French and German counterparts. Yet the opening throes of the Great War had seen it involved heavily in a more traditional sense. Reputedly the first British troops to fire a shot in anger, the first to sight the enemy and the first to kill a German, the mobile nature of the opening weeks of the conflict saw them somewhat in their natural element. However, by 1916, circumstances and technology had overtaken them on the Western Front at least. The rise of the airman saw them taking on the traditional cavalry role of reconnaissance, the static nature of industrial warfare rendering the reality of a charging body of horsemen obsolete. The cavalry fought dismounted, or languished at the back waiting for an opportunity to ride into action. In all history, cavalry had been proudly instrumental in warfare; now their influence was waning in front of them.

At the beginning of August, William Fenton's regiment was in bivouacs almost as far back as Amiens. But, if there was no need to use them in their dwindling, traditional sense, there was categorically never enough manpower available on the Western Front. Thus, on the 5th it was not unusual that William was summoned to join a digging party. Recent work carried out by the battalion had included helping to build an ammunition railhead at Corbie, but on this occasion the men would be going right up to the front lines. As they went about their work, the party came under a bombardment of enemy artillery and a shell plunged into their ranks. Three men were killed outright and William Fenton was mortally wounded. Although he was taken to a nearby casualty clearing station, the 23 year old died later in the day and was laid to rest at Dernancourt Communal Cemetery, plot J.25.

6TH AUGUST
Lieutenant Arthur William Staples Pratte

10TH LINCOLNSHIRE REGIMENT

NEAR ANNIHILATION ON 1ST JULY did not necessary ensure that a battalion would have finished playing its part on the Somme. The 10th Lincolnshire Regiment went into action ahead of Billy Disbrey and the 11th Suffolks on that fateful day and were nearly destroyed by La Boisselle, suffering some 500 casualties in a day. It was unspeakably traumatic for a group that had been drawn from those with local ties, many of them associated with a single school.

On formation, the men hadn't liked the sound of a Pals battalion. They were dubbed the Grimsby Chums instead and among their number was 22-year-old Arthur Pratte, a clerk and in his spare time an immensely talented violinist. He enlisted on 17th September 1914 and was immediately granted a commission, largely due to his seven years' experience with the Grimsby Municipal College OTC as a colour sergeant. The school's OTC was in camp in Staffordshire at the outbreak of war under the command of the headmaster and of Arthur's father, William. They packed up and returned to Grimsby, determined to raise at least a company out of the college's old boys. On the first evening, more than fifty indicated a willingness to join and in a matter of days they had some 200 men at their disposal, including teachers. The unit began to expand past this company and into a full battalion, thanks to posters put up about the town and when other schools contributed towards their number.

After months of training, months of living and working together, this close-knit band was in tatters on the evening of 1st July. Arthur and his fellow survivors were withdrawn to tents in a wood to the rear, where reinforcements arrived to replace the friends and family wiped out when they attempted to carry out their doomed offensive. Most of these new men were unfit or conscripts, and they dropped in in small groups from various regiments who could spare them, such

as the Northamptons, the Middlesex or the South Staffords. The ties of community brought from Grimsby had been broken. The emotional impact of losing so many of their number, family, friends old and new, those whom they had come to know so well during the training and deployment, was shattering. The survivors with the battalion were still enveloped by grief at the beginning of August.

A little over a week after their divisional commander, General Ingouville-Williams, was killed they went back into the line. The whole area was gruesome; apparently some of the sandbags had been weighted with human parts. The commanders of Arthur's battalion slept for three nights in a dugout that smelled bad, only to realise when they decided to clean it that they had been sleeping on the bodies of three dead Germans. The nearby woodland, what was left of it, was strewn with piles of corpses. 'The smells, the noise, the unnatural shapes, and the bloody mess of the shell-torn bodies! Life at Bazentin was unpleasant!'

On 4th August Arthur Pratte and the rest of his battalion moved up to relieve the 11th Suffolks in the front lines to the north-east of Bazentin-le-Petit and small groups immediately went out bombing, although the weight of the enemy barrage was too much with which to contend. Arthur had been put in charge of A Company, the one that had originally been full of old boys from the Municipal College. On 6th August he was standing talking to another officer in a trench when a shell sailed into range and sprayed them both with shrapnel. Arthur was killed instantly; his friend died within half an hour. The colonel wrote to his father, who was by now with the 11th Lincolns, 'Your boy was killed instantaneously,' he told him, 'Murphy dying a few minutes later. Your son has been with us since the beginning and I feel his loss very keenly. So few of our original officers are left.' His company commander also had some kind words to say. 'Your son was the essence of coolness and courage. I shall miss him as a friend.'

The battalion had been in the trenches just under a week and their stint had exacted a miserable toll on the survivors of 1st July and the strangers who had been sent up to make good their losses in the intervening month. Nearly 200 men were gone from the strength of the battalion again. The shadow of the Grimsby Chums, growing ever fainter, marched back out of the lines to trenches on the other side of Mametz Wood.

Arthur Pratte had married his sweetheart Annie, a teacher at the Municipal College, on 25th May 1916 before returning to France to

Lieutenant Arthur Pratte (*front row, third right*). (Authors' collection)

embark on the Battle of the Somme. He had survived a mere two months after their wedding. Arthur originally lay where he fell. In 1934, he was recovered and identified by the Imperial War Graves Commission by his officer clothing and his regimental badges. His father had been dead some twelve years and never knew of his recovery, and his widow had been remarried for thirteen years. Arthur was finally laid to rest at London Cemetery and Extension, plot II.D.19 and when his mother passed away some eight years later it was in the knowledge that her boy rested in a proper grave in France.

7TH AUGUST
#2687 Private Ernest James Holland

14TH BATTALION, AUSTRALIAN INFANTRY FORCE

ON 4TH AUGUST THE AUSTRALIANS went forward again and this time, with adequate time to prepare, they finally conquered the OG Lines. When the 2nd Australian Division was subsequently relieved on the 6th, they had suffered almost 7,000 casualties to be able to lay claim to the crest of the ridge beyond Pozières, They had secured for Gough's army a view over Courcelette and Martinpuich, beyond the German second line out toward Bapaume 5 miles away, but now the time had come for yet another group of their countrymen to be fed into the battle.

From Victoria, Ernest Holland enlisted at 33 and, leaving a wife and newborn son behind, sailed from Melbourne in August 1915. A veteran volunteer who had also served in South Africa, Ernest was in Gallipoli by the end of the year and shortly before Christmas was another of the high number of troops being evacuated sick to Egypt. He suffered multiple minor illnesses before his battalion was sent to the more friendly climate of France on the Cunard liner SS *Transylvania*, landing in Marseilles in June 1916.

Approaching Pozières with the 14th Battalion, Ernest marched up in bad light, guns raging beyond, cutting the Australian lines to pieces.

Pozières (as it appeared to the Australians on their arrival in July 1916). (Authors' collection)

The relief was so confusing that, although the men thought they were occupying a supporting position, they were actually in the front line. New to the trenches, there was no chance for Ernest and the rest of his battalion to settle in. Before dawn on 7th August the Germans counter-attacked. Shortly after 4am the enemy came at him and his companions in force. They overran confused Australians unfamiliar with their surroundings, who were sitting in their own old positions, and moved on to try to take back Pozières. A British barrage managed to disperse the supporting German troops assembling behind the first wave and, after some desperate hand-to-hand fighting, the scrap ended in a complete victory over the opposing troops who had advanced up to that point.

This was the to be last counter-attack made on Pozières by the Germans, but despite having helped to fight off the enemy, Ernest Holland had become one of the thousands of men consumed by the Somme battlefield seemingly without a trace left behind. In 1922, his wife was still hopeful that there might be some news of his final resting place, asking for photographs of his grave. The military authorities were sympathetic but, as they explained, exhaustive efforts had been made to find the remains of those still on the battlefield. 'It must reluctantly be concluded that the Grave Registration Units have not succeeded in locating the [soldier].' In this instance, Lizzie Holland was told that it was the intention of the authorities to erect a memorial to those with no known grave. She was then left, a young widow and mother, to attempt to rebuild her life.

When the Villers Bretonneux Memorial to the missing Australian contingent was unveiled by George VI in 1938, however, Ernest Holland was not on it. Two years previously an anonymous grave had been found near Pozières containing two men. Clothing, boots and titles revealed that they were Australian, and one was named as an officer of a machine-gun regiment by his leather identification tags. The tags belonging to the other were illegible, but he had on him a pocket book with a clasp engraved with the letters 'EJH'. A search was begun to find Ernest Holland's widow.

In November 1936, Lizzie, by now remarried and living in Tasmania, received a letter informing her that the Imperial War Graves Commission had finally found her first husband near Pozières. He had been carefully exhumed for reburial, and his new grave would have a fitting headstone placed over it. More than twenty years after his death, Ernest Holland was finally laid to rest at Sucrerie Military Cemetery, plot I.JJ.20.

8TH AUGUST
#F/936 Private William Webber Walter Gerrish

17TH MIDDLESEX REGIMENT

Former Aston Villa player Private William Gerrish. (Authors' collection)

THE ATTACK ON GUILLEMONT ON 30th July had not yielded any kind of significant progress. The situation was reviewed at a conference on the following day, when General Rawlinson said that the village should only be attacked again after thorough preparation. Guillemont, Ginchy and Falfemont Farm must be taken to help forward the French advance to the British right, but Haig was still attempting to make a stand against wasteful attacks of the attritional kind that were not yielding adequate results in return for the casualties incurred or the material used. Billy Congreve's father, still in charge of this sector, said that for this to be observed he would not be able to attack Guillemont again until 8th August. In light of a mandate from Haig on conserving resources and attacking only when commanders on the spot were ready, so it would be.

Preparations began in force. Ammunition was gathered and the artillery continued to try to pick away at their counterpart German batteries to the east. The enemy had brought up numerous reinforcements and guns, and strengthened their existing positions so that, although they were inevitably tired after the gruelling bombardments to which they had been subjected, the idea that they would be pushovers was far from accurate. Sadly for those about to be thrown into battle too, the plan differed little from that which had failed on both 23rd and 30th July. Irrespective of how much more effort was put into communications or artillery preparation, British troops would still be walking towards incredibly well situated German machine guns.

The Footballer's Battalion arrived in the area on the night of 5th August. Still with them after the fighting at Delville Wood was William Gerrish, a 27-year-old player who had spells at Aston Villa, Bristol Rovers, Chesterfield and Preston North End behind him and who had enlisted in the 17th Middlesex in February 1915. Detailed orders were issued less than forty-eight hours after the relief. William was to advance south to the area around Waterlot Farm, which lay about halfway between Delville Wood and Guillemont, then move south towards the outskirts of the village itself, past the train station and the railway embankment. Guillemont itself would be the task of the battalion to their right. The attack was to be preceded by a hefty seventeen-hour bombardment of heavy artillery, which began with a vengeance at 9am on 7th August. The British gunners also made six 'Chinese attacks', which were occasional flurries of increased fire, to confuse the Germans about when the inevitable assault would come and ease the path of William and his fellow troops. They lasted for fifteen minutes, spouting a mixture of shells that jumped backwards and forwards furiously, implying that the infantry were about to burst forward. At 9pm the artillery paused while the attacking troops got into position. Straightaway the Footballer's Battalion began sending out patrols to check the German trenches to see how strongly they might be held on the other side of Waterlot Farm. They came back with the worrying news that the lines were full of enemy troops and that the bombardment appeared to have done little damage to their defences. The torrent of shellfire then resumed at midnight, other guns also targeting the German lines elsewhere, attempting to draw attention away from the front at Guillemont. The rampant barrage continued all the way up to zero hour.

An easterly wind threw dust and smoke from the German artillery's intense fire into William's face as he waited to attack. At 4:20am the 17th Middlesex climbed out of its jumping off trenches to crawl out in front and minimise the distance to be covered. Shortly after dawn the first troops got to their feet and went forward. The battlefield was cloaked in thick mist with visibility limited to about 10 yards, meaning that the troops could not actually see their objectives. As a result, on the right of the 17th Middlesex, troops lost direction coming out of the trench

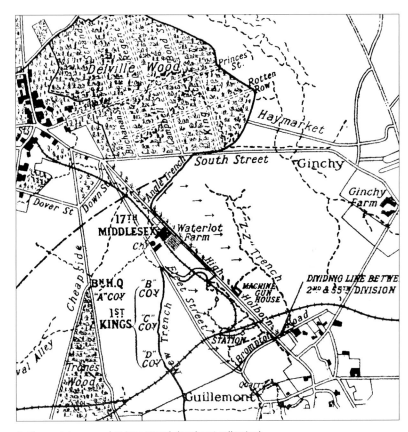

Guillemont, Longueval, Trônes Wood. (Authors' collection)

dug especially for launching the attack and ended up veering off to the south, missing crucial strong points that were to have eased the path of their advance once put out of action. As the British pushed on, it appeared that the enemy retreated into deep dugouts in the ruins of the village, with numerous entrances, and that after the initial wave of attack had passed over, they emerged carrying machine guns and were able to shoot their attackers in the back.

The neighbouring troops had been unable to claim Guillemont itself. William Gerrish's battalion was in Z-Z Trench, to the north, as planned, ready to try to fight its way down to meet them. However, it was under heavy fire too, being mercilessly enfiladed by machine guns and hit with bombing attacks. The situation was spiralling rapidly out of control. The men of the 17th Middlesex became lost; the green signalling flares that should have been shooting up to let them know the troops around them had arrived at their objectives were absent and communications were dire.

At 5am a runner shot into the battalion's headquarters to report that the original attacking party had been entirely bombed out of Z-Z Trench. The commanding officer promptly ordered a company to send out half a dozen bombers and a handful of men with fixed bayonets. They were to go along an old trench towards an imposing German-held building, a strong point known imaginatively as Machine-Gun House, to meet up with their neighbours, who were supposed to have taken it as part of their second objective. Half an hour later his party had nearly reached the spot, but couldn't get any further, although they were still attempting to bomb their way out of trouble. One single Lewis gun had managed to get back into Z-Z Trench. In the assault on the village itself, troops had made some progress towards Guillemont before being held up by the rate of German fire. Those who got furthest forward were stuck in isolated shell holes with no support, their front raked continuously by machine guns. This was to prove the extent of the success experienced in the advance on Guillemont on 8th August 1916. When a German counter-attack came in the village, the troops inside were in no position to withstand it. Fighting hand-to-hand, clinging on despite a lack of drinking water, many of them carrying wounds and having run out of bombs and ammunition, they were finally overwhelmed.

Despite the effort put into additional preparation efforts to maintain communications, the results of the day were dismal. Whole companies simply evaporated. The battalion suffered more than 200 casualties in one day. Guillemont was still in enemy hands and, once again, the battlefield lay littered with the bodies of hundreds of men who had been cruelly thrown in to try and claim it as part of a small force. One of those who vanished on the field of battle, William Gerrish's death was eventually officially accepted a year later as having occurred on 8th August 1916. He was unmarried and left behind a 6-year-old son named Horace. His body, if recovered, was never identified and he is commemorated on the Thiepval Memorial, Pier & Face 12d/13b.

9TH AUGUST
#21452 Private Walter Vurley
7TH LINCOLNSHIRE REGIMENT

Private Walter Vurley. (Authors' collection)

MEANWHILE, SLIGHTLY TO THE NORTH-WEST, the saga of Delville Wood continued. After the attacks of the Footballer's Battalion and the Royal Fusiliers that claimed the lives of William Jonas and Corsellis Lawton, the Germans were in a ragged state inside. Although infantry fighting had fallen into a lull, they couldn't even get their wounded out as the furious British barrage continued to rain down.

Rather than volunteer to fight at the onset of war, 27-year-old Walter Vurley had, until conscription came into force, done his bit for the war effort by quitting his job as a baker's journeyman near his home in Upwell, Norfolk, and going to work in a munitions factory in Scunthorpe. Enlisting in the Lincolnshire Regiment in 1916, he arrived on the Western Front in July and was posted to the 7th Battalion, which had helped to capture Fricourt early in July, suffering some 350 casualties. Like Walter, many of the men coming to replace them were fresh from home with no experience at all. There would be no chance to introduce them gradually to trench warfare or life at the front, as had been the case when the battalion first arrived. They were going straight into battle. At the end of the month Walter's division was on orders to be ready to move at three hours' notice to resume fighting.

When he arrived on 1st August, the Germans were still in possession of sections in the north and east of Delville Wood. The British occupied most of Longueval, but at the end of the July the enemy had still been lurking in the orchards at the northern end of the village. Walter's battalion struggled to get into the line, 'for it was not easy to locate the forward positions, and the Germans were very close'. The enemy had been moving up artillery on a front of some 4 miles around the salient formed by Longueval and Delville Wood, which enabled them to fire upon the position from three sides. But this salient had to be held at all costs until a renewed advance would straighten out the British line by pushing it forward to the right of the wood. Unfortunately for him, Walter Vurley's fate was to be one of the men sent in to cling to this perilous position.

The whole scene was a mess, crammed with guns and ammunition 'and impedimenta of all sorts [that] had necessarily to be crowded together'. Casualties immediately began to mount owing to the enemy's shellfire, and on the 7th the Lincolns took a step closer to the action, moving into reserve trenches to support a battalion of Sherwood Foresters. Walter held steady in terrifying conditions, waiting to see what orders would come. One company of the 7th Lincolns accumulated almost 100 casualties just sitting in this position for twenty-four hours on 8th August, such was the rate of the German artillery fire.

That night Walter and his battalion were ordered to go up through Longueval to relieve the Sherwood Foresters. Conditions were indescribable, 'almost to the breaking point of endurance'. Only the south and west parts of Delville Wood were clear of the enemy. There was next to no protection: 'the line was at best a series of detached fragments of old German trenches, with between them strings of shell craters, improvised into posts.' The area was 'a mass of broken trees and fallen branches ... with shell holes everywhere, and a tangle of undergrowth, bristling here and there with rusty barbed wire'. The air was foul with gas, which had been used during the relentless shelling: '[it] hung in the hollows, and drifted among the undergrowth.' Then there were the bodies. In the stifling, tropical heat that had characterised much of the battle for the wood there were piles of corpses littered everywhere and maimed body parts, all clad in a mixture of field grey and khaki. 'I never remember having seen so many dead in so small a stretch of ground,' wrote one witness. Decay set in within hours in

Delville Wood Cemetery, Longueval. (Andrew Holmes)

the summer weather and these unburied, blackened men had now lain discarded for weeks.

Walter and his battalion had completed their relief by 7:30am the following morning. On 9th August they were busy digging a new trench through the orchard on the outskirts of Longueval, to connect the British line with a post that their predecessors had managed to establish. Enemy artillery was very active and the Germans also showered them with indirect machine-gun fire. Snipers were also prevalent as Walter, a novice to the Western Front, attempted to work. By the end of the day, a deadly combination of shell and bullets had claimed his life, illustrating just how quickly valuable manpower was being exhausted on the Somme. Walter Vurley had been run from Britain, through France and into the line, where he was killed in action in just three weeks. He was with his battalion for precisely eight days. He had not survived long enough to go into battle, to help attempt to advance the line or press on with the offensive, but died simply digging a trench to try to stave off German attempts to claim back ground that had been lost. Walter's body, if recovered, was never identified and he is commemorated on the Thiepval Memorial, Pier & Face 1c.

10TH AUGUST

#2511 Private Owen Stanley Tolman

26TH BATTALION, AUSTRALIAN INFANTRY FORCE

Private Owen Tolman. (Australian National War Memorial)

DESPITE THE FACT THAT AUGUST would not contain a major offensive on the Somme, high casualties continued to mount. As well as the sick being evacuated from the line, casualty clearing stations were inundated with a constant stream of wounded men; those hit by stray bullets, maimed by the never-ending shellfire and taken ill in the dreadful squalor of the trenches.

Born in Hobart, 24-year-old Owen Tolman, a dockside worker, had enlisted at Claremont, Tasmania, in July 1915. With the 26th Infantry Battalion, he was one of those who had relieved the exhausted 1st Australian Division at the end of July after its capture of Pozières. When they arrived, Owen and his counterparts found their predecessors lying in the bottom of the trenches, the parapets littered with dead men. All looked exhausted and were at the end of the limits of their endurance.

On 27th July four waves of Owen's battalion lined up shortly after 11pm, the objective at that time still being the OG Lines. As midnight passed, Owen was moving steadily forward to the 26th Battalion's designated start position. Suddenly the enemy opened fire on them with machine-gun and rifle fire, although a large percentage of it was too high to hit anything effectively. They began their attack. As Owen and his battalion advanced, the men encountered first advanced posts, connected underground to the German lines, and then a shallow trench lightly manned and only partly protected by wire entanglements. In the darkness the men became somewhat confused. Troops veered to the left, and the men on their right became mixed up with Owen and his companions. The formation of waves set up to advance melted away into small groups as they climbed over uneven ground and attempted to avoid enemy shellfire.

Despite their troubles, Owen and his fellow Australians in their isolated groups managed to get as far as the undamaged and cumbersome wire entanglements in front of the enemy's second line and a few men even managed to enter their defences. There was no way of contacting headquarters, and no co-operation with their own artillery. In the face of the wire and a fiercely defended position, the 26th Battalion began to retire again, confused as to whether orders to do so had been issued or not. Having established that any gains in the enemy line were meagre and not sustainable, and that other troops had been ordered to withdraw, the same order was officially given to Owen's battalion. For the most part the men ended up right back where they started.

Casualty clearing stations behind the line were swamped with the wounded. That day No. 3 CCS, situated at Puchevillers, admitted 370 officers and men and on the next 178 more. Owen arrived with 233 more troops on the 29th, another busy day, as men continued to be treated, succumbed to their wounds or were transferred on to ambulance trains to be sent on to base hospitals and beyond that, Blighty. Numbers continued to be high, spiking even more in the first week of August as admittances reached nearly 600 men per day, including nearly 100 Germans. All the while, Owen remained under their care, too badly hurt to be transferred. When the 26th Australian Infantry Battalion was withdrawn from the lines on the 7th it had suffered more than 650 casualties, including Owen Tolman. He succumbed to his wounds on 10th August and was laid to rest at Puchevillers British Cemetery plot I.F.61.

11TH AUGUST

#5604 Private George Wain

1ST NORTH STAFFORDSHIRE REGIMENT

BORN IN STOKE-ON-TRENT, GEORGE WAIN was a regular who had been serving his country since before the turn of the century. Having initially worked as a miner before joining the army at 18, George had been stationed in India at the outbreak of the Boer War. In 1899 he was one of those mobilised with the 2nd Battalion and sent to South Africa. He took part in a scorched earth campaign and occupation in Transvaal in 1901, as well as seeing action at Cape Colony and during De Wet's invasion of the Orange Free State as a lance corporal.

As a reservist, George rejoined the colours on the declaration of war in 1914 and embarked for France in September. Quite remarkably he had not been wounded nor taken seriously ill at all during the war. Thus far he had served uninterrupted all the way through to the Somme, coming unscathed through actions on the Aisne, at Hooge, particularly nasty German gas attacks and the ongoing slaughter at Delville Wood.

Peronne Road Cemetery.
(Andrew Holmes)

Following the failed attempts on Guillemont, George's battalion of the North Staffordshire Regiment moved up to take over trenches in front of the village while planning went on for a renewed attack. The 11th August was a fine, hazy day and blissfully void of all but a few shells falling on the support trenches. That evening though, most of the battalion was ordered out in working parties to go out in front of its trench and dig a new one closer to the enemy. After George and the rest of the parties had left, word came through to cancel their work order as the troops on their right were about to attack. It was too late to warn the likes of George Wain and bring them back. Now under fire, he and his fellow troops took cover in a trench and waited it out, while being heavily bombarded by the German artillery. The flurry of activity over, digging resumed as planned at midnight, but having survived everything else that the enemy could throw at him for two years, George had been killed by a tragic lack of communication. Thirty-six years old, he was originally buried with a number of other casualties in the Briqueterie, to the south-west of Bernafay Wood. In October 1918 the men were exhumed and finally laid to rest at Peronne Road Cemetery, plot II.B.35.

12TH AUGUST
#96187 Sergeant John Edwin Dawson

47TH BRIGADE, ROYAL FIELD ARTILLERY

JOHN DAWSON WAS A 26-YEAR-OLD factory worker from Sheffield, the son of a furnaceman. One of the first men in the country to rush to the colours, he enlisted in August 1914 and found himself in the Royal Field Artillery, the largest of all the variants of British artillery serving in the war. They were armed with horse-drawn 18-pounder field guns, batteries that fired mainly high-explosive or shrapnel shells, which sprayed hundreds of metal spheres in mid-air.

John embarked for France in May 1915 and, although not present when the Battle of the Somme commenced, at the beginning of August his division was routed south. On the afternoon of the 8th, John and his

fellow gunners arrived at Dernancourt, to the south-west of Albert in fine weather and the whole of the divisional artillery parked in one big space in the open. The following day the battery commanders went forward to reconnoitre the gun positions they were to take over past Fricourt and at the south-west corner of Mametz Wood. That night John Dawson and the other batteries began relieving the Highland Division's gunners ahead of them.

The casualties began to mount immediately, with one officer killed and another wounded on their first day in action on the Somme. By the morning of 11th August the relief had been completed and the guns formed into two batteries of six pieces each. Their role was simple; they were to keep firing day and night. The targets that John was given were the enemy trenches and support lines in the south-east part of High Wood and they dutifully kept up a steady rate of fire, attracting retribution from the German guns, which laid an intense barrage on the British lines.

The batteries themselves also came under fire as they continued their relentless bombardment to pave the way for the infantry and on 12th August John was killed by enemy fire. He left behind a wife, Emma, and two children, Charlie aged 4 and Evelyn, aged 6. 'Your husband was one of my best Sergeants,' wrote his commanding officer, 'and was very popular with all the ranks in the battery. He was always so cheerful, and kept everybody happy. His loss will be felt very deeply by all of us here.' John Dawson was laid to rest at Flatiron Copse Cemetery, plot I.B.26.

A gun team work their 18-pounder wearing gas masks. (Authors' collection)

13TH AUGUST

Lieutenant Lewis Thierry Seymour

2ND YORK & LANCASTER REGIMENT

Lieutenant Lewis Seymour. (St Edward's School)

NORTH OF THE ANCRE, MAINTENANCE work and the subsequent sporadic torment of each other continued to add to the casualty figures on both the British and German sides of the line. Near Beaumont Hamel troops rotated in and out of the trenches. There would be no major offensive in the sector for the rest of the summer, but infantry patrols and raids were regularly carried out and there was always labour-intensive work to be done.

Lewis Seymour was born in 1893 in Hyderabad, where his father was forging a career towards being Superintendent of Lands, Records and Agriculture in Sind with the Indian Civil Service. The family's home in England was Oxford and Lewis was first educated at the Christ Church Choir School before winning a scholarship to St Edward's, where he was not only a bright academic but a talented sportsman too, representing the school at both cricket and rugby.

Before the war he had served with King Edward's Horse, with whom he stayed in 1914. In the spring of 1915, though, Lewis made the move to the York & Lancaster Regiment, where he saw intense action in the Ypres Salient and became imprisoned in a section of trenches for three days and nights without food and water after helping to retake them from the enemy. After a spell at home as a machine-gun instructor at Strensall in Yorkshire, a specialist in Lewis guns, he returned to the front in April 1916 with his battalion.

Lewis' battalion marched to Mailly-Maillet Wood on 9th August as it prepared to take over the holding and maintenance of a section of the line at the northern end of the Somme battlefield. Their spell in the trenches was plagued by a gusting wind when they relieved a battalion of The Buffs north of Hamel. A lack of offensive activity by no means meant a relaxing stint ahead of them. By both day and night Lewis and the other officers escorted working parties out into no-man's-land for a spell of hard labour. The York & Lancasters struggled to dig a new communication trench and improve the British position as they were plagued by *minenwerfer* and gas alerts. The situation became bad enough that on 12th August the unit began to request artillery support to silence the enemy. On the 13th the battalion did so again, as Lewis took a party out to a particularly dangerous spot. As his men dug, a German mortar was fired that claimed the life of their 23-year-old officer. His commander told his family that Lewis 'was a keen and capable officer and I miss him very much'. Another victim of attritional war on the Western Front, Lieutenant Seymour was laid to rest at Englebelmer Communal Cemetery, plot II.B.5.

14TH AUGUST

Captain George Robert Hitchin

2/1ST WEST LANCASHIRE FIELD AMBULANCE, ROYAL ARMY MEDICAL CORPS

GEORGE HITCHIN WAS A BURNLEY native who volunteered to contribute to the war effort straight away in 1914. Educated locally and at Manchester University, as soon as George came forward to offer his particular expertise as a doctor, his local territorial division in Lancashire was clamouring to give the 37 year old a commission. Unmarried and well known in the Wetherby district, George had acted previously an assistant to a local practitioner before he eventually journeyed to the Western Front to see active service.

A dressing station under fire at the southern end of the Somme battlefield. (Authors' collection)

The West Lancashire division to which he was assigned had carried out the failed attack on Guillemont on the right of the Footballer's Battalion on 8th August. George had joined it just beforehand to replace an officer going off to work at a hospital to the rear and he began work at one of the divisional field ambulances. The main dressing station set further forward was situated on the western outskirts of Maricourt on the way to Peronne and there the medical personnel worked twelve-hour shifts, 6 until 6, with two officers leading each. Both shifts also had a warrant officer who controlled the cars coming in from the advanced dressing stations even closer to the lines, a messing sergeant with a staff of orderlies, a dispenser, two clerks and cooks for making hot tea and drinks for those passing through or remaining under treatment.

The Fourth Army would carry on assaulting Guillemont in an attempt to wrestle this critical objective from German hands, noting in particular that the major issues affecting their ability to seize this prize were how to maintain communications and how to manoeuvre around the crippling enemy machine guns that were hidden in shell holes and amongst the rubble.

On 10th August rain hampered any attempts to continue offensive action and the next attempt on the village was postponed until the 12th. A preliminary bombardment led up to zero hour at 5:15pm, whereafter troops made it to their objective in half an hour. Unfortunately for George Hitchin's division though, the French on their right, with whom they were attacking, failed to secure Maurepas Ravine in their sector to the south. This meant that the British troops were left isolated, enfiladed from the right by enemy fire. Their new position was clearly untenable and the men had to be withdrawn after nightfall.

George's field ambulance had an advanced dressing station up in Dublin Trench, to the south-east of Montauban and facing Bernafay Wood, where he was put to work during the battle, assisting the wounded as they came in and evacuating them back to the main dressing station if necessary. Throughout the 12th and in the days following, it was filled with the wounded brought in from three collection points even closer to the fighting or from the regimental aid posts that belonged to each unit and were also situated nearer to the front lines.

It was dangerous work for the men of the Royal Army Medical Corps. Since their arrival and throughout the failed attack on Guillemont that began on the 8th, George's field ambulance had lost eleven men who were hurt as they brought in injured soldiers. On the 14th George was continuing to treat the wounded troops brought before him when a shell struck the dressing station at 6:30pm and tore it apart, killing him as he worked.

In its division's spell at Guillemont, the 2/1st West Lancashire Field Ambulance had treated seventy officers and 986 men, 821 of those during the two main failed attacks on the village. Most of their patients had been passed further to the rear for more comprehensive treatment. Nineteen had died with them. The line had advanced, but still Guillemont had not fallen. Fighting on the Somme was proving a battle of attrition with artillery pounding away and ill-conceived strategy seemingly failed to take advantage of any weakness that the enemy might suffer as a result of the shelling. Captain Hitchin was laid to rest at Dive Copse British Cemetery, plot II.F.25.

15TH AUGUST
#4535 Private Richard Henry Osborne

1/1ST BUCKINGHAMSHIRE, OXFORD & BUCKINGHAMSHIRE LIGHT INFANTRY

BACK IN THE MIDDLE OF the battlefield, with the OG Lines finally conquered, the plan now was not to push eastwards, but north toward Mouquet Farm and then on to Thiepval, isolating it from this direction instead of repeating the eastward thrust that had failed so dismally on 1st July. The farm, which was to become a notorious spot known as 'Mucky Farm' to the Allied troops nearby, had been an advance HQ for the Germans prior to the battle and was one of the listed objectives that British troops had got nowhere near to on the opening day of the Somme campaign. By now it had been fairly knocked about, but was 'protected by almost every barrier against attack that could be devised by human ingenuity'. In addition, the Germans had constructed tunnels around their trenches in the area, leading well into no-man's-land. 'The system was well devised, and many weeks passed before it was understood in its completeness by the Allied forces.'

The only son of a coast watcher from St Ives, Cornwall, Richard Osborne was a 31-year-old tin dresser born and educated in the village of Nancledra, some 3 miles inland. He enlisted in 1916, after the advent of conscription, and was another of the reinforcements arriving on the Somme, reaching the front in mid-July to serve with a Buckinghamshire battalion.

Richard's outfit had not been involved in the initial assault in the Pozières sector, playing a supporting role, but with the division having sustained nearly 3,000 casualties, it was withdrawn from the line at the end of July. Now, just two weeks later, Richard and the rest of the Buckinghamshire men were about to be sent for again to take on a troublesome objective to the north-east of Pozières and on the left of the Australians, who faced the ruins of Mouquet Farm. Skyline Trench was priceless because, as its name suggested, it commanded a comprehensive view from the top of a spur. British troops had got into it, but the German artillery had them marked and all but two small garrisons had to withdraw down the other side of the slope to evade enemy shellfire. When the inevitable counter-attack came therefore, most of them were overrun in their small numbers and the British lost almost the whole trench again.

Attempts to retake it failed and on 14th August Richard Osborne's battalion was ordered up to help push the line northwards to come up level with Mouquet Farm. Their journey into the fray was difficult enough. Such was the barrage that had pummelled the top of the ridge that they were forced continuously to climb over banks of earth churned up by shellfire. After this tiring journey, Richard and his fellow men moved up to attack communication trenches at 10pm, laden with bombs on their way towards the enemy.

They worked up these trenches effectively, chucking their haul of explosives and, after some fierce hand-to-hand fighting, had cleared most of Skyline Trench itself by dawn on the 15th. The trenches Richard found himself in were a state, having been assaulted consistently by artillery. The German infantry had not put up much of a fight. Apart from the throwing of a few bombs, the enemy mostly ran away down the reverse slope of the hill and away from the Buckinghamshire men.

By the middle of the afternoon though, the new British occupants had had to withdraw back to the heads of the communication trenches. As of midday the Germans had laid down a three-hour bombardment of shells of all calibres and mortars. 'It seemed as if all the destructive power of Germany had got to work on this trench.' It was the heaviest barrage that the battalion had ever endured and the Buckinghamshire men suffered almost 200 casualties. Any further attempt during the day to conquer Skyline Trench got nowhere. Killed while bomb throwing, 31-year-old Richard Osborne was never seen or heard from again. His body, if recovered, was never identified and he is commemorated on the Thiepval Memorial, Pier & Face 10a/10d.

16TH AUGUST
#8842 Private Albert Victor Atkins
1ST NORTHAMPTONSHIRE REGIMENT

THUS FAR THE 1ST NORTHAMPTONSHIRE Regiment had spent August to the rear at Henencourt, to the west of Albert. The men's days were a combination of sports contests (tug of war, relay races and sprints), general exercises that encompassed the art of musketry or bayonet fighting and precise training for night operations on an elaborate, brigade level. Among their number was a 26-year-old labourer from Northampton named Albert Atkins, who had enlisted in 1908.

Albert had done more to potentially damage himself than the Germans had managed so far. He had had to attend a court of enquiry in November 1915 after he and some accomplices managed to get hold of a box of pear-shaped bombs and decided it would be good sport to throw them back and forth to each other. Fifteen minutes later, predictably, one had gone off when one of the men stooped to pick it up, wounding three, and the blame was put on Albert for fetching the box in the first place.

Long since suitably admonished, on 12th August 1916 Albert Atkins' battalion received orders that it would be moving back into the line the following evening. Gathering their kit, the men did just this, passing through Albert and out the other side, where they bedded down for the night. On the afternoon of the 14th they carried on moving towards the fighting. They went into support lines to the left of High Wood and began digging frantically under enemy fire to improve their trenches and fashion adequate protection from the German artillery. The next day Albert and his battalion rested as much as possible until 5pm, when the Northamptonshire men moved up and relieved a group of Sussex troops on the front line.

Patrols were immediately pushed out and an attempt was even made to storm a German trench, taking the enemy by surprise. It failed. On the morning of the 16th, the officer who had led the raid crawled back into the front line with information as to the enemy's disposition, having spent the night in a shell hole in no-man's-land. He was 'absolutely confident' that should the Northamptons receive the order to attack, then they would be successful.

Planning began immediately. That night Albert moved forward with his company to attack the trench in front of them, men of the Royal Sussex Regiment operating on their right. All involved seized their objectives, dashing forward in the dark and then digging furiously to consolidate their position. But the enemy was not about to stand by idly. The Germans launched a counter-attack on the Sussex battalion, forcing it to evacuate its position, and then began bombing systematically down the trench towards Albert and the rest of the Northamptons. The men fiercely stood their ground and managed to halt them, resisting all the bombs thrown at them. For their trouble, the 1st Northamptonshires lost seven officers and forty-two men, including Albert Atkins. It was a high price to pay for an extremely limited gain, and indicative of actions along the Somme front as a whole at the time. Albert was commemorated on a special memorial in Bazentin-le-Petit Communal Cemetery Extension A.8. He was laid to rest within the cemetery, but the exact location was not documented accurately.

Memorial headstone for Private Albert Atkins. (Andrew Holmes)

17TH AUGUST
#19 Private Arthur Leonard Smith

1ST AUSTRALIAN FIELD AMBULANCE, AAMC

TO THE NORTH-WEST, THE AUSTRALIAN contingent had their sights firmly set on Mouquet Farm. Tending to the health of his countrymen as they advanced towards this perilous objective was 25-year-old Arthur Smith. His enthusiasm to fight in the war had been evident when he enlisted before the conflict was two weeks old in August 1914. A railway signalman from Haberfield, Sydney, Arthur, the son of a greengrocer, was immediately routed into the Australian Army Medical Corps and one of the field ambulances belonging to the 1st Australian Division. He joined his unit in time to witness the Gallipoli landings, where scores of wounded lay on the landing beach crying for attention from overworked medical men. By the end of the year he had become yet another victim of inherent sickness and disease in the unhealthy climate of the Dardanelles and was evacuated before his comrades, rejoining them at Alexandria having made a full recovery in March 1916. By the end of the month Arthur had disembarked in France. While the Australians grew accustomed to the Western Front, his family had already suffered tragedy when his younger brother, Stanley, had died of septicaemia at a casualty clearing station further north after a brief illness on 29th June 1916.

Bombardments in the direction of Mouquet Farm had been going on since 6th August. Two days later movement towards it began, ready for a full-blown assault on this enemy strong point. The previous occupants had got the line within striking distance, but in doing so, in just over a week they had lost nearly 5,000 men. The returning 1st Division was not at full strength, despite reinforcements coming in during its respite. The men were expecting to fight again, but it was still with dread that they returned, 'in much the same spirit in which a boy accepts that of an inevitable disciplinary thrashing'.

The ground was terrible: 'the flayed land, shell-hole bordering shell-hole, corpses of young men lying against the trench walls or in the shell holes.' It was an eerie sight:

Private Arthur Smith (*right*) at Gallipoli. (Australian National War Memorial)

Some – except for the dust settling on them – appeared to be asleep; others torn in half; others rotting, swollen, and discoloured ... the air fetid with their stench or at times pungent with the chemical reek of high explosive.

The landscape had become featureless. 'The whole area resembled one big, ploughed field.' It was nearly impossible for battalions to ascertain where they were going. 'An immediate result was that the perplexed troops and their commanders frequently found it impossible to determine their position, even in the daytime.' At night, especially during a barrage, reliefs and parties of carriers or workers sometimes became completely lost.

Plans were already under way to swap out the Australians, who had seen quite enough of Pozières and the surrounding area, and bring in the Canadian Corps; but that would not be until the end of August. In the meantime, the Australians' work was far from done. Objectives had still been allotted for them to secure before their departure. The terrain was difficult: a narrow front on the summit and western slope of a ridge, so cramped that one or two battalions were enough to cover it going forward. Here the Australians were to make a significant attack in the third week of August.

On 14th August Arthur Smith's field ambulance unit moved en masse down to the Brickfields at Albert ready to set up to operate fully from Bécourt, 5 miles to the south-west of Pozières, the following day. Arthur's unit was then carefully spread out behind the battlefield. The field ambulance was frequently taking in men from other units where necessary to boost its numbers, and the nature of the work meant that the twenty-two officers and nearly 600 men on its strength as August progressed divided up their thirty-five motor ambulances and nine horse-drawn wagons and worked broken down into various teams at five different locations leading up to Pozières and as far forward as one of the OG Lines.

With no major attack taking place, the sheer ferocity of the German barrage and the havoc it wreaked on the ranks of the Australian units in the line was illustrated when Arthur's field ambulance took in nearly 350 men in its first two days of operation at Bécourt. Australian preparations for the upcoming offensive were also being hampered by counter-attacks coming from Fabeck Graben, a significant German line that ran eastward away from Mouquet Farm, and medical men such as Arthur worked around the clock to treat and evacuate the wounded. He had been sent out with a team to set up a link in the chain of evacuation on a sunken road to the north of Contalmaison, which ran north-east towards Martinpuich, a position that was acting as both a regimental aid post and an advanced dressing station for the wounded, who had mainly been maimed by the shellfire at the front. Little stretcher parties of four or five worked constantly to collect the wounded from the open ground and in range of the enemy barrage, 'often, for want of a Red Cross flag, under a white handkerchief or other rag'. On 17th August, as Arthur's field ambulance processed another 257 cases, he was killed at his post.

In just six weeks around Pozières, the Australians had suffered nearly as many casualties as they had in the entire Gallipoli campaign. Originally buried at the site of the dressing station, Arthur Smith was eventually exhumed for a proper burial in 1925 as the battlefield was cleared and laid to rest at Pozières British Cemetery, plot IV.L.50.

18TH AUGUST

#1745 Sergeant William Isaac Cannon

1/6TH ROYAL WARWICKSHIRE REGIMENT

OPERATING ON THE LEFT OF the ANZAC troops at the northern end of the battlefield, 23-year-old William Cannon had not begun his war service in the infantry. From Wallingford, Berkshire, and one of seven children, he enlisted at Reading and originally served in a cyclist company. A porter for the Great Western Railway, but an ardent Territorial in peacetime, William had recently become attached to an infantry battalion of the Royal Warwickshire Regiment on the Somme.

William had been doing well since his arrival and had impressed his officers. The beginning of the month found the battalion in training to the rear, but in mid-August it would be required to go forward again. William departed with his men, having received another promotion for which he had been desperate. 'Got the other stripe,' he told his parents proudly. 'It was weary waiting for it but I have got it at last.' When he signed the bottom of his letter, he did so with precisely thirty-one kisses arranged in a pattern for them and reminded them of his rank again: 'Sergeant.'

On 16th August Sergeant Cannon and his battalion arrived at Ovillers and proceeded to relieve a battalion of the Gloucester Regiment in the line. A German counter-attack the following day was stopped by an artillery barrage, but a number of men were wounded. On the 18th, it was the turn of the Warwickshires to attack. Artillery of all calibres had managed to isolate their objective. Smoke came from opposite Thiepval, laid down as cover for them by the division next door. Under a surprise barrage, William led his men forward on the right of the attack at 5pm.

A view of the area around Mouquet Farm. (Authors' collection)

What ensued was referred to as a 'heartening success'. Encountering some initial resistance laid down by German machine guns, the men of one company had to throw themselves into a nearby trench or shell holes. But, persisting, they then made good ground, taking all their objectives. In the act of pushing them back though, Sergeant Cannon was leading his platoon towards the enemy when he was struck by a German bullet. As well as capturing its objectives, the 1/6th Royal Warwickshires seized six German officers and 245 men, including a large number of NCOs. The cost to the battalion was 150 casualties. 'His death was deeply regretted by the company and by the officers especially myself,' wrote William's company commander to his parents. 'We tender our deepest sympathy to you for your loss. Your sorrow may be somewhat alleviated by the fact that he died like a hero and a true Briton.' William Cannon was originally buried to the east of Authuile Wood. In 1919 he was carefully exhumed by a Canadian Graves Detachment clearing the area and finally laid to rest at Pozières British Cemetery, plot IV.F.5.

19TH AUGUST

#8943 Lance Corporal Morgan William Hughes

10TH ROYAL WELSH FUSILIERS

THERE WAS ONLY ONE CONCERTED effort at operations during August in which a significant number of troops were engaged, and in charge of the French contingent, General Joffre was not happy at the lack of progress in the Somme Campaign. On the 12th he met Haig and they agreed on a joint offensive for British and French troops from the river up to High Wood on 18th August.

From Bangor, Morgan Hughes had worked as a farm labourer before travelling to Cardiff to enlist in the Royal Welsh Fusiliers in 1905. The army had sent him abroad with his battalion and he had spent nearly six years prior to the war serving in Burma and India. Returning home in 1912, he had married two years later and had a young son before he journeyed to the Western Front. As the war progressed, Morgan began to serve in one of the New Army battalions and was in Billy Congreve's brigade the day he was killed at Longueval, being wounded himself. In mid-August the 10th Royal Welsh Fusiliers were employed as working parties for trench improvements and carried out practice attacks in the rain. On 14th August they began moving up to put their new training into action, having to halt on the way as the enemy was shelling the valley ahead. Delays caused considerable congestion of men all along their route and Morgan and his battalion did not get into their new trenches until after dark; a highly unsavoury prospect.

During the attack of the 18th, yet again the area around Guillemont was to be one of the objectives. Morgan's battalion would be attacking Lonely Trench, an isolated line to the east of Maltz Horn Farm at the very southern end of the British Front, on the way to Falfemont Farm. In the wet days leading up to the attack, the battalion's senior officers went up over the deteriorating ground to look at the state of the trenches, then once their men had taken up residence on the front in general, they then investigated the specific objectives they faced. At 5pm on the 17th the Welshmen were issued with flares, smoke bombs, tools and wire cutters.

There were complications with the preliminary bombardment, owing to how close British troops were to targets, but promptly at 8pm Morgan Hughes moved off to attack towards Falfemont Farm with his battalion. As they made their way up to form lines on tape laid out for them out in no-man's-land, German shells rained down. The men were in position ready for 10pm when suddenly an order came to delay the assault by half an hour. It was impossible, argued Morgan's commanding officer. The men were already over the parapet and waiting; there would be no time to tell the artillery, ready with their timetable, and so when their shells began pounding no-man's-land all the element of surprise would be lost and his troops would not be adequately protected.

And so the 10th Royal Welsh Fusiliers went forward in the dark towards the German lines. All along their front they found themselves pinned down by enemy fire. The Kaiser's men had been waiting for them and they lay in front of the German trenches, behind wire and a screen of bombs being thrown for them. A platoon of the King's Own Royal Lancasters was sent up to try and push through. In the meantime, the commanders of the Royal Welsh Fusiliers sought to achieve at least something and ordered a party of supporting troops to dig a new forward trench where the tape had been placed prior to the attack.

At 4am the men were ordered to go forward again. Through the dawn hours on 18th August the Welshmen, along with men of the Lancasters, the Suffolks and the West Yorkshire Regiment, all tried to beat down German resistance, but before 6am Battalion Headquarters had received word from the men in the lines that they had failed again. The ordeal for Morgan's battalion was not yet over. Two fresh companies came up and preparations were made to attack once again.

The 18th August was periodically wet and miserable. Many of the men were novices and not accustomed to being confined to trenches under shellfire. It appeared that they may be making progress on their objective, for Germans were seen leaving the southern end of Lonely Trench. Ominously though, when Morgan's battalion advanced again mid-afternoon, they vanished from view into a cloud of smoke and dust thrown up from shellfire. As soon as they breached the parapet the Welshmen came under heavy machine-gun fire that scythed down and cut through the ranks and their officers. Shrapnel shells burst overhead. Contact aeroplanes were taking signals back, pigeons were being carried up into battle. The battalion had even taken coloured flags up to mark the furthest points reached but on 18th August it was all to no avail.

La Neuville British Cemetery.
(Andrew Holmes)

Awaiting progress reports, headquarters was ominously silent. Morgan Hughes' battalion managed to rush the southern end of Lonely Trench and some of them also reached the road to Combles beyond. Unfortunately the troops on their left could not get forward and the 10th Royal Welsh Fusiliers, for all their hard work, taken in flank, had to withdraw.

As afternoon faded to dusk and the day ended, German shelling was heavy and accurate. At about 9pm, a staff officer went up to the captured line and found a mixture of troops, including the remaining Welshmen, consolidating their gains; the trench crammed with men. To the south the French were being counter-attacked back towards Maurepas Ravine, dragging back elements of British troops too. All the ground that had been gained initially was being lost. Lonely Trench remained in German hands, a stubborn obstacle in the way of the Allied advance.

During the night of the 18th, parties were extended over the ground on which the attacks had taken place and men collected the wounded, including Morgan Hughes. He had been shot in the back, but such was the confusion of the battle that nobody knew when. As he was carried away from the battlefield, shrapnel continued to explode overhead. In all, the 10th Royal Welsh Fusiliers lost more than 320 men. Morgan died at a casualty clearing station on 19th August. He left behind his wife, Elizabeth, and son Henry. He was laid to rest at La Neuville British Cemetery, plot I.F.74.

20TH AUGUST

#S/6585 Private Murdoch MacRae

11TH ARGYLL & SUTHERLAND HIGHLANDERS

BORN NEAR OBAN, 29-YEAR-OLD MURDOCH MacRae was a baker with an established history of serving in the militia before the war. He waited until November 1914 to join the army and then rapidly took care of his affairs, enlisting on the 17th in a battalion of the Argyll & Sutherland Highlanders and marrying his sweetheart Mary Jane the following day.

Having arrived in France in October 1915, by mid-August the following year Murdoch and his battalion were bivouacked at Albert, receiving drafts to replace those lost in their last stint in the trenches and attempting to avoid the enemy's high velocity shells by scraping small niches in the riverbanks and drawing covers over themselves with old sacking and waterproof sheets. Thankfully a number of their new recruits were sorely needed specialists and tired officers were switched over with those who had remained in the rest camp the last time everyone had gone into the lines.

On 19th August, Murdoch MacRae and the other Highlanders relieved another battalion overnight, picking up casualties immediately. With the troops next along they were sent out from their own front line to discover if the trench ahead was occupied. The British had noticed that lights being sent up only came from the trenches behind and, indeed, when patrols reported back it was to state there was little or no movement in the line in question. And so it was decided to occupy it by peaceful penetration, dispensing with any artillery preparation, 'which, in addition to putting the enemy on his guard usually brings forth a severe and continuous barrage from the enemy'.

It was a dull, cold morning on 20th August as the Argyll & Sutherland Highlanders finalised their preparations to take over the abandoned enemy line. That evening the battalion began to file up to claim it, told by the occasional wounded Saxon that they came across that the Germans had left days ago. As his comrades began this heartening take

over, though, Murdoch MacRae was mortally wounded and, although evacuated back to a casualty clearing station, the 29 year old died before the day's end. He was laid to rest at Heilly Station Cemetery, plot III.F.12.

21ST AUGUST

#1762 Corporal Henry Arthur Biggs

3RD RIFLE BRIGADE

HENRY BIGGS WAS A LONG-SERVING regular who had seen plenty of the war before the onset of the Battle of the Somme. From Plaistow, East London, he had originally been a seaman before enlisting in the Rifle Brigade at the age of 18. His service had taken him throughout the Empire. A rowdy recruit in his early days in Egypt, Henry was often confined to barracks for minor offences: playing football when forbidden in Egypt, losing his tartan trousers and allowing his bedding to become infested with vermin. By the time that the Great War was declared though, Henry was in his mid-twenties and had settled down to become a disciplined and well thought of soldier, commended for his good conduct. He had been serving for some time with the 4th Battalion of his regiment and was in India in August 1914. It sailed from Bombay in October and was on the Western Front by Christmas, where the miserable winter weather affected the rank and file forced to live in the trenches. Henry had to be admitted to hospital in January 1915 with frostbite, returning in time to receive a gunshot wound to the thigh in the spring. He was evacuated home, found time to get married while he recovered and when he sailed for France in February 1916 he joined the 3rd Rifle Brigade, his original unit having departed for Salonika.

On 16th August, Henry and his battalion relieved men of the Royal Fusiliers in the Guillemont sector ready for the strong assault of 18th August. The 3rd Rifle Brigade was ordered to attack two lines of enemy trenches on its front. The preceding artillery barrage was accurate and effective, and when Henry and the rest moved off they managed to stay right up close against the protective barrage and

The effects of the Battle of the Somme on the high street in Guillemont. (Authors' collection)

completely surprised the enemy. They took seventy prisoners, including an officer, and a pile of 'booty', among which was two machine guns. Some of the enemy troops actually came out to greet them, and were so enthusiastic to be captured and away from the Somme that they willingly went to the rear to be processed without even needing an escort.

Going over ground that had come to haunt men such as the Footballer's Battalion just two weeks earlier, the likes of Henry Biggs found that Machine Gun House fell to them, and that Z-Z Trench was a far simpler objective than had been feared after previous experience. Sending in higher numbers of troops and planning for possible eventualities paid dividends, as did extensive use of smoke bombs and grenades to clear dugouts, and Lewis guns were thrown up in front to play on shell holes as the enemy attempted to use them for cover in order to retreat. The ground north of Guillemont was in British hands.

By 19th August the situation for Henry Biggs and his companions had returned to normal, but on the 20th the enemy kept up persistent shelling, with a focus on the new British positions. Plans were now fully under way for a major new offensive in the middle of September. One of the objectives that had been designated as essential before this could take place was, of course, Guillemont. Consequently, on 21st August Henry Biggs and the rest of the 3rd Rifle Brigade were ordered to help secure the Western side of the village.

That morning, parties of both Henry's battalion and men of The Buffs occupied most of Z-Z Trench leading down to Guillemont and went forward under a heavy barrage towards the village. Under a smoke screen discharged by the neighbouring division to cover his flank, Henry advanced from the station. The attack was failing. The Rifle Brigade attackers were met by accurate fire from Wuttemberg troops opposite and could not hold their position. When they fell back and were relieved, Henry was not among their number.

The battalion's efforts since the 18th had caused some 300 casualties. Henry Biggs had left his wife, Hannah, pregnant when he returned to the front in February 1916. She had given birth on 25th July, the day after Henry reached the Somme with his battalion. Their daughter, Joan, was just over three weeks old when he was killed. Twenty-eight-year-old Henry, who had never laid eyes on his little girl, was originally buried near where he fell. When the battlefield was cleared after the war he was exhumed and finally laid to rest at Delville Wood Cemetery, plot XXI.G.9.

22ND AUGUST

#11989 Lance Corporal Alfred Chiswell Huntley

6TH SOMERSET LIGHT INFANTRY

ALFRED HUNTLEY WAS A WELL-KNOWN face in Weston-super-Mare, where his father was the owner of the Beach Restaurant and Hotel overlooking the seafront. A renowned swimmer and member of Bath Harriers running club, he was educated locally and at Trowbridge High School before leaving to become an apprentice at a confectionery firm in Bath. The 21 year old volunteered at the height of the recruiting boom in the first week of September 1914 and arrived in France the following May, where he had since become a member of a Lewis gun section with his battalion.

It was the fate of the 6th Somerset Light Infantry to become the latest troops to be acquainted with Delville Wood and its environs, where the Germans had now been forced back into the north-east corner. In mid-August, Alfred and his cohorts had spent several nights sending up large working parties to the remains of the wood, sometimes wearing goggles owing to lachrymatory shells falling in the area. In just maintaining what tenuous hold Rawlinson's force had over the remnants of Delville Wood, Alfred was to be severely wounded on the 16th while digging new trenches in the hours of darkness with his fellow men. He was evacuated back to a casualty clearing station.

Within two days the rest of the battalion would be thrown into action in another limited attack aimed at trying to push the Germans out of Delville Wood. Harassed by their own guns firing short, repeatedly bombarding the British trenches and causing casualties, 'our men in the end were more afraid of our guns than the German'. When the barrage lifted, the Somerset men occupied most of their first objective, then the second and third. They seized some 200 German prisoners, who 'were in a very demoralised condition and surrendered without even putting up a fight'. Then the battalion began consolidating their gains.

When the 6th Somerset Light Infantry was relieved on 21st August, the survivors paraded in front of the brigadier, who congratulated the men on their fine performance in Delville Wood. It would matter little to Alfred Huntley, for the 21 year old was to die painfully of his wounds the following day. He was laid to rest at Heilly Station Cemetery, plot III.F.2.

23RD AUGUST

#15414 Corporal Thomas Herbert Birks

11TH KING'S ROYAL RIFLE CORPS

MEANWHILE, BACK AT GUILLEMONT, THE fight for the village went on. On the day that Henry Biggs was killed trying to seize it, 21st August, the 11th King's Royal Rifles came up to relieve troops from his division in front of this problematic objective. Among their number was Thomas Birks, a labourer from Sheffield. Thirty-seven years old when he enlisted in September 1915 at Winchester, Thomas had a wife and children at home.

Despite the fact the battalion was taking over the line in wet, sticky conditions, the relief passed off quietly and there were no casualties amongst the riflemen as they entered the trenches. The plan was to have Thomas' battalion attack Guillemont from specially dug trenches on their front on 24th August, as part of a larger attack with French co-operation on the right of the British line.

On the evening of the 23rd, though, the Germans put down a heavy barrage on the British support lines to block reinforcements coming up and attacked Thomas and the 11th King's Royal Rifles in their trenches with more than 100 men. Beginning with throwing bombs, the enemy managed to get close to Thomas under cover of morning mist. The British artillery countered, but could not stop the enemy's advance. The rifles themselves managed to fend off the attack by rifle and machine-gun fire, and no German found his way into the British line, but the scene was one of utter confusion. Bullets splayed all over the place, indiscriminately cutting down men of the King's Royal Rifles and enemy alike. In the chaos, Thomas was hit.

The trenches were badly blocked with troops who were sent up to reinforce the riflemen and the wounded being evacuated. Under continuing heavy artillery fire, the parties who were sent up to dig the new trenches and prepare for the attack on the 24th could do nothing. The following day's operation was cancelled.

The 11th King's Royal Rifles had suffered casualties of more than 100

men, most of whom were now missing. Thomas Birks was hurriedly evacuated and admitted to a casualty clearing station with bullet wounds to his head, side and his right knee. He did not survive the day. One source lists his death as accidental, which suggests that perhaps he was hit by British fire. Thomas left behind his wife, Sarah, and their three children, Ethel, 14; Alice, 12; and 5-year-old George. He was laid to rest at La Neuville British Cemetery, plot II.A.54.

Corporal Thomas Birks's grave at La Neuville British Cemetery. (Andrew Holmes)

24TH AUGUST
Soldat Florian Morel

1ER REGIMENT D'INFANTERIE,
6E ARMÉE FRANÇAISE

TO THE RIGHT, THE ATTACK of the 24th would still go ahead in the French sector, with a now minimal contribution from a British division supporting their left flank. The French assault at the beginning of July had somewhat routed both the first and second German positions in their sector. In some places they had advanced 6 miles and they had got tantalisingly close to Peronne. The enemy lost 12,000 men as prisoners, eighty-five guns, twenty-six *minenwerfer* and 100 machine guns. 'It was the most beautiful success since the Marne.' Then the Germans had steeled themselves, brought in thousands of reinforcements and attritional warfare had set in.

Florian Morel was a 23 year old from Annay, near Béthune. His home town was under German occupation, so serving with the 1st Regiment d'Infanterie, which had a large contingent of men whose homes were now behind enemy lines, he had a particularly fierce motivation for defeating the Germans.

On 18th August the French attacked, alongside the British. After a steady bombardment that was not raised to a crescendo prior to the infantry assault in the hope of confusing the enemy, the men set off behind a creeping barrage. It was a disappointing endeavour. In charge of the French, Joffre appeared to be furious. The French contribution to the day, he thought, was absolutely insignificant. As far as he was concerned, the British had 'the right to be unhappy and somewhat surprised' at the lack of support that they had received. It simply would not do to give them cause to complain about the conduct of their French allies. A significant new attack was now planned, but before it could be carried out certain objectives needed to be claimed properly, including the village of Maurepas, which, just to the right of the British sector, had proved a significant aggravation to the French Army for some time. The French held part of the village, but on the following day would be looking to rip the north-eastern section from the enemy.

As the Battle of the Somme began, Florian had been busy to the south-west of Reims. His regiment had been doing back-breaking work on their trench lines when, in the third week of July, they received orders to leave and relocated to 25 miles south of Amiens. Florian had been digging or sitting still for weeks and so for him and his countrymen a stringent programme of physical training began. There were daily exercises: four hours in the morning, a break and then four more hours in the late afternoon. The regiment began by training in sections, with general fitness in mind. With upcoming operations planned, they then expanded their practice, first in companies, then in battalions as rehearsing the attacks grew grander in scale.

There was time for relaxation and the odd luxury. Showers were put up in a nearby barn, and there were constant medal presentations, reviews and concerts. At the beginning of August the 1st Infantry Regiment undertook even more elaborate manoeuvres, the largest of which was a fake attack on Hardevillers, including overnight operations, with one session that went on for sixteen hours. A week later, prepared for their part in the Battle of the Somme, Florian and his regiment had begun the move back towards the front.

Like their British counterparts further north on the battlefield, the French were suffering from the effects of constant rain, their sector becoming 'a quagmire, a swamp'. On 19th August, Florian finally moved

Left: Bombers of the 1st Regiment d'Infanterie at work at Maurepas. (Authors' collection)

Below: Detail featuring Florian Morel's name from the village war memorial at Annay. (Andrew Holmes)

MONTAIGNE ROGER
MOREL CHARLES JBTE
MOREL CHARLES
MOREL FLORIAN
MOREL NARCISSE
MOREL THEOPHILE
POLVECHE LIÉ

into the Maurepas sector, his regiment relieving a Zouave one. They went into the line the following day. 'Gusts' of artillery fire were prevalent as the battalions went about improving the position and, as the day of the attack approached, violent bombardments rained down on Maurepas and the surrounding area, with all calibres of gun in action.

The countryside was in ruins. One village nearby:

Looked like a sea, whose enormous waves had suddenly been frozen and on which floated an extraordinary debris of all kinds: stone blocks, twisted metal, charred beams, bricks, broken tiles, pieces of furniture, clothing, mattresses ripped open, plowing instruments, military equipment, logs, weapons, posts, ammunition, wheels, demolished cars … everything was confused, pell-mell, in an infernal mess.

Everywhere there was evidence of Frenchmen who had attempted to claim the spot before them. Blackened, swollen corpses, heads, arms, legs; everywhere were scattered rifles, boxes, ammunition, knapsacks, helmets 'scattered in heartbreaking order'. On 23rd August there was hectic air activity about Florian and his regiment. Men that were sent out into the unoccupied part of Maurepas to reconnoitre were heavily fired on.

At 5:45pm on 24th August two battalions of the French 1st Infantry Regiment went forward to hardly any enemy artillery response at all. As the men climbed upon the parapet, one of the battalion commanders issued a rallying cry as they went forward: 'Now my friends, forward for France!' As soon as Florian left the trenches he and his comrades met fierce opposition. 'Machine guns begin to spit.' The Germans had distributed them throughout the ruins of Maurepas, hiding them in destroyed houses. Fighting was close and Frenchmen assaulted from house to house through the village. Throughout the 24th, through the hours of darkness and into 25th August, the situation remained unclear.

The village was in such a ruinous state that the men hardly noticed when they arrived. One officer asked, 'Where is Maurepas?' The reply was humorous. 'Maurepas? But you are here. This is it!' There were just a few mounds and some rubble to show where the village had been. 'Broken bricks, rubble, pieces of rafters', but nothing at all like a solid wall. 'What a sad picture!' Strewn through the debris of furniture and masonry were huge shell holes, 3–4m across and 1m deep. Everywhere was littered with agricultural implements and smashed beams.

Despite meticulous artillery preparation, Florian Morel and his regiment had advanced into heavy German shellfire and fierce resistance. Maurepas, however, was finally secured in its entirety. In the aftermath, a road within the town was cleaned and made traversable for traffic. An ambulance was set up against the side of a crumbling house to deal with the wounded carpeting the area. Florian was not among them. The 23 year old was never seen or heard from again. In the aftermath of the war, the French decided that, rather than erecting large-scale memorials to the missing, they should be commemorated on memorials in their home town. Florian Morel's name appears on one in the communal cemetery at Annay.

25TH AUGUST
#RMA/13227 Gunner George Pitt

ROYAL MARINE ARTILLERY,
HOWITZER BRIGADE

TWENTY-YEAR-OLD GEORGE PITT, FROM ACTON in West London, had joined the Navy before the war at the age of 16 after a brief career as an instrument maker. Immediately designated as a gunner, for the first year of the war he had been on the battleship HMS *Monarch*.

After a brief spell at home in 1915, George returned to the Royal Marine Artillery, in which he had served before going to sea, and in January 1916 joined the Royal Marine Artillery Howitzer Brigade in France. This consisted of massive 15in howitzers with a range of some 5½ miles that operated as individual units, with a large crew of sixty men. Each individual shell weighed the equivalent of eight or nine average men, and the guns themselves required a number of tractors to be moved. Fashioned between the Coventry Works and the Royal Navy, they were, quite simply, monsters.

In mid-April the gun team went through a complicated process of loading tractors, the howitzer train and their equipment and overseeing its move down to the south coast. On the transport, horse boxes had been fashioned to keep the giant components of their howitzer under cover for the journey to the front. It was not until the beginning of

A 15in howitzer of the kind used by George Pitt's gun team in the Royal Marine Artillery. (Authors' collection)

the following month that the laborious process of parking it had been finished. The scale of operations meant that May in its entirety was spent working from 8am until 5pm, making magazines, digging trenches for cables, and fashioning dugouts for their own guns and others belonging to the Royal Marine Artillery.

Finally, in the middle of June, George and his fellow gunners were ready to carry out the back-breaking work of collecting giant shells. It took two days to sort out the ammunition, 'most of it being coated with dry linseed oil, making weight and other markings mostly indecipherable'. A total of 200 rounds was received. By 25th June George and the crew were registering their howitzer on Mouquet Farm, which at the time was a German headquarters and a target for 1st July. Other objectives in their sights before the beginning of the attack were Thiepval and St Pierre Divion, before work was hampered by a damaged air cylinder that put the gun out of action for two days, causing George and his men to fire their ammunition from a different gun instead.

The howitzers' deadly rounds were fired in bursts of an hour or two, eight to twelve rounds at a time, on 1st July, although it was difficult to observe what they were hitting as so many guns were firing at the same time. With no gun of their own in working order, George Pitt and the rest of his team became bona fide workhorses well into August. While the other gun crews continued to fire their behemoth guns, George could do little more than carry out a supporting role, helping to lay platforms for the ones that were still operational and reinforcing roads ready for the progression of their tractors. When it came to moving, George assisted with making sure that stores were sent to

Shell of the type used by the Royal Marine Artillery. (Authors' collection)

the workshop out of the way, and that gun parts and platforms were clean and debris free. A spare ammunition wagon was fashioned into a makeshift travelling store and armourer's workshop.

On 20th August George Pitt and several personnel were dispatched to help the 70th Siege Battery of the Royal Garrison Artillery. For five days they prepared gun positions and dugouts under fire. On the last of them three of the Royal Marine Artillery men were in direct range of German shells. One had to be evacuated with shellshock, another was slightly wounded and George Pitt was killed instantly by a German shell. The 20 year old was laid to rest at Mesnil Communal Cemetery Extension, plot II.D.14.

26TH AUGUST
#13324 Sergeant Albert Cowell
8TH LOYAL NORTH LANCASHIRE REGIMENT

BACK AT THE NORTHERNMOST REACHES of the battlefield, despite movement around Mouquet Farm, the village of Thiepval was still firmly in German hands and guarded the ridge beyond from any eastward approach. Additionally, the competent tactical movement that had dictated events at Pozières the month before was now absent and lacked the same direction.

One of those destined to try to silence the formidable Leipzig Salient during continued operations was 20-year-old Albert Cowell from Cleveley near Blackpool. A spinner, he enlisted in Chorley enthusiastically on 2nd September 1914 with a stiff little finger that was overlooked by a compliant medical man. Albert had thus far survived everything that the Germans could throw at him, but he had almost managed to kill himself. At the beginning of 1916 he picked up a German grenade as a souvenir while out with a working party. Souvenir hunting was responsible for many an accident among young men on the Western Front when it came to meddling with dangerous weapons. Having managed to convince his officer that he had done a bombing course, knew what he was doing and should be allowed to keep his grenade 'for instructional purposes', Albert was left to his own devices. He was showing it to a friend when it went off. Several people were knocked down in their shared billets and he suffered wounds to his right leg, but nobody was maimed permanently or killed and Albert rejoined his battalion a few days later. A court martial reasoned that yes, his wounds were self-inflicted, but seemingly that it was through stupidity and not malicious intent, and his punishment was light.

On 23rd August 1916, Albert and his battalion marched past Aveluy Wood and up to support positions behind troops in the Leipzig Salient, where his company was ordered to conceal itself in nearby dugouts. The following day it was attached to the 3rd Worcestershire Regiment and ordered to seize a nearby trench at 4pm. The ground gained on one side exceeded the objectives and a barricade was erected. Staying close up against the creeping British barrage, no difficulty was experienced in crossing no-man's-land. In fact, almost all of the casualties were caused by British shellfire when men strayed too close to its protective curtain.

The Germans found their British attackers on top of them before they could man their parapet or bring their machine guns into action. The enemy then made a good, stubborn effort at resistance but suffered heavy casualties when the combined battalion engaged them in bomb fighting, flinging their explosives down into the entrances of dugouts and dispensing with the defenders inside. The attack was a success. Two machine guns were captured along with large piles of rifles, equipment and bombs.

Rain cascaded down on top of Albert Cowell and the Lancashire men on the night of 25th/26th August, an inch of water turning the chalky ground into a sea of white mud. The troops waded up early the next morning to take over different trenches from a battalion of the Wiltshire Regiment in preparation for an attack on the Salient.

Throughout the day they were informed the trench that comprised the battalion's objective was held by less than 100 Germans, who were starving and ready to surrender. Men from Albert's company were selected to make the attack on a small scale under one lieutenant and at 6pm they rushed forward following a small local bombardment with trench mortars. The Germans responded with heavy shell and machine-gun fire and many of the attackers fell approaching the enemy lines. The survivors entered the German trench and were surprised to find it strongly held by very determined troops. A fierce fight ensued, in which the Loyal North Lancashire men were heavily outnumbered. A lieutenant led two more companies up to help and some progress was made, but the few men he left behind were suddenly subjected to an enemy counter-attack on the British position behind.

The lieutenant saw that to go and attack was too risky and that his priority was now not to aid the attack, but to make sure that his own position was not overrun and captured. The Germans attacked the British line in force, but the North Lancashire men beat them off several times, and the enemy suffered heavy losses. Fierce shelling continued for the next few hours and then at intervals throughout the night. The failed attempt on the Salient had cost the Loyal North Lancashire battalion nearly 300 casualties, including Albert Cowell, who failed to return. His body, if recovered, was never identified and he is commemorated on the Thiepval Memorial, Pier & Face 11a.

27TH AUGUST
#306830 Private Joseph Shearman

1/8TH ROYAL WARWICKSHIRE REGIMENT

JOSEPH SHEARMAN WAS A 38-YEAR-OLD steel polisher from Handsworth in Birmingham. Long estranged from his wife, he was raising his teenage daughter alone when he was compelled to enlist in January 1916. In the spring Joseph's absent wife had passed away and within a few weeks, before his departure for the front, he had married again, his new bride, Annie, a local widow with two toddlers. Once on the Western Front, by 24th August Joseph was in the vicinity of Skyline Trench undergoing a rigorous programme of training that included trigger pressing, bomb throwing, judging distances and bayonet fighting in preparation for the battalion's next stint in action to the south of Thiepval. When these sessions were finished, the men went up the front lines in working parties in grim weather, being heavily shelled in Skyline as they worked to improve and repair it in muddy conditions. Any rest from physical labour was punctuated by lectures and demonstrations.

On the morning of 27th August final preparations were under way with the men stocking bomb dumps and carrying up ladders to their jumping off trenches. The ladders were not in the right location and it was mid-afternoon before the men had got them into place. It was later suspected that this confusion gave the game away to a certain extent, for half an hour later Joseph and the rest of his battalion moved up ready to attack and the enemy appeared to know that they were coming.

'The men moved out of our trench in splendid style, there was not a single waverer among them!' Despite the apparent enthusiasm of the Warwickshire men though, the damaged nature of the ground they were attacking meant that their objective was indistinct. As soon as the barrage began pummelling it further Joseph and the rest of the troops lost sight of their destination and men began to veer off in the wrong direction and lost touch with the rest of the battalion. Officer casualties

Men of the Royal Warwickshire Regiment at rest on the Somme. (Authors' collection)

wrought even more confusion on these unfortunate men, who found themselves leaderless in the midst of battle. Others ran into the British barrage straightaway, or overshot their objective completely and fell into the second phase of their own artillery bombardment. Any men who reached the correct objective were bombed out of it again and forced to retire, taking heavy losses. The 1/8th Royal Warwickshires had suffered almost 200 casualties. Annie Shearman was seven months pregnant when Joseph disappeared into the confusion. Their daughter, Nancy, was born in October 1916, seven weeks after her husband died. Her elder daughter died less than a year later at the age of 4. Joseph Shearman's body, if recovered, was never identified and he is commemorated on the Thiepval Memorial, Pier & Face 9a/9b & 10b.

28TH AUGUST
#16936 Private James Kennedy

13TH ROYAL SCOTS

IN EARLY AUGUST A DIVISION of Scottish troops had taken over the area to the left of High Wood. The trenches were in a disgusting condition thanks to a combination of the recent fighting and shelling in the area, and due to the constant rain. On arrival, the line consisted of shell holes strung together and shallow ditches. They were going to have to 'work like Trojans' to gain any cover.

Among the new occupants of the sector was a 29-year-old labourer from Alloa serving with the 13th Royal Scots named James Kennedy. Enlisting in January 1915, James had been ever present on the Western Front since the summer of that year and, when his time on the Somme began, was as yet unharmed physically, despite the horrors of the Battle of Loos at the tail end of 1915.

James' early days next to High Wood were comparatively quiet. He and his companions were to get straight to work in spite of the maintenance that needed doing on their lines, raiding trenches 'and otherwise annoying the enemy'. The Germans opposite appeared to be confused at this point, having suffered numerous small setbacks. James and the rest of his battalion spent their time working hard to link their

forward line with an old British trench behind. The Switch Line in front of them running out of High Wood had turned out to be empty, so it had been occupied and they slung out new posts in front of it.

The 13th Royal Scots were not involved during operations on 18th August, but came up the following day to relieve a battalion of the Highland Light Infantry that had been part of the assault. Their three-day stay in the trenches was uncomfortable, not only on account of the weather but because they were harassed by German gas shells. Casualties mounted until James and his fellow Scotsmen were relieved again on the 22nd. There was to be little respite for the 13th Royal Scots. Now James was employed as part of constant work parties, wading through mud as the battalion accumulated more losses all the while carrying supplies back up to the front lines. The cycle of exhausting work continued when, on 27th August, James Kennedy's company was sent into the firing line with another to relieve a battalion of the South Wales Borderers. Casualties began to mount again immediately. Eleven men were killed and another nine wounded just taking up their new positions. The trenches were in a neglected state and almost uninhabitable. In full view of High Wood, James and his comrades were under constant heavy shellfire from the enemy guns in that direction as 28th August dawned. Fourteen men of the 13th Royal Scots were wounded that day, and two killed, including James Kennedy, another victim of the daily attrition on the Somme. James left behind a wife, Catherine, and three sons: James, 9; John, 3 and 1-year-old George. His body, if recovered, was never identified and he is commemorated on the Thiepval Memorial, Pier & Face 6d/7d.

29TH AUGUST
#7396 2nd Class Air Mechanic Reginald Alfred Hobbs

ROYAL FLYING CORPS

REGGIE HOBBS HAD ONLY TURNED 14 two weeks before the assassination of Archduke Franz Ferdinand in Sarajevo that would prove the spark that ignited the Great War. A North London boy, from Edmonton, Reggie's father was a local butcher and dairyman with a

Members of the Hobbs family pose outside their shop before the war. (Private collection)

large premises that included a shop and space for livestock. The middle of five children, Reggie kept himself busy with a variety of different interests. He liked his football, especially Spurs. He went to a show, perhaps at the Tottenham Palace or the Edmonton Empire, at least once or twice a week to see shows such as *Alias Johnny Valentine*, *Queen of the Redskins* or *The Monk and the Woman*. More devout than his elder brother Stanley, he sang in St Martin's choir and the Hobbs family loved their seaside holidays, in Hastings, for example.

Despite having a weakness in his eye that made him unsuitable for office work, Reggie was a bright boy, winning a scholarship to the Latymer School in Haselbury Road. He had always had a keen interest in aviation and noted key events in his diary, including watching Hawker on part of his flight around Great Britain and keeping a lookout in the newspapers for updates when Gustav Hamel disappeared. After giving up work as a clerk, he would, rather predictably given the family line of work, become a butcher's assistant, although not for his father.

The war was, naturally for a boy of Reggie's age, exciting and of huge interest. His brother Stanley was a pre-war regular, joining the cavalry in 1912, and the family anxiously waved him off to war in August 1914. Reggie had left school by this point and was a Boy Scout in his spare time. He enquired straight away as to the kind of government work that he could do to help, such as volunteering as a messenger, and worked out of the local police station as a despatch rider in the early days of the war. He walked along the Embankment with his mother, watching the searchlights, and waited for Stanley's stingy efforts at letters home. Although still 14, by November Reggie was making enquiries about joining the army himself. He enquired about the Territorials, but they said they were full. He was pointed in the direction of the Royal Garrison Artillery, but he was not keen, so Reggie went to see the London Yeomanry. He got as far as a riding test but then was told that, at 5ft 6in, he was an inch too short as the unit had upped its minimum height requirement. After Christmas he went to enquire about the

Army Veterinary Corps and the Army Personnel Centre, but his enquiries came to nothing. Perhaps the reason why he could not secure a place in the services was because he was obviously underage.

At New Year the Hobbs family sat at home and drank a toast to Stanley at the front, and Reggie settled for joining the Athletes Volunteer Force for home service at the end of January 1915. A month later he was also working as a special constable. His father followed a month later and they had practice skirmishes at White Hart Lane. When the wounded arrived at The Edmonton Poor Law Infirmary, which had been turned into a military hospital, Reggie and his father would be called out to help with their arrival. When the Zeppelin raids started as 1915 wore on, they were called out for those too, cycling about to maintain order or keeping watch on the roof of the Tottenham Hospital.

Now aged 15, by July Reggie was still bent on military service. His mother was compliant, making at least one visit with him to make enquiries. She would rather know where her son was, and in what capacity, than end up with a runaway on her hands and no clue what he was up to. Reggie went to Whitehall to ask about the requirements for joining the Royal Flying Corps or the Royal Naval Air Service. He knew immediately it was the choice for him. It took several meetings, some of which his mother accompanied him to, but he passed the medical and, claiming to be 19, Reggie enlisted on 4th August 1915 and left for Farnborough the following day.

A wireless learner, it took Reggie only five days to get a trip up in an aeroplane. Shortly afterwards, he was sent back to London to the Polytechnic for Wireless Training in Regent Street. There, the pupils did two hours of sending and receiving in the morning, lectures, drill and parade, before more sending and receiving in the afternoon to get up to speed. At the end of October, young men from Reggie's course began to leave for the front. Reggie was up to a reasonable speed of sending twenty-five words per minute, but it would be a further seven months, probably on account of his youth, before he found his way to France. By then 16, Reggie Hobbs' job as a wireless operator for the Royal Flying Corps would see him well to the rear with 3 Squadron. 'I am many miles from the firing line,' he reassured his family, 'but occasionally can hear the guns in the distance.'

As it turned out, Reggie was not one to shy away from danger. At the end of August there was a shortage of wireless men available to work with the Royal Horse Artillery and he volunteered to help in Caterpillar Valley. The commanding officer was fairly comfortable that Reggie was working in a safe place, but on 29th August 1916 he was operating at a set in a shed near the battery as it fired. A violent thunderstorm raged throughout the afternoon. Shells began to crash down nearby as the German artillery attempted to register on the guns, but the 16 year old refused to take any additional cover and carried on working cheerfully.

Reggie Hobbs (*left*) with his elder brother Stan (*right*). (Private collection)

A short time later a large calibre shell came barrelling through the roof and burst inside. A doctor nearby rushed to him, but Reggie was beyond help. Both his legs had been blown off, along with one of his arms. He never regained consciousness.

Stanley had recovered the details of his brother's injuries and intended to keep them from the family until he was coaxed to part with them. 'I think the sad news ... must have turned me mad for a bit,' he admitted. 'I wrote to Mother and Father as soon as I got Mother's letter but I don't know what I put in it.' Their mother was in pieces, convinced that she was to blame for letting Reggie go to war. 'If you had stopped him,' Stanley assured her, 'he might have run away to the infantry or somewhere, and [you might have] never heard from him, or even of his death, again.' He was taking a philosophical approach. 'I quite believe that what is to be – will be – and nobody can stop it.' Stanley was determined to have his revenge on the enemy as soon as possible. 'Cheer mother up all you can,' he told his sister. 'Nobody is to blame, and I am sure if he heard her say it he would not like it.'

Sixteen-year-old Reggie Hobbs was wrapped in a blanket and laid to rest at Quarry Cemetery, plot V.G.19. Stanley Hobbs would survive the war. In 1917 another member of 3 Squadron had finally got up to put a cross on Reggie's grave, which was no longer in quite such a perilous spot. He sent Reggie's mother a photograph, 'hoping that you will excuse ... reopening the wound that his death must have caused'.

30TH AUGUST
#R/16519 Rifleman Cyril Kirby Bentley

12TH KING'S ROYAL RIFLE CORPS

ATTEMPTS ON GUILLEMONT HAD FAILED on 23rd July and then on the 30th, when Arthur Facer was mortally wounded with his machine-gun company, and again on 8th August, when William Gerrish fell with the 17th Middlesex. On the 18th, Morgan Hughes had been mortally wounded during his attack and, although Henry Biggs got into Z-Z Trench to the north of the village with his battalion of the Rifle

Brigade a few days later, Guillemont was still in German hands. Plans to try again on 24th August had to be abandoned when the likes of Thomas Birks were hit by a German counter-attack the day before and left the area unprepared for an assault.

But Guillemont was still a crucial objective and preparations were now under way to attack the battered remains of the village again. This time, those troops flinging themselves against a mass of rubble and German machine guns would include Cyril Bentley, a 31-year-old barman originally from Bishop's Stortford, Hertfordshire, but now living in North London. Cyril enlisted in November 1915, when he travelled to Winchester to join the King's Royal Rifle Corps.

To the north of Beaumont Hamel, Cyril and his battalion had begun the move south towards the Guillemont sector in mid-July. They reached the front line on 26th August, relieving a battalion of the Somerset Light Infantry. It had been raining for days and the trenches were in a woeful state. The area was also prone to heavy artillery fire that was dominated by gas shells and made trying to get any work done in the wretched conditions near impossible. 'The trenches were deep in mud and water, and were constantly being blown in; some of the communication trenches were impassable ... so that it became a most difficult matter to bring up rations.' The state of the Carnoy-Montauban Road nearby was so bad at this juncture, that on 29th August thirty-seven vehicles became sucked into the mud and broke down.

To make matters worse for Cyril, after a short preliminary bombardment on the 29th, the Germans attacked the 12th King's Royal Rifles, although they were easily bombed back before any of the Kaiser's men reached their lines. The following day the enemy would try again, but were once more repelled, this time with machine-gun and rifle fire.

The next British attack had been planned for lunchtime on the 29th, but the state of the trenches and the weather, punctuated by violent thunderstorms, were both so bad that it was postponed. The Germans continued to shell Cyril and his comrades. At 6pm, as thunder and lightning raged, they counter-attacked his battalion in numerous small parties of about half a dozen men. More could be seen forming up nearby. The King's Royal Rifles opened up a galling machine-gun fire and jumped to their rifles, scattering the attackers, and then the situation calmed down for the night. Cyril resumed sitting in his wet, muddy trench as conditions deteriorated further. 'No-man's-land [was full of] dead bodies which had been lying out for weeks and the state of the whole line was foul ... there was no time to let the men rest, for they were constantly trying to improve the conditions. They were so tired that it was doubtful just how effective they would be when they attacked Guillemont again.'

The fresh attack on Guillemont had been postponed until 30th August, but conditions were such that it was put off once again, for it was impossible to move at all in the trenches that lay forward of Trônes Wood. The Germans had also increased the intensity of their artillery fire and bludgeoned not only the front lines but the areas around Bernafay Wood to the rear. Stored in the northern part of it were dumps of small arms ammunition and bombs, and both were blown sky high. It was a miserable day for Cyril and his fellow riflemen. Many of them were buried alive by shellfire and a patrol that went out ran headlong into a band of Germans. During the course of the day Cyril was wounded by enemy fire and evacuated away from his miserable plight, but it was to no avail and he died later that day. The troops allotted to the next attempt on Guillemont had suffered so badly in their four-day stint in the lines that they had to be moved back into reserve and new men selected to carry out the assault. Cyril Bentley left behind a wife, Edith, and was laid to rest at Corbie Communal Cemetery Extension, plot II.B.48.

31ST AUGUST
2nd Lieutenant Henry Augustus Butters

109TH BRIGADE, ROYAL FIELD ARTILLERY

IN 1916, THE UNITED STATES had not yet entered the war. It was, however, not wholly unusual to find Americans serving in the British or French armies. One officer's family were distinctly unimpressed at his choice to do so, but 24-year-old Harry Butters of California summarised his reasoning succinctly in a letter home:

I find myself a soldier amongst millions fighting for all I believe right and civilised and humane, against a power which is evil and which threatens the existence of all the right we prize and the freedom we enjoy. It may

seem to you that for me this is all uncalled for ... but I tell you that not only am I willing to give my life to this enterprise ... but I firmly believe ... that never will I have an opportunity to gain so much honourable advancement for my own soul or to do so much for the world's progress.

Harry was raised partly in Cape Town and educated for a time at Beaumont College, a Jesuit school in Windsor, before returning to the US. He was 6ft 2in, a giant among his British colleagues and the only son of a successful businessman, who occupied his time with mines and

2nd Lieutenant Henry Butters on horseback. (Authors' collection)

railways. Keen on horses and cars, 'a crack shot and a fine polo player', Harry had a bubbly personality and was vibrant and engaging. 'To talk with him was to receive a new and promising revelation of the mind of young America.' One notable personage quite taken with him was Winston Churchill. 'I met him quite by chance in his observation post neat Ploegsteert and was charmed by his extraordinary fund of wit and gaiety,' the future prime minister recalled. 'His conversation was delightful, full at once of fun and good sense … A whole table could sit and listen to him with the utmost interest and pleasure.' The pair hit it off so well that on leave, Harry was invited to dine with the Churchills and accompany the politician on a trip to the theatre.

Harry had arrived in England early in 1915 to join the British Army, vehemently believing that German ambition and aggressiveness must be crushed. 'Yes, my dearest folks, we are indeed doing the world's work over here, and I am in it to the finish.' On being commissioned, he spent a few weeks in the infantry with a battalion of the Royal Warwickshires, but his technical mind called for something more and he transferred to the artillery. By August 1916 he had already spent quite some time at the front, and in the spring of 1916 had suffered a breakdown, about which he was frank and open. 'This comes as rather a jolt,' he said. 'But I am forced to realise that it is by no means a sudden shock.' He was moved back to work with the Divisional Ammunition Column further to the rear, supplying the batteries with their shells and the infantry with their bullets. He wrote home of his experience. 'Men stand up to [the war] in various ways,' he explained. 'The strength of religion, lack of imagination or natural phlegmatic temperament, a sense of humour and an ability to bluff one's self out of it, are the usual means of endurance.' But something in him had snapped and he acknowledged he needed a rest. He admitted that his state of mind was troubling. 'I lived with some very dark thoughts, indeed, before coming out of it.'

After a week he claimed to be on the mend, but all too soon casualties among the officers in front might mean he would have to be recalled. 'Already,' he wrote, 'although the sound of a shell sends my heart action up … I am beginning to take a more normal view of things. The moments of depression come farther apart, and the rest of the time I see things in a much more endurable light.' Harry was contemplating leaving to work with anti-aircraft guns, a safer prospect than an artillery brigade, when at the end of July his stepmother's son died. Twenty-year-old Gerard had survived the gruelling onset of the battle around La Boisselle, only to be

killed on 22nd July. A month later Harry wrote to her to let her know that the inevitable had happened. Casualties in the brigade meant he would have to rejoin one of the batteries. He still didn't feel himself, 'but it can't be helped and it's surely what I'm here for after all,' he reflected.

On 25th August Harry's brigade moved into the dangerous position in Caterpillar Valley, where it immediately suffered four casualties.

Harry Butters' headstone at Meaulte Military Cemetery featuring the inscription that he requested for himself. (Alexandra Churchill)

The following day the unit was registering on targets to the south-east of Guillemont before the weather took a turn for the worse and began to interfere with infantry operations towards the village. More casualties mounted among the artillery as the rain lashed down. Bombardments were ordered, then cancelled again. In the meantime, German reinforcements had arrived.

As the month drew to a close, enemy batteries unleashed a fierce torrent of shells on the British lines, which usually meant a counter-attack was coming. It was launched on the 31st, the first fine day for more than a week. As the Germans pushed the British back into the environs of Delville Wood, to the north-east of the battery, the enemy's gunners hammered the British artillery in Caterpillar Valley. All day and into the night the shellfire on batteries such as Harry's was unrelenting. The bombardment included gas shells, and so all day long Harry directed gunfire in his mask. Shortly after 11pm he was taking a breather in a dugout near the gun positions. 'The Germans were putting over a heavy barrage of gas shells and the air became very poisonous and oppressive,' one of his fellow officers explained. 'Harry said "it's time we moved out of this" and went out. Immediately he was outside a gas shell hit him direct.' His companion removed his gas mask to check the extent of his injuries, but Harry was already dead. The enemy bombardment had claimed nineteen men of his artillery brigade in a single day.

Preparing for the idea that he might have to go back up to the brigade, Harry had written to a chaplain friend, leaving instructions for a 'cheery' letter to be written to his sister in Piedmont if the worst should happen. 'How I got it, what I was doing, when I went up ... location of grave, etc., etc. ... Please reiterate to her how much my heart was in this cause, and how more than willing I am to give my life to it. Say all the nice things you can about me, *but no lies* ...' He also had instructions for his burial. 'Try and have the Roman Catholic padre plant me and you can tell her that, it will give her greater consolation than anything, and please put after my name on the wooden cross, the bare fact that I was an American. I want this particularly, and want her to know that it has been done so.' They followed his instructions to the letter. Harry Butters was placed in a coffin and buried by a Roman Catholic Chaplain under a Union Jack. As many of his officer friends as could get away stood as a trumpeter played the last post. Harry Butters 'an American citizen' was laid to rest at Meaulte Military Cemetery, plot E.27.

1ST SEPTEMBER
#L/9501 Private Percy George Sharland
2ND QUEEN'S (ROYAL WEST SURREY) REGIMENT

PERCY SHARLAND WAS BORN IN Bromley, Kent, but raised in West Surrey at Haslemere. In 1909 he abandoned his job as a labourer, made the short trip to Guildford and, aged 19, enlisted in The Queen's (Royal West Surrey) Regiment. Before the war his service took him all over the globe to places including Bermuda and Gibraltar. He was stationed in South Africa in 1914 and arrived back in England in September, before the battalion embarked to join the British Expeditionary Force on the Western Front. His first stint in the Great War was cut short by a nasty gunshot wound to the elbow that saw him evacuated home from the 1st Battle of Ypres, and Percy's convalescence was lengthy. He was not fit to return to the front until March 1916. Barring a slight shrapnel wound to the shoulder blade since, he had thus far come through the Battle of the Somme without major injury when The Queen's was ordered to relieve troops at the southern end of the battlefield in the last week of August.

A bitter struggle was going on past the eastern edge of Delville Wood. The area was dominated by the 'Alcohol Trenches', a tangle of defences dubbed with names including Hop, Lager, Pilsen, Beer and Ale. The weather was awful as Percy and the rest of the battalion carried out training and then prepared to march up towards Delville Wood on 31st August. That afternoon the Germans released a torrent of shells and then launched three separate counter-attacks on a battalion of the South Staffordshires in the Alcohol Trenches. They stood firm through all of them until at the last they were forced back into the wood behind. A heavy barrage fell on its eastern side when Percy Sharland's battalion began arriving to reinforce the Staffordshires in the evening.

On 1st September Percy was among those ordered to help seize back the ground lost on the previous day. At 5am the Surrey men began attempting to bomb through the eastern fringes of Delville Wood, but the trench they were moving along was too shallow and provided scant cover. German machine guns in positions outside the wood harassed Percy and his companions as they made their way long. Under a hail of bullets they had to settle for establishing a bombing block part way back to the lost position and digging a new length of trench behind it at right angles to try to prevent the Germans from forcing them back any more.

For the rest of the day, Percy Sharland and the rest of The Queen's were under a merciless enemy artillery barrage. Telephone wires were repeatedly cut and getting information back and forth the battalion was reliant on messengers, who were forced to run a gauntlet of enemy fire. One company's flank was uncertain of their next steps, and the men edged about with their backs pressed against their trenches to squeeze past the crowds cowering within in order to bury the fallen, clear the line and form stores of accessible ammunition and bombs. The attack of The Queen's may have failed, but in just a few days' time Delville Wood would finally fall permanently into British hands. Exposed to the constant bombardment on the 1st, Percy Sharland did not survive the day. His body, if recovered, was never identified. The 26 year old is commemorated on the Thiepval Memorial, Pier & Face 5d/6d.

2ND SEPTEMBER
#9191 Private Frank Ernest Bindoff

22ND MANCHESTER REGIMENT

TWENTY-ONE-YEAR-OLD TWINS FRANK AND HERBERT Bindoff enlisted at the end of 1915. Until the War Office could provide the resources to train them, both walked the streets of their native Brighton wearing armlets to fend off criticism and indicate that they had already joined the army. Both six footers, both clerks in their home town, the brothers joined the Royal Sussex Regiment when they were finally mobilised at the beginning of March. They embarked to join the 2nd Battalion of their regiment at the end of June 1916, but on arriving at a base in France found that a different fate was awaiting them.

Privates Frank (*left*) and Herbert (*right*) Bindoff. (Authors' collection)

The 22nd Manchesters had been mauled on 1st July, first over at 7:30am as part of the division that successfully captured the village of Mametz by the day's end. They had contributed to the limited success of the opening day of the Battle of the Somme at a cost of almost 500 casualties. When the twins arrived on the Western Front, they were some of the first reinforcements to be sent out to depleted units on the Somme. On 8th July, along with seventy-five others of their Sussex battalion, they were reallocated to the 22nd Manchesters and two days later joined them with hundreds of other men gleaned from another Manchester battalion, the Middlesex Regiment, The Royal West Kents, Royal Fusiliers, and even two men of the Border Regiment sent to make its numbers up after their fight at Mametz.

On 25th August, General Rawlinson had met with his corps commanders in the morning and read them a letter from GHQ that emphasised the importance of securing key objectives 'without delay' in order to prepare for the new large-scale offensive due in mid-September. As a result, on the 3rd his army would try to secure all the desired start line positions for this attack in the opening days of the month. One of these was the village of Ginchy. To the north-east of Guillemont and set on a high plain, it formed a forward position in the German defences.

Thus far Frank and Herbert Bindoff's experience of fighting the Great War was some twenty-four hours of hell inside High Wood. In divisional reserve as the Battle of Bazentin Ridge commenced on 14th July, the following day the 22nd Manchesters blundered about inside the wood, during the ill-conceived attack as Lorimer Headley died advancing to the side of it. Less than a week after receiving all their reinforcements, the Manchesters suffered almost another 250 casualties.

Then the division went, deservedly, to rest. For the rest of July and the whole of August, the Bindoff twins acclimatised to their northern battalion together. They trained and watched as the Manchesters absorbed yet more reinforcements. On 31st August they left Fricourt to return to the trenches. The battalion passed back through the area around Mametz to hold the line ready whilst other troops prepared to make the attack on Ginchy on 3rd September.

The twins entered the front lines on the 1st and immediately came under heavy German shellfire as they improved their surrounding by digging latrines and repairing blown in and wet trenches. Throughout the night Frank and Herbert were bludgeoned by lachrymatory shells and poisonous gas as they tried to work. The enemy, it seemed, was aware of an impending attack and was determined to prevent it from coming to pass. In a four-day stint before they were relieved, leaving other troops to capture Ginchy while they furnished carrying parties in support, the 22nd Manchesters had lost another 100 men. Included among them were the Bindoff twins, killed by the same shell during the hellish artillery bombardment laid down by the enemy.

On Coventry Street in Brighton, on the opposite side of the railway lines from Preston Park, the twins' widowed mother was beside herself. Not only had her two sons been killed on the same day, but by the same shell. The two boys were deemed missing, but there was seemingly no hope, for almost immediately they were classed as having been killed in action, or having died of the wounds shortly after the shell landed. Kate Bindoff could not understand why Frank should have a grave and yet Herbert be lost to her, destined to have his name carved on to the Thiepval Memorial. Herbert's mortal wounds were described to his mother by the fellow soldier that buried him, but if when the isolated graves in the area were tidied and the fallen brought together Herbert was among them, his body was never identified. It is likely that he still lies somewhere on the battlefield. His twin brother was originally buried in Ginchy, but as the battlefields were cleared Frank was eventually laid to rest at Delville Wood Cemetery, plot XVII.C.3.

3RD SEPTEMBER
2nd Lieutenant William Alexander Stanhope Forbes
1ST DUKE OF CORNWALL'S LIGHT INFANTRY

2nd Lieutenant 'Alec' Forbes. (Private collection)

OTHER OBJECTIVES ON 3RD SEPTEMBER were to include, naturally, Guillemont and Falfemont Farm, the much fortified German strong point to the south-east of the village. If the Fourth Army could reach as far east as the ground running between Ginchy and Leuze Wood then it would be almost upon Combles, beyond which lay the original German third-line system. Haig was convinced that such preliminaries were well within the power of the troops and artillery available if matters were planned with the proper diligence and care. Rawlinson decided to bring in a new division to take the area south of Guillemont and among them, coming into the line and relieving the Bantam division, was the 1st Battalion of the Duke of Cornwall's Light Infantry.

From Newlyn, Penzance, Alec Forbes was the son of a recently widowed artist, both parents having been founder members of the Newlyn School. An architectural student before the onset of war, Alec had failed to prove himself fit enough to stand the rigours of military life, but by a convoluted route found his way through the Railway Transport Commission and into his local regiment. Twenty-three years old on the Somme, by August Alec found himself joining his battalion and among the last Brits on the battlefield, before the French assumed the line holding the ground east of Maurepas thanks in part to the effort of Florian Morel on his right. The sector was quiet, the ferocity of battle having temporarily died down in the area except for shelling on certain positions.

On 2nd September the Cornwalls moved up into the line ready for the following day's battle as the preliminary bombardment raged. Before dawn on the 3rd, Alec had led his men to their assembly trenches and the battalion sat ready to attack Falfemont Farm and Leuze Wood to the south-west of Guillemont. It was a poisonous area. A few days earlier the French had secured Angle Wood to the south and the German second position to the south-east of Falfemont Farm, but fire from the farm still halted further progress. The German occupants, armed with machine guns, could wreak untold havoc on any attackers from this stronghold. For that reason, at 9am on 3rd September, troops to the right of the Duke of Cornwall's Light Infantry attacked the farm before the onset of the main advance to try to silence it. This 'roused the Hun' and the Germans responded by bombarding the British line, including Alec and his companions in their assembly trenches. The enemy managed to hold firm as Rawlinson's troops were forced to try to conquer the farm without accurate artillery support. Within an hour, the attack on Falfemont Farm had petered out. The consequences would be harsh for those waiting to carry on the advance, who would now face these machine guns, and for the French, who could not hope to capture Combles with this position held up by hostile troops.

In the meantime, Alec Forbes was making final preparations for zero hour. Instructions were issued and the artillery ploughed on, subjecting the Germans to 'a methodical and effective bombardment'. At noon, the 12th Gloucesters on the right and the Cornwall men on the left attacked the spur south of Guillemont. The artillery pounded their first objective in preparation for their arrival as they moved off in four waves behind a competent, disciplined creeping barrage. Alec and his men kept close behind it and the leading two waves poured into their initial objective.

With British troops dropping into their defensive lines, the enemy began laying a brutal barrage down on the advancing Cornwalls, 'but quite undeterred our men pressed on steadily to their objective'. In the face of galling machine-gun fire, the men showed excellent marksmanship as they picked off the culprits. However, the battalion was losing many officers, many of whom had only been with the Cornwalls for a matter of weeks. At this juncture, as the young subalterns led their platoons on, they fell, killed instantaneously or collapsing to the ground mortally wounded. Twenty-three-year-old Alec Forbes was among their number.

Without him, the advance continued and the line from Wedge Wood up to the south-eastern corner of Guillemont was captured. The Germans were showing far less resistance than had been expected, again in large part due to the Cornwalls' marksmanship. Next to them, the Gloucesters suffered the brunt of the untamed machine-gun fire that poured out of Falfemont Farm, but the third objective fell. Consolidation began, along with the sorting of troops who had become helplessly muddled in the frenzy of the advance.

It had been a day of mixed fortunes for Rawlinson and his army. Another attack on Falfemont Farm in the evening failed, the German machine gunners inside still fiercely determined to stand their ground. To the north, Guillemont was finally captured, or at least the pitiful remains of it. This was the only outstanding success of 3rd September. Any gains made around High Wood or Ginchy were cancelled out when the Germans counter-attacked in force and pushed the British back again. Lieutenant Alec Forbes was laid to rest at Guillemont Road Cemetery, plot I.A.1.

4TH SEPTEMBER
2nd Lieutenant Charles Lewarne Teape

9TH DEVONSHIRE REGIMENT

2nd Lieutenant Charles Teape.
(Authors' collection)

TO THE NORTH OF ALEC Forbes and his battalion, another young officer was also among those assaulting one of Haig's designated key objectives. Charles Lewarne Teape was the only son of a clergyman, who presided over the church of St Michael's in Devonport. Born in Surbiton and educated at St John's School, Leatherhead, Charles was a keen cricketer in the second XI, with 'a good eye' but a poor fielding record. As an academic he was more successful and was entered for Pembroke College, Cambridge, for 1915. Instead of going up to university though, Charles applied for a commission at the age of 18. It was quite some time before he arrived at the front. After first training at St Albans he then went on to become a bombing instructor. It was a role in which he excelled and Charles was consequently sent to be adjutant to the commandant of the Southern Area Grenade School at Lyndhurst, where he was most diligent and well-liked by his fellow officers. It was not until mid-August 1916 that Charles Teape was sent to France and joined the 9th Devons on the Somme. He found a daunting task waiting for him.

Having watched his army fail to seize desired objectives on 3rd September, and with positions still outstanding that were deemed essential for the onset of the rapidly approaching offensive in the middle of the month, Rawlinson reacted by doing exactly what he had been warned against. Despite strict instructions not to waste resources on small-scale attacks, he now ordered these on local targets that were still outstanding, namely Ginchy, which the Bindoff twins' division had entered, but failed to hold on to the day before. His army began to repeat the same pattern of behaviour that had been causing Haig to lose patience with his subordinate.

On 4th September Charles Teape and his battalion would be sent up to try to secure Ginchy once and for all. The Germans had now reoccupied it in some force. The Devons had spent 3rd September in reserve before orders arrived in the evening to move as quickly as possible by bus to Mametz. As the night wore on, Charles and his comrades bumped across broken ground on the way to do battle.

In the early hours the Devons were collecting picks, shovels and water from Bernafay Wood as they hurried on, lurching frustrated around a quarry and Mametz looking for misplaced bombs. The situation was uncertain but British troops apparently still remained inside Ginchy and

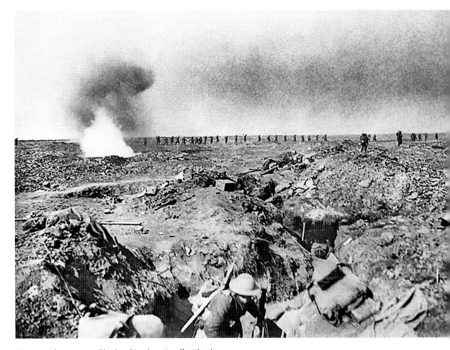

Troops advance on Ginchy. (Authors' collection)

as a result there would be no artillery bombardment to support them and help silence the German occupants. There was simply too much of a risk that it would inflict casualties on its own soldiers. Charles was ordered him to seize one of two trenches off the south-east corner of Delville Wood, standing directly en route to the village, and from here he and his company attacked the southern end of Ginchy.

As soon as they moved off, No. 2 Company's commanding officer was struck down and Charles swiftly and coolly took over. He seemed impervious to the shocking bombardment being levelled on the Devons as he quite calmly led the whole company on towards its objective. The battalion managed to get to the outskirts of the village, but the German machine-gun and shrapnel fire was so accurate and so devastating that they could get no further. Charles had begun to reconnoitre their surroundings when a shell flew into Ginchy and burst right underneath him. He was killed instantly, as the Devons began falling back to their starting positions. The attack on Ginchy had failed.

His parents received a pile of correspondence from the officers who survived the encounter. 'Although he was only with the regiment such a short time,' wrote one, 'he won the esteem of men and officers alike. He was a fine, brave officer in every way and very cool under heavy shellfire.' Charles Teape had survived just three weeks on the Somme. Originally buried where he fell, to the east of Ginchy, the 20 year old was later laid to rest at Delville Wood Cemetery, plot VI.M.1.

5TH SEPTEMBER

#6029 Sergeant George Lee

156TH BRIGADE, ROYAL FIELD ARTILLERY

BEHIND THE BATTLE FOR GINCHY the artillery were doing everything they could to help the infantry to progress. At Montauban there was a father and son team serving with the Royal Field Artillery named George and Robert Lee. Nineteen-year-old Robert had already been serving in the army when war was declared and had arrived on the Western Front as early as August 1914 with the 3rd Brigade of the Royal Horse Artillery. In the meantime, his father carried on as the landlord of the Star and Garter on New Cross Road. In early 1915, however, 44-year-old George travelled 2½ miles to East Dulwich to join a new artillery unit that was being raised in Grove Vale.

While Robert continued to serve abroad, the new 156th Brigade of the Royal Field Artillery began recruiting on 3rd February 1915 and had all the personnel it needed in seven weeks. Nicknamed 'the Camberwell Gun Brigade', in July the army took over responsibility for equipping and clothing the unit and issued it with four 18-pounders. The men continued to live at home and each day George left to take part in initial training, which progressed locally in Dulwich and at the Harrods Institute in Bermondsey. Artificers went to Woolwich, men who were to be cooks went to a school in St John's Wood, and Lady Bathurst even gave French lessons locally. George Lee left for Bulford at the beginning of August. Properly outfitted with guns on their arrival, the brigade began practising with their new weapons in November at Larkhill. Orders arrived just a month later: the brigade was to proceed overseas. On 12th December 1915, George Lee joined his son on the Western Front.

The brigade saw in the new year by undergoing a meticulous introduction to the front by partnering up with the artillery of one of the regular divisions to learn how to ply its trade in a fighting environment. In March it was in action properly, although still attached to another division. George's battery was cutting its teeth by firing on the north bank of the La Bassée canal, where it crossed with a German front-line trench. Here it remained until the end of April and every opportunity was taken to send the officers and men off on gunnery courses and anything else that would get them ready for the summer campaign.

The orders to move to the Somme battlefield came in July, by the middle of which the brigade had reached Corbie. On the 15th George marched through the ruins of Fricourt just after dawn. The guns began firing on the 17th from a position next to Mametz Wood. By the 20th the brigade had been tasked with helping the infantry as they tried to seize High Wood again. They had spent the previous morning registering their targets, and now George and his fellow gunners let rip on the splintered trees and the trenches branching off to the north-west. Their collection of 18-pounder guns launched 2,000 rounds in a bombardment that started at 1am. For the rest of the day they maintained a constant barrage at a slower pace to protect the infantry as they attempted to consolidate any positions gained.

Graves of Sergeant George and Private Robert Lee at Dartmoor Cemetery. (Andrew Holmes)

Three days later, on the 23rd, as Horace Callaghan was going forward at Pozières and other attempts to gain ground went off at different intervals, the 156th Brigade had changed from divisionally allocated to corps artillery. This meant they were no longer directly responsible for the protection of the infantry, but searched the back areas and approaches to the enemy front. German retribution was scathing. On 25th July the wagon lines to the rear were so heavily shelled that they had to be sent back behind Fricourt. Four days later George helped to fire another 1,500 rounds at the rear areas behind High and Delville Woods in just three hours.

August was somewhat quieter than this frantic introduction to the Somme, but notable for the Lee family. During the month, eighty-one men were drafted in to join the 156th Brigade, among them George's teenage son, Robert. From now on, father and son would serve side by side. As August ran its course, there were sporadic flurries of intense counter-battery fire laid down by the German artillery. George and Robert had to contend with the issues that arose from their guns being used constantly and not maintained properly, as many were put out of action when springs and other components failed. Replacement guns had to be hauled in, those that were not in use by other divisions, while their own were sent to the workshops at Heilly for repairs.

On 30th August heavy rain fell, rendering trenches used as cover and gun pits that had only been constructed hastily almost uninhabitable. George and Robert suffered from the same monstrous barrage that killed Harry Butters the following day, 'thousands of lethal shells' falling about them and releasing noxious fumes so that they too had to pull on their gas helmets to avoid being exposed as their work continued. At the beginning of September the brigade was yet another based in the Caterpillar Valley area, where life for an artilleryman was extremely dangerous.

On 5th September the men of A Battery, 156th Brigade suffered a huge blow; four men killed by enemy shellfire at once, including both George and Robert Lee. George's widow, Fanny, had lost both a husband and her only son on one day. They were laid to rest alongside each other at Dartmoor Cemetery, plot I.A.35.

6TH SEPTEMBER
#S/13261 Private Andrew Ballantyne

2ND GORDON HIGHLANDERS

Andrew Ballantyne. (Authors' collection)

THE FIERCE BATTLE FOR GINCHY would continue. The Devons still had a part to play in the aftermath of Charles Teape's death, but joining the fray were the 2nd Gordon Highlanders and among their number was another only son, this time of a mill foreman from Hawick. Born in Galashiels, on the Scottish border, Andrew Ballantyne was educated locally at Gala Public School and at Wilton Public School. After completing his education, he moved to London and was working as a wholesale drapery warehouseman with Messrs Cook, Son & Co. at St Paul's Churchyard when the war began in 1914. He enlisted in October the following year and began training in Aberdeen, arriving in France at the beginning of June 1916.

Like the 9th Devons, the 2nd Gordon Highlanders were in reserve on 3rd October. Half an hour after Charles Teape was ordered to move, Andrew Ballantyne's battalion was ordered into lorries and began the journey up towards Mametz, arriving not long after dawn on 4th September. That night, after the failure of the Devons to take Ginchy, Andrew's battalion was ordered towards the village just before midnight. It had received orders to attack before dawn, but the guides were late in arriving to show them up to the starting points and, following the failed assault of the 4th, the congestion in the trenches coupled with the bad weather all conspired to ensure the Highlanders would be lucky to even reach their jumping off trenches in time for dawn, let alone be ready to attack Ginchy.

The authorities had decided that the next attack should be a surprise one launched in the dark, so Andrew Ballantyne was given a twenty-four hour reprieve when the assault on Ginchy was postponed. The rest of the day was spent in preparation as the battalion was heavily shelled while waiting to charge at the ruined village. Two companies made the initial advance on 6th September as Andrew waited behind. Led by inexperienced replacement officers in the dark, across completely unfamiliar ground, the waves of Scotsmen veered off in the wrong direction almost immediately and had to return to their assembly trenches to start again.

The battalion commander, Major Oxley, came up himself to reorganise his charges and at 5:30am they went off again, supported by the Devons. For his trouble the major received fatal bullet wounds to the head and stomach. Struggling over shell-pocked ground, slipping on slick mud, the men got to within 50 yards of the trees bordering Ginchy before the enemy opened a torrent of fire on them. Snipers in the ruins concentrated on bringing the Highlanders' officers to ground. Without their leaders, the men began to scatter. The assault on the village ground to a halt, the approach to the western side dominated by German machine guns.

Rumours abounded that the enemy was counter-attacking, but an officer who had assumed command rightly concluded that these were false. He could do nothing, though, about the vicious sniping coming from the wrecked masonry about the village whenever a man dared to show his head. To compound the misery of Andrew and his comrades, British shells began to fall short in their midst. 'One shell from our own side is more demoralising than two from the enemy's.'

Andrew Ballantyne and the 2nd Gordon Highlanders were to resume their attack in the afternoon. A further bombardment was levelled on the area and punctually at 2pm the men went forward again with further support from the Devons. Isolated parties got in to the village, but the ruins of Ginchy were rife with spluttering machine guns. The Germans bombarded the spot viciously. Concentrating particularly on the western side of the village, they managed to ensure that no reinforcements could get up. To add to the devastating effect of the enemy shelling, Andrew and his fellow Highlanders had

edged and bombed forward. This was to their credit, but it brought frightful consequences in confused circumstances with patchy lines of communication when they transpired to be well beyond the line that they had reported themselves as holding and came under their own artillery barrage.

The Highlanders were scattered across a wide area and in many cases were now leaderless. A bombing officer managed to collect and reorganise all the men that he could find, urging them to ready themselves defensively for the inevitable counter-attack that was to come. When it arrived, 200 Germans advancing towards them, it proved too much. Still under artillery fire from both sides, and unable to hold their positions when it appeared that everyone was against them, the tattered remnants of the Gordons and Devons began to abandon their hold on Ginchy during the late afternoon and retreat towards their own front line. By 5am the following morning they had been relieved by the 22nd Manchesters.

For Andrew Ballantyne and the 2nd Gordon Highlanders the attack had been a frustrating disaster. Rushed up to the front and into action, their preparation was almost non-existent. The unfortunate loss of their company commanders early in the day left the attack without cohesion and they were simply spread too thinly on a significant objective. To compound the misery inflicted upon the Scotsmen on 6th September, many of their casualties had been caused by the British guns owing to the perennial struggle to maintain adequate communications in the midst of battle.

With his company, Andrew had got well forward with a number of his comrades. They reached a spot within about 80 yards of the German front, so far as they could make out. Amidst the horrendous shelling, he and the rest of the company were attempting to dig from shell hole to shell hole, forming a continuous line of defence. An officer organising the enterprise shouted some orders towards one hole, which Andrew happened to be in. He made a fatal mistake on hearing the officer's voice, looking up and exposing enough of his head to present a target to an enemy sniper. The 21 year old fell dead in Ginchy. 'Personally, I miss poor Andrew more as time goes on,' wrote one of his officers. 'He was a thorough young gentleman.' Andrew Ballantyne was buried near where he fell, but his grave was subsequently lost and his body, if recovered again, was never identified. He is commemorated on the Thiepval Memorial, Pier & Face 15b/15c.

7TH SEPTEMBER
#6008 Private John Dyson Allison

1ST/4TH YORK & LANCASTER REGIMENT

Private John Allison. (Private collection)

WHILE BATTLED RAGED AT GINCHY, casualties were still mounting at the northern end of the battlefield as Gough's army attempted to make progress too. An assault needed to be made on Thiepval and on the Schwaben Redoubt, a particularly menacing German strong point on top of a hill that looked down on Thiepval and to the ground on both sides of the River Ancre.

To move forward Gough's men needed to secure St Pierre Divion and the Strasburg line that ran up to the village. On 3rd September two brigades of the West Riding division lined up as Thiepval was shelled with ammonal and gas to silence the enemy troops protecting the surrounding area from within. At 5:13am they went off and seized a decent amount of the enemy front line amidst smoke and mist. Then fire came from the Schwaben Redoubt and parts of the sector still occupied by the Germans. Elsewhere, the attack could not get forward at all and soon, out of bombs and missing nearly all their officers, the troops now occupying the enemy front line had to withdraw. The two brigades involved had lost 1,200 men. Initially they had been ordered to attack again in the evening, but this was cancelled because the men were in no condition to advance.

It had been a frontal assault that the Germans saw coming, made by new arrivals with dubious amounts of training or by exhausted men.

Born in Halifax, John Allison lived in Elland, in between his hometown and Huddersfield, and worked as a woollen piecer in a local textile factory, tying together broken threads during the weaving process. He had been a territorial in the Duke of Wellington's since 1912 and at the outbreak of war was mobilised swiftly, arriving in France in the summer of 1915. He was at the front for six months before being invalided home to a hospital in Sheffield with a severe case of trench foot. John was not ready to go back to active service for seven months and he embarked at Folkestone in August 1916. On reaching a depot at Étaples, rather than rejoining his unit, he was sent to join the Hallamshire Battalion of the York & Lancaster Regiment.

John's new battalion had not been used during the failed attack of 3rd September. With thirty-one officers and more than 800 men, the Hallamshires had remained to the rear in the Thiepval sector until they were called forward when the attack faltered to relieve troops in the line. Casualties in the battalion had begun to mount almost immediately, thanks to German howitzer shells. The knowledge of the old hands that they would once again be sent out in working parties to Thiepval Wood in filthy weather was utterly demoralising. On 6th September, John Allison arrived with fifty-one other reinforcements taken largely from his old regiment.

At 2am the following morning the enemy began a rancorous bombardment of the York & Lancaster line, sending over a storm of poisonous gas and high explosives. Then came burning oil drums and chlorine gas fired from trench mortars. For three hours it went on, fire and brimstone, shaking the ground, caving in trenches and mutilating all in its path. More than 100 men became casualties, including John Allison.

He had survived a matter of hours on the Somme. John had married his sweetheart, Nellie, two days after Christmas in 1915 while at home wounded, and she was a few weeks pregnant when he was killed. Their daughter, Phyllis, was born in 1917. John Allison was originally buried in Paisley Avenue Cemetery to the south of Thiepval Wood. This was later cleared and those interred relocated. He was finally laid to rest at Lonsdale Cemetery, plot X.H.6.

8TH SEPTEMBER

#58176 Sapper
William Wallwork

16TH DIVISIONAL SIGNALS COMPANY, ROYAL ENGINEERS

TWENTY-YEAR-OLD WILLIAM WALLWORK WAS FROM Bolton. In peacetime he was a telegraphist for the Post Office, and so when he enlisted in his hometown in November 1914, his knowledge of Morse Code and of wireless operation made William a perfect candidate for a very specific role on the Western Front. The idea of signalling on the battlefield was as old as war itself and all manner of methods had been used since the age of antiquity: torches, smoke, beacons, shutters and flags. Communications were revolutionised by Morse Code in the nineteenth century, then the electric telegraph, and the army made the most of Marconi's wireless invention almost immediately at the turn of the twentieth century. In 1908 the Signal Service was formed as part of the Royal Engineers and for the most part it was to provide communications during the Great War by way of a signals company attached to each division.

As with every other form of military technology, equipment and innovations advanced rapidly during the war. Signal companies would incorporate wired telephones, which required the upkeep of miles of cable exposed to enemy shelling, wireless kits and the use of despatch riders to maintain communications on the Western Front. They also used more traditional equipment, such as lamps flashing messages in Morse or mirrors using the reflection of the sun to spell out signals.

William was placed in the company belonging to the 16th (Irish) Division and after training at Blackdown and Hitchin he embarked with the unit in December 1915. Moving anywhere was a trial for the likes of William and his fellow signallers. Each relocation brought with it a new system of telephony with which to become acquainted, setting up equipment and troubleshooting, all without letting essential communications lapse on the battlefield.

A few hours before Andrew Ballantyne had gone forward on 6th September with the 2nd Gordon Highlanders, the Irish Division had fully come into the line and the men had had a piecemeal involvement in earlier attacks on Ginchy. The division spent 8th September busily getting ready for the next day's attack. Men were gathering in the Guillemont area, while battalions busily dug trenches and formed carrying parties. Teams of stretcher-bearers worked hard under fire to bring in the wounded still lying in no-man's-land after the last attack on Ginchy. A few were lucky enough to rest as they awaited nightfall and the order to begin moving up.

Signallers attend to telephone wires on the Somme. (Authors' collection)

Each of the division's three brigades had its own section of signalmen and William and his cohorts had been run off their feet since arriving in the Ginchy sector. The lines of wire that the signallers had run out to brigades from Divisional HQ were long, up to 3 or 4 miles in some cases, and were in very poor condition owing to shellfire and traffic. Time and labour constraints meant they could not do a lot about such a vast and constant issue while the infantry were in the trenches and they were busy elsewhere, but William and his fellow sappers had laid some alternative cabling routes to try to work around the problem. They hadn't even managed to bury their cables to as good a standard as they would have liked. Ideally they would have laid them safely some 6–8ft down in the areas that were being most fiercely shelled, but the division only had one little section of cables buried and they were hardly underground at all.

William and his companions had been luckier with telephone lines laid further forwards towards various battalion headquarters in their sector. They had stayed mostly intact, for 'it was found that even a shallow trench gave very considerable protection to lines laid therein, as compared to lines which had to cross the open'. As far as the most forward cabling was concerned, it was useless, for every time it was laid it was simply cut to pieces again almost immediately. The signals men simply gave up, 'as communication by runner was quicker and satisfactory'. Visual signalling was also pointless. Their lamps were cumbersome and kept getting smashed, and for all the effort they entailed, near Ginchy the dust and smoke from constant explosions meant that nobody could see any successful transmissions.

William was under no illusions about the peril that his job entailed. He had handed his paybook and some money in before heading up to the front on the 8th, with the words, 'take care of these until I come back, you never know your luck in these parts'. Artillery fire on both sides was constant during the day, along with enemy snipers seeking to pick off men one at a time. During the course of the day William was killed, his body retrieved and brought back for burial as final preparations were concluded for the upcoming attack. He was just 20. His mother Alice chased the War Office in desperation to know where her boy was buried, 'since his and our sacrifice is so great, and we hope in future to be permitted to visit the spot which to us is so dear'. Her 'Dear Boy' William was laid to rest at Dantzig Alley British Cemetery, plot I.E.4.

9TH SEPTEMBER

Lieutenant Thomas Michael Kettle

9TH ROYAL DUBLIN FUSILIERS

THOMAS KETTLE WAS 36 YEARS old on the Somme. He was the son of a Dublin farmer and one of the founders of the Land League. Having finished at University College Dublin, Tom was elected as Nationalist MP for East Tyrone in 1906 by a narrow margin of less than twenty votes. He had retired from parliament four years later, however, when he was elected to the Chair of National Economics of Ireland at his alma mater. A member of the Irish Bar, now with a wife, Margaret, and a daughter, Betty, Tom now made his living mostly as a journalist and writer.

A member of the original Executive of the National Volunteers and a staunch supporter of Irish Independence, Thomas was in Belgium when war was declared, obtaining arms for the Nationalist cause.

Lieutenant Thomas Kettle. (Authors' collection)

Irish troops return from the capture of Ginchy.
(Authors' collection)

On 2nd August he saw people in the streets of Brussels tear newspapers from the vendors' hands to read the latest on the great European conflict. He stayed in Belgium working as a war correspondent for the *Daily News*, this overtaking his original purpose for being on the Continent. Tom believed fiercely that people should know what was happening. 'Our duty,' he claimed, 'is not to banish the memories of war as we have experienced it, but to burn them in beyond effacement, every line and trait, every dot and detail.' He travelled the Western Front to be able to do it, including visiting GHQ in France.

As a man who had given out anti-recruiting leaflets during the Second Boer War on the streets of Dublin, Tom had developed surprising opinions in the eyes of many and went so far as to join the army in order to go and fight the enemy himself. Neutrality, in his opinion, meant that evil won. 'He considered that Ireland had a duty not only to herself, but to the world and an obligation to follow the road of honour and justice.' He also believed that doing this would help lead to the implementation of Home Rule. He travelled the country tirelessly expounding this point of view. Opponents labelled him a recruiting sergeant and he received a

multitude of abusive correspondence, usually anonymous. His answer? 'Ireland was on the side of England because England was on the side of God.' The crimes committed against Belgium must be accounted for. 'I care for Liberty,' he admitted, 'more than I care for Ireland.'

Tom left Dublin on the evening of 14th July 1916 for the front. 'I am calm and happy,' he told his brother soon afterwards, 'but desperately anxious to live.' He had seen modern, industrialised warfare, been bombarded by artillery and knew 'what an outrage it is against simple men'. It was enough to convince him that working for peace when the war was finally over was a worthy way to spend the rest of his days. As September dawned, the front was taking its toll on Tom but he refused to go on sick leave and declined offers of a staff appointment in order to stay with his men.

Since the onset of September all the troops of the 16th (Irish) Division had been in action under other commands, attached to various other formations. Now, weak in numbers and tired, Tom and the other survivors were back under their proper authority. His brigadier made it clear that his men, including the 9th Royal Dublin Fusiliers, would need to be relieved as soon as the next assault had taken place on Ginchy, as they would not be fit for anything else. By the night of the 7th the men were digging assembly trenches ready for the resumption of the assault on the village on the 9th. Placed in charge of the remnants of B Company, Tom advanced into position alongside a fellow officer. The stench of the dead on the road on the way up was so bad that they smeared foot powder on their faces. The support trench was finished; the men steeled themselves for battle. Everything was set for the Irish to take their turn in attacking Ginchy.

The 9th September dawned. A priest sat with the Catholic officers and gave general absolution as zero hour approached. Then, in the early evening, the line advanced under the artillery barrage on the first objective, the platoons spread out 40 yards apart. Still Tom waited to go forward in support. Just after 5pm, the 9th Royal Dublin Fusiliers made their attack, advancing to help clear the western side of the village. German troops were surrendering, fleeing towards Flers and Lesboeufs. So excited were some of the Irishmen that they needed to be reined in so they could consolidate the ruins of the village instead of charging after them. Finally, Ginchy had fallen. Tom's brigade would claim the honour of having captured the village, but he would not be with them.

'I was just behind Tom when we went over the top,' wrote a young subaltern. 'He was in a front position and a bullet got over a steel waistcoat that he wore and entered his heart.' Kettle had fallen right at the beginning of the advance. His companion pressed a crucifix into his hand, and within a minute he was gone. He commented, 'this is the seventh anniversary of my wedding, I forget whether seventh or eighth.'

The Germans made several attempts to recapture the village on the 9th, all of which were unsuccessful. When the surviving Irishmen marched out of Ginchy, a piper walked in front of them, playing a lament for those who had not returned. Much was made of the political loss to Ireland of Tom Kettle's death, but his own thoughts were simpler. If he was not to come home, Tom wanted his wife to know that 'there was never in all the world a dearer woman or a more perfect wife and adorable mother'. He couldn't help but think of their little girl. 'My heart cries for you and Betty, whom I may never see again ... If the last sacrifice is ordained think that in the end I wiped out all the old stains. Tell Betty her daddy was a soldier and died as one. My love, now at last clean, will find a way to you.' Lieutenant Kettle did receive a burial on the field of battle, but his grave was subsequently lost. If recovered again, his remains were never identified and he is commemorated on the Thiepval Memorial, Pier & Face 16c.

10TH SEPTEMBER
2nd Lieutenant Edward Cazalet

1ST WELSH GUARDS

2nd Lieutenant Edward Cazalet. (College Library, Eton College)

IT WAS THE 1ST WELSH Guards who would bury Tom Kettle when the battalion began arriving in the early hours of 10th September to relieve the Irishmen at Ginchy. The unit had only come into existence by Royal Warrant in February 1915 and among their number as the Guards Division arrived on the Somme was 22-year-old subaltern Edward Cazalet.

Educated at Eton College and Trinity College, Cambridge, 'Doodie' was one of four children and grew up at the family home in Fairlawne, Tonbridge. He had contributed a year to the OTC at school, but was not of a particularly military temperament. Nonetheless, Edward applied for a commission in The Buffs on the outbreak of war. Having applied to transfer into the new Welsh Guards, by the beginning of 1916 he was stationed at the Tower of London and spent time guarding Roger Casement before his execution. In mid-July Edward left Southampton and joined the 1st Battalion in the Ypres sector. Less than two weeks later the Welsh Guards were ordered south, where they were accommodated on a large farm. There they trained in open warfare for the upcoming offensive on 15th September, undergoing several battalion field days and a larger scale brigade one. All their endeavours were a trial and of dubious use because the local countryside was covered in crops in full growth and Edward and his men were forced to file around the side of them in the middle of mock battle so as not to do any damage.

Molly Cazalet with her first born, Edward (College Library, Eton College)

Edward despised the squalor of the front. 'It is rather cold,' he wrote to his mother in early September, 'with the result that there are hardly any flies! That is only to say about 1,000 in my room instead of 100,000.' The trenches, of course, were worse. 'I can't get a moment's sleep,' he complained from them in August when he was plagued by rats. 'The German shells, etc. are nothing as compared to the incessant scratch, rubble, squeak, etc. of this beastly vermin.'

The Cazalets were extremely close and he missed his family, especially his mother, Molly, dearly. Edward's letters were interspersed by quick notes that reminded them constantly of how much his parents, brother and sisters were always in his thoughts. 'I just long with my heart and soul to be with you,' said one. 'This is just to tell you that I love you more than ever,' he scribbled in another to Molly. A third was included in a last letter before the battalion was sent into the line at Ginchy: 'My own darling, this is only a line to tell you that I love my mother ... and that I long to be with you and all my family.' In turn, Molly Cazalet adored her first born and could not do enough for him and his companions at the front. She was sending copies of *The Spectator* to a friend of his and Edward caught sight of one in his tent. 'I could have kissed it,' he told her, 'as I knew my Mummie had read and touched it!' As well as sending

Edward regular orders from Fortnum & Mason, his mother wanted to send parcels to the men, as well as gifts to his particular friends. Edward gave her an address for his soldier servant. 'He would like some food I know.'

Although Ginchy had been taken by the Irish Division, the situation was not secure on the evening of 9th September. Nevertheless, the Guards Division was ordered to take over the line. Edward and his fellow officers were instructed to dump all excess kit in a nearby barn ready to move up. They passed up congested roads, past clumps and rows of guns, the concentration of which in such high numbers the Guards had never seen. On arrival, Edward Cazalet's commanding officer went to Bernafay Wood to see the brigadier of the Irish 49th Brigade, who was apparently in charge of the 48th too in the chaos following the battle, to arrange the relief that was supposed to take place. It was envisaged that this would not happen until the situation was actually secure and the commanders fully informed as to the disposition of troops. However, in line with statements made before the attack, the Irish brigadier asked for a relief at once for his exhausted men, who had been without respite for days.

This was less than ideal for the incoming Guards, who would be taking over the line when the fighting had yet to fully die down, in the dark, and in an area they were completely unfamiliar with and had not yet reconnoitred. But this was agreed and that night the Welsh Guards were informed that they would be taking over the left-hand side of the line in Ginchy, temporarily coming under the command of the Irish Division until the situation was resolved the following morning.

Edward's company commander had gone away sick, so they were short of officers. Guides met them at Bernafay Wood and led them through Guillemont and then on to Ginchy. Edward's company was to form the left of the line and it arrived to assume its position in frightening circumstances. The 48th Brigade began filing away at midnight, past Welsh Guards Battalion HQ, which was on the outskirts of Guillemont. Then Edward and his comrades were alone. Ginchy was shrouded in complete darkness, out of which came spurts of rifle fire from different directions. Germans shot out from among the ruins, but thankfully for the terrified Welsh Guards, those they encountered personally surrendered at once.

It was nearly impossible to find the right positions. Instead of facing north-east as planned, Edward was facing north-west on the outskirts of Ginchy. The whole scenario was a mess. No. 3 Company had managed to get in touch with the troops on its left, but its diligence was causing problems because the rest of the battalion was off point. Edward's company was stretching the whole line back. The enemy kept popping up and firing at them, then vanishing into the night as the Welshmen fumbled in the dark looking for the troops on their flanks. There was still barely any light at 7am. The Grenadier Guards were not on their right where they should have been, it seemed, and the Prince of Wales Company was still looking for them when the Germans attacked suddenly.

The counter-attack came from the north, the enemy's movements masked by mist. There was a bitter and confusing struggle, and rabid hand-to-hand fighting. There were many examples of desperate scrapping as the Germans tried to force their way back into the village. A Private William Williams 'was seen to dispose of several of the enemy, until with a furious thrust he completely transfixed a German and was unable to free his bayonet'. Undeterred, 'he knocked another down with his fists, and seized yet another by the throat, when they both fell into a shell hole. More Germans rushed up, and the gallant Williams did not rise again.'

Inch by inch, the Guards repulsed the counter-attack, but as they did so a shell burst claimed the life of Edward Cazalet. Mortally wounded, the 22 year old survived just a few moments before passing away. His soldier servant was devastated. He fussed over his fallen officer. They had had a conversation several days earlier and so he was clear on what should be done. Edward was taken back down the line for burial alongside another Old Etonian of the battalion who had also been killed. A French master who had left Eton immediately on the outbreak of war to act as an interpreter had found himself attached to the battalion. 'I have just been to the funeral,' he wrote to Edward's younger brother Victor, who was also serving in the army. 'I am so cut up about these losses of my dear young friends that I cannot write more.' In all, in taking

over the line at Ginchy, ill-prepared to stave off enemy counter-attacks, the Welsh Guards had suffered more than 200 casualties.

In 1927 the father of one of the survivors of 10th September read the name of a female MP with a familiar name – Edward's sister, Thelma. He felt compelled to pen a letter:

Every time I see your name in print, I am sadly reminded of the very tender action of a young officer in the Welsh Guards bearing your name, who just before he himself was killed found time to show much sympathy to a son of mine who had been seriously wounded. Noticing my son wiping away the blood coursing through his lips with his coat sleeve, Cazalet took out his own handkerchief and placed it in my son's hand, and observing at the same time that he was shivering violently, he rapidly ran to his dugout and brought his own [blanket] and tenderly wrapped it round my son who by then had been laid on a stretcher.

This small act had never been forgotten by this man, who had mourned the loss of his son in the early 1920s when he never recovered from his experiences in the war:

I can never express the sorrow and gratitude that fills my heart at the sound of your name. If you are any relation of Lieutenant Cazalet would it be asking too much of you to let his parents know of their boy's last gallant and loving deed?

The Cazalet family were deeply religious and had put much money into St Giles' Church in Shipbourne. A memorial service for 22-year-old Edward was overseen there by the Bishop of Rochester. The congregation sang his favourite hymns and read his favourite psalms. Edward Cazalet was laid to rest at Citadel New Military Cemetery, plot II.A.4.

11TH SEPTEMBER

#TF/1473 Private William Oscar Jannaway

1/8TH MIDDLESEX REGIMENT

BORN IN PORTSMOUTH, WILLIAM JANNAWAY was a 20-year-old labourer for the Brentford Gas Company when he signed up for his local Territorials in 1911. At the outbreak of war he had been working at Messrs Beldam's factory, 'where he was held in high regard by all the firm', but on mobilisation William's battalion of the Middlesex Regiment was sent to Gibraltar. There he remained for six months before a brief spell at home followed by redeployment to the Western Front. William's period of service expired in 1915, but he immediately enlisted again for the duration of the war. The onset of the great Somme offensive was a complicated affair, with men to be moved, prisoners to be supervised and guard details to fulfil, and so there was a great need for military policemen. William was attached to them for just this purpose for the first two weeks of July, until returning to the 1/8th Middlesex in time for the rest of the battle.

By 11th September, at the same time that Ginchy was being furiously fought over, the southern forces of Rawlinson's army were also trying to secure ground before the onset of the new offensive; attacking ground beyond Guillemont, including Leuze Wood. Known as 'Lousy Wood' by the British troops, it straddled the road from Guillemont to Combles north of Falfemont Farm, a commanding position with views to the north and east. This had to be achieved despite commanders being hampered by a lack of reinforcements because men were being held back for 15th September.

To the rear, William Jannaway and his fellow Middlesex men trained for forthcoming operations, before, on the 9th, they went up into support lines while the rest of their London division made an attack. Thus far the division had made attempts to attack towards Combles, but the enemy had counter-attacked with a high proportion of bombers and forced them back, resulting in only partial success. The following day, the 10th, William's battalion commander went up to reconnoitre a route up to the forward trenches that he and his fellow Londoners would occupy. At 7:30pm that night the battalion began to take over the line opposite Leuze Wood.

At 4:50pm on the 11th, William's battalion received orders for two companies to attack trenches on the Ginchy/Morval road, where there was a little salient strongly held by the enemy, in order to link up with the Guards on their left. The Guards would support them as they attempted to cut it off, wiping out the German occupants, until the rest of the battalion could hold firm and provide support. However, throughout the rest of the afternoon the enemy placed a heavy barrage on and behind Leuze Wood and the Middlesex men could not get everybody arranged for the attack, so it was postponed for a few hours.

At zero hour William and his comrades surged forward and took their objective, but the troops on the left did not conform as expected and so they were forced to give up the position they had won as the enemy began to come at them wielding bombs. At a cost of almost 200 casualties, the Middlesex men had claimed 50 yards of trench.

William Jannaway fell at the outset of the attack, mortally wounded as he was climbing over the parapet of his trench, chucking bombs as he went. Officially reported as missing until 1917, there was little doubt as to what had happened to him, according to the Middlesex's chaplain. 'He was one of the brave lads who fell on that terrible night ... He was a good lad and a real soldier.' William left behind a wife of less than a year, Maude. His body, if recovered, was never identified and he is commemorated on the Thiepval Memorial, Pier & Face 12d/13b.

12TH SEPTEMBER

#118074 Private Robert Henry Killip

2ND CANADIAN MOUNTED RIFLES

ALL OF THE TROOPS THAT began making up Canada's contingent on the outbreak of the Great War were volunteers. The first group of more than 30,000 offered their services in just a few days and of those, 60 per cent were of British birth. Canada was also experiencing a depression in 1914 and many men were out of work. Some appreciated the wage, or if they were expats perhaps saw it as a route home. Others were experienced men who had fought in the Boer War; adventurers who could not resist the great European conflict. By the time the Canadians arrived on the Somme they numbered more than 100,000 men in four divisions. The first three had been resting since June after a monstrous time in the dreaded Ypres Salient, but still providing working parties and undergoing training. One of these was 25-year-old Robert Killip. Born and raised on the Isle of Man, he emigrated aboard the *Empress of Ireland* in 1912, sailing into Nova Scotia. Having departed Britain a farm labourer, on the outbreak of war he was a rancher in Alberta, where he enlisted at Pincher's Creek, a rural new town south-west of the Rockies.

Until they arrived on the Somme, the Canadian forces' experience of fighting in Europe had been very much characterised by defensive warfare. Life had become monotonous in Belgium and so there was excitement about venturing over the border. Many of the men spoke French and the knowledge that they had crossed the Atlantic to fight the Germans made them fascinating to the natives. As planned, the ANZAC troops on the Somme were being withdrawn and replaced by the Canadians, command passing to the latter on 3rd September. At the beginning of the month, Robert Killip was at Abeele undergoing training when orders came to say that the 2nd Canadian Mounted Rifles were to leave immediately and entrain for the battlefield. On the 7th Robert travelled via Saint-Omer, Étaples and Boulogne and arrived north of Amiens at 3:30am the following morning. Three days later, more orders came to clamber into motor buses that jolted and lurched towards Albert. Twenty-four hours on, having arrived, Robert and the rest of the men drew forty-eight hour rations and departed for the trenches. The Mounted Rifles were about to find themselves in the Mouquet Farm sector, where their compatriots had already been standing their ground for a week or so, despite heavy barrages and counter-attacks. The artillery bombardment rarely let up, but Haig wanted his Canadian troops to have time to settle in before undertaking any major offensive operations.

On the night of 11th/12th September, in 'inky darkness' the Canadians came into the line to find dubious looking trenches scratched into the unfamiliar ground. Robert's battalion relieved the 10th Canadian Infantry near Pozières, a shade over 700 men with twenty-two officers. Two companies went into the front line, leaving one in support and one in reserve. The relief was completed relatively swiftly, without mishap and patrols were immediately sent out into no-man's-land. The men even managed to set out advanced posts ahead of their front line.

The Canadians were constantly sapping to get ready for upcoming operations and the Germans were trying to wreck their efforts with shells, machine guns and bombs against working parties, anything they could to deter efforts, causing mounting casualties. From the moment they came into the line, Robert Killip's brigade was subjected to heavy shelling, 'the Germans evidently having become aware of the fact that new troops were arriving in the sector'. Before they had had any chance to settle in, a sudden attack was launched by the enemy at Robert's battalion. They were driven back, with the ground left covered in German bodies, but the Canadians had suffered too.

Less than twenty-four hours after arriving in the trenches on the Somme, Robert Killip was mortally wounded. Admitted to a field ambulance with a fractured skull caused by gunshot wounds to his head, there was nothing that medical personnel could do to save him. By 13th September, having assumed command ten days before, the Canadian contingent had already suffered casualties of almost 100 officers and more than 2,700 men. Robert Killip was laid to rest at Albert Communal Cemetery Extension, plot I.N.19.

Canadian troops move off with their picks and shovels to consolidate a position. (Authors' collection)

13TH SEPTEMBER

2nd Lieutenant Godfrey Derman Gardner

9TH SUFFOLK REGIMENT

TIME WAS RUNNING OUT FOR Rawlinson's army to get to their chosen start line before 15th September and troops were still trying frantically to secure objectives to pave the way for a momentous breakthrough advance. On the 9th there had been another ill-fated attack towards High Wood, but it still evaded the general's men. To the south the intended advance towards Combles had faltered, although Falfemont Farm was now in Allied hands. The Earl of Cavan was overseeing the corps of the Fourth Army that met with the French and under his command was a 34-year-old musician named Godfrey Gardner. Born in West London, on the outbreak of war Godfrey joined one of the city's territorial battalions before applying for a regular commission and finding himself transferred to the Suffolk Regiment.

Music was in Godfrey Gardner's blood. His father was a professor of music and Godfrey, one of the youngest of more than a dozen children, followed his lead. Educated at the Philological School, he went on to the Guildhall School of Music, Queen's College, Oxford, and the Royal Academy of Music. He was a member and organist of the Royal Philharmonic Society, an organist at Holy Trinity, Paddington, and St Giles', Cripplegate. He also found time to fulfil his role as a professor of music at the School for the Blind in Swiss Cottage. Once in France in 1915, Godrey arranged numerous events and entertainments for the men in addition to his official duties. He organised the music for the Easter services at Talbot House. Named after a fallen young officer, this 'Every-Mans Club' in Poperinghe near Ypres was the brainchild of an army chaplain named 'Tubby' Clayton and a refuge for the British soldier. Opened at the end of 1915, rank was left at the door. There was a constant supply of tea, rooms where the men could relax and read, and a chapel at the top of the house where visitors could seek solace and try to forget what was going on nearby on the battlefield.

The Thiepval Memorial. (Andrew Holmes)

Clayton said of Easter Day 1916: 'I shall always regard it as the happiest of my ministry.' They had planned ten services, not having a clue if anyone would be able to make it at all, but the day far surpassed their expectations. The house was busy from 5:30am with worshippers. Godfrey laid on music for the occasion and was helped by members of the Welsh Guards' Choir. At lunchtime they went off in a group to a headquarters for another service before visiting a battery of gunners bearing hymn books and a harmonium for Godfrey to play.

During the month of August 1916, Godfrey's battalion rotated in and out of the trenches at the northern end of the Somme battlefield. By the end of the month though, the 9th Suffolks had travelled south and on 11th September moved into the trenches running from Leuze Wood to the edge of Ginchy, partly relieving William Jannaway's division and partly Edward Cazalet's. Patrols revealed no enemy troops immediately south-east of Ginchy and Godfrey's battalion was among those ordered to attack. At 6:20am on 13th September, the 9th Suffolks went forward in conjunction with another battalion to attack the Quadrilateral, a well-protected German stronghold to the east of Ginchy. When the men reached the 400 yards of open ground running up to the German wire entanglements in front of the Quadrilateral, the battalion was held up by machine-gun fire amidst mist and low cloud.

The attack ground to a halt. A reserve company was ordered up to join them but, owing to the German machine-gun fire, they could not attack. A third attempt went forward at 6pm but the 9th Suffolks could still not penetrate the Quadrilateral. A new trench was dug by the battalion and this enabled them to get in touch with the 2nd Sherwoods on the left and the 8th Bedfords on the right, but for the honour of sitting half a mile forward of the morning's position, Godfrey's battalion had suffered heavy casualties. A total of 212 men were gone from the ranks of the 9th Suffolks. Lord Cavan had decided that enough was enough, his men would attack from where they already were on the 15th. There was nothing to do now but prepare and then wait it out until zero hour. More than half the Suffolks' officers had become casualties during their attack, including Godfrey Gardner, who was killed in action while leading his men and buried where he fell. Lieutenant Gardner's body, if recovered, was never identified and he is commemorated on the Thiepval Memorial, Pier & Face 1c/2a.

14TH SEPTEMBER
#15965 Private Francis Henry Halfacre

1ST/8TH DUKE OF WELLINGTON'S WEST RIDING REGIMENT

Private Francis Halfacre. (Authors' collection)

BEFORE THE WAR, FRANCIS HALFACRE had been a point boy for the Tramways Company. A 25-year-old North London native, he enlisted in March 1915 and served at Gallipoli, landing at Suvla Bay in August of that year. By July 1916 he was on the Western Front. Arriving on the Somme, Francis' division came into the line on 7th September, the day that John Allison was killed on the right of Gough's army.

Gough had been ordered to take good care of his resources because, frankly, with the offensive due to resume in force to the south of him in twenty-four hours, there weren't any to spare. Commanders beneath him were still orchestrating smaller assaults if there was some profit to be had but, on Gough's remit, they were not placing any more than two battalions into any attack at once. On this premise it had been decided that Francis Halfacre's battalion could be used in limited endeavour to make some useful progress on the higher ground to the south of Thiepval.

On 11th September he and his comrades were in huts attempting to clean themselves up and training nearby, but at 8am on the 14th the men were ordered to depart and relieve the 6th York & Lancaster Regiment in the Hindenburg Trench to the south of Thiepval. At 6:30pm they were ordered to attack the Wonder Work, a star-shaped strong point guarding the south of Thiepval that lay in front of the British lines. There were two companies, with a third in support and the last in reserve. The British artillery barrage was spot on. The West Riding battalion reached its objective, taking the German front line and 250 yards of a nearby trench alongside a battalion of the West Yorkshires, and then the *Wunderwerk* along with a portion of the German line as far as the Thiepval road. Their left flank was secured by more Yorkshiremen and the attacking companies immediately began digging themselves communication trenches linking their new position to existing ones immediately.

It was a short, decisive action. The two battalions involved carried their initial gains with few losses, but those engaged had then lost some 700 men in trying to dig in in their new positions, mostly at the cost of enemy shelling, which came down furiously once the Germans had lost ground. Francis Halfacre was mortally wounded by this enemy barrage and was laid to rest at Lonsdale Cemetery, plot VI.L.5.

15TH SEPTEMBER
Captain David Henderson

1/19TH LONDON REGIMENT

SINCE THE SUCCESS OF 14TH July, Rawlinson's army had advanced only 1,000 yards on a 5-mile front. This had been achieved in all manner of smaller scale attacks conducted in a comparatively disorganised manner when his previous success was taken into account. To achieve these gains his men had suffered more than 80,000 casualties and his standing with Haig had fallen significantly as a result. All now rested on the resumption of the offensive proper on 15th September.

The Battle of Flers-Courcelette had been a long time coming. Rawlinson had been aware since mid-August that Haig wanted a large-scale offensive on the original third German system. By the latter's reckoning, in mid-September the Germans would be thoroughly worn out by British and French endeavours, so it was hoped that this was the time to make a decisive breakthrough and try to win the Battle of the Somme. By the end of August, leaders at home had begun to question

the mounting casualties on the Somme. Did the ends justify the means? But Britain had fully committed herself to this enterprise and there was no question of simply abandoning it and starting somewhere else. Rawlinson was immediately put to work planning this new offensive.

Haig rejected his first attempt; it wasn't bold enough for his liking. Rawlinson's standing was low enough after the previous weeks' endeavours that he wasn't in a position to argue, or at least he did not. A new plan was submitted on 31st August and Haig was much keener; Rawlinson had outlined a 'weightier thrust' all along the Fourth Army line. Morval, Lesboeufs, Gueudecourt and Flers were to be seized as soon as possible. These were the closest points of the original third line, which were by now the Germans' front system. It was now an overly ambitious plan. Just like 1st July, the Fourth Army would be trying to break through three lines of defence at once in order to send the enemy running for home. Once again, when the troops had got into the enemy system, the cavalry were marked to be ready and waiting to deploy into the gap at an opportune moment. Haig had three more armies to the north on alert ready to add to German woes, and at one point there was even a plan for feigning a landing on the Belgian coast to stretch the enemy's resources to the utmost. He was going to have another shot at conquering the Germans on the Western Front in 1916.

According the attack the reverence it warranted, fresh troops would be brought in for this grand new offensive. Among them was the 47th London Division, which comprised battalions from all over the capital: Blackheath, Woolwich and Clapham, as well as those with special affiliations: The Post Office Rifles, the London Irish and the Civil Service Rifles. Serving in one of them was the 27-year-old son of Arthur Henderson, leader of the Labour Party, a future winner of the Nobel Peace Prize and, in the midst of the First World War, the first Labour Cabinet member. Prior to the war, his son David had acted as an assistant to John Hodge, an MP in charge of the British Steel Smelters' Trade Union. He was also very active in the Brotherhood movement, the youngest member of the National Council and Assistant Honorary Secretary of the London Federation. In short, following in the footsteps of his father, David was a shining future hope for the Labour Party: 'one of those strong attractive personalities that impress themselves on people and events.'

David Henderson joined the Public Schools Battalion in September 1914 and was later transferred to the Inns of Court Officer Training Corps and given a commission in February 1915. He was promoted to captain in June, but both of his younger brothers had seen active service with the Honourable Artillery Company and understandably David, whose service had all been home based, applied for a transfer to do so too. He was later attached to the Middlesex Regiment, but was transferred to the 19th London Regiment, created on Camden High Street at the beginning of the war. On his arrival on the Western Front, he was 'full of brave, cheery, enthusiastic optimism', David was given his own company after only twenty-four hours in the trenches.

His battalion started marching south towards the Somme on 1st August and a month later they began training for an assault near High Wood using a flagged course. The 15th September was to begin with four stages of attack, moving trench to trench and methodically taking objectives: green, brown, blue and red lines on the map, the last of which Rawlinson ambitiously reckoned on getting to by noon. Then, of course, when a gap had been forced in the German line, the cavalry would be waiting to gallop into action.

Formal orders and instructions were issued on 11th September. David Henderson's division was allocated the attack on and around High Wood and the wood itself was among the first objectives. Once the first line had been taken, the 19th Londons were among those ordered to pass through the initial attackers and proceed down the other side of the hill towards the German rear positions.

The preliminary bombardment opened on the 12th, the most severe since 1st July. The Londoners were filing into the line, through Albert, past fields full of waiting cavalry and massed groups of guns banging away at enemy targets far in the distance. On 13th September the junior officers of David's battalion reconnoitred the front line they were to attack. High Wood was off to the side and allotted to another battalion. By now it was a wood in name only, with 'ragged stumps sticking out of churned up earth, poisoned with the fumes of high explosives'. There was a total absence of landmarks. 'Imagine Hampstead Heath full of cocoa powder, and the natural surface folds further complicated by countless shell holes each deep enough to hold a man, and everywhere meandering crevices where men live below the surface of the ground.' The objectives for 47th Division were limited when compared with some of those going forward in terms of distance, but this did not diminish their importance. High Wood was a significant prize. Possession of their first objective would give the British Army observation all the way out towards Bapaume.

Shared grave of Captain David Henderson at London Cemetery and Extension. (Andrew Holmes)

At 1:40am David Henderson and his company moved to their assembly positions. The trenches detailed for this were pitiable, troops having been unable to dig them properly because of enemy attention. Zero hour was at 6:20am and Rawlinson's men poured forward. Ahead of David, the leading battalions advanced into no-man's-land, but were held up by machine-gun fire and could go no further. The assault of High Wood had also been held up by enemy machine-gun fire, 'in spite of the reckless bravery of officers and men, whilst a confused struggle continued and losses grew heavy'. The men of the London Division were being grievously punished for an error on the part of their corps commander, who thought that the opposing lines were too close together at High Wood and so had ordered no artillery bombardment before the men went forward to help silence German machine gunners and ease their path.

Zero hour for David Henderson was 7am. In mist, the 19th and 20th London battalions left their assembly trenches and bent their heads against heavy enfilade fire from the left. They came up behind the stalling men in front of them and the four battalions became congested inside High Wood, piled on top of each other. Here, the wood, the first objective, was still not secured, let alone the reverse of the slope beyond, allocated to David and his men. The trenches were so full of wounded and dying men, that the 19th Londons could not get forward. At this point the battalion's commanding officer decided to leave his headquarters to try to restore order. He clambered out of the communication trench, calling upon men to follow, and was killed almost immediately by a machine-gun bullet.

While efforts were made to clear the surrounding trenches of the dead and wounded, a barrage was requested. Bombing attacks were organised to work up the flanks of the wood, but it was the brigade's trench mortars that decided the fate of High Wood. They launched a quite incredible 750 mortar rounds into it in just fifteen minutes. The rapid rate of fire blew the enemy away in terms of morale, as well as physically. German occupants began to surrender. Hundreds of prisoners were collected, along with several machine guns and two howitzers. The enemy were pouring out of the western side of the wood and into British hands, some of them did not even need an escort as they willingly went away into captivity, desperate to get away from the place. They had had enough. After two months of bitter fighting, High Wood fell.

By 11am it was reported as being clear of the enemy. Collections of men from all units were pushed up to consolidate it. The scene was so chaotic that it was decided to pull everyone together and form just one battalion. Each trench was placed under the command of a separate officer. In fine weather, the rest of 15th September was spent counting their losses and reorganising their survivors while consolidation of the first objective continued. For now, the other three were forgotten. The losses to the 47th London Division were catastrophic, nearly 5,000. The 19th Londons had suffered casualties of more than 300 men, including David Henderson.

His death was overshadowed on the political scene. The war did not take into account party loyalty, and on the same day, serving with a battalion of the Grenadier Guards, the prime minister's son, Raymond Asquith, had fallen. But in the week following his death, a memorial service was held for David at the Wesleyan Church in Clapham and a message of condolence read out on behalf of the King and Queen. Captain David Henderson was laid to rest at London Cemetery and Extension, plot 1A.A.14.

16TH SEPTEMBER
Lieutenant Reginald Charles Legge

D COMPANY, HEAVY BRANCH
MACHINE GUN CORPS

THE FACE OF A MODERN battlefield would change forever on 15th September 1916. Caterpillar tractors had been used to shift heavy artillery pieces since 1908 in the British Army. The idea of a tank had been around before the onset of the Great War and, as ever, the Royal Engineers would be instrumental in its innovation. A determined major named Swinton had been trying to get the concept of a 'machine gun destroyer' off the ground since 1914. With Winston Churchill also pushing something similar in the Navy, research began, but ground to a halt when results were not encouraging. By the summer of 1915, though, the idea had reached exalted ears and Swinton now began to garner attention from GHQ and the War Office. By February 1916, his brainchild was undergoing secret trials at Hatfield in front of Kitchener and high ranking politicians. A hundred of the prototype were ordered and in May the Heavy Branch Machine Guns Corps came into being, intended to comprise six companies of twenty-five tanks with twenty-eight officers and 255 men allotted to each. All of this was unknown to the enemy, for it had occurred under a shroud of secrecy: 'one of the most remarkable exhibitions of patriotic restraint in the whole course of the war.'

Haig had been kept fully informed about this new-fangled invention. He was 'eager to employ them as soon as a sufficient number were ready'. To waste the element of surprise would have been criminal by introducing them one or two at a time, so it was in September 1916 that they would make their debut. It was the stuff of which dreams were made: an armoured vehicle that could withstand small arms fire or red hot splinters from shells; armed with two mobile 6-pounder guns and several travelling machine guns and capable of simply rolling over trenches, through wire entanglements, or crashing through walls. And what would it be able to do to the enemy machine-gun nests from which advancing men were torn apart? There would also be the effect on morale. This was a machine that the enemy did not even know existed that would amble towards them breathing fire and crushing all in its path. Rawlinson and Gough were given notes on tactics to decide how to use the tanks when they were making their battle plans for September. They were told the strength of them lay in getting tanks close to the enemy and employing them in conjunction with the infantry. They were told that they should be used against woods, villages, strong points and machine guns that were giving the troops particular problems. Thus, on the eve of the Battle of Flers-Courcelette, dozens of tanks were ready

A C Company Mark I tank in September 1916. Note the 'tail', a feature that was later abandoned. (Authors' collection)

back in England, attested at the end of November 1915 into the ranks of the Buckinghamshire Yeomanry. Later, Reginald applied for a commission in the regular army, citing his first choice as the Royal Sussex Regiment, but when the Machine Gun Corps began touting for officers to man their new tanks he made the transfer to the Heavy Branch in the spring of 1916.

By the end of August, Reginald had trained at Burley and Thetford and the men had begun overseeing their precious cargo aboard heavy trains bound for the coast. D Company's tanks were ready for unloading at Rouen as September dawned and, despite the secrecy that was maintained around these new additions, shrouded in their tarpaulins, plenty of exalted personages such as Haig and General Joffre came to gawp at them 'in embarrassing numbers'.

On the night of the 13th, the tank crews collected petrol, oil, water, rations and ammunition ready for their debut. The following day Reginald and the other officers reconnoitred the route they were to take up to the trenches, discovering that it was much damaged by shell holes and cut up by communication trenches, all of which they would need to traverse. 'To move tanks over this ground in the dark would mean heavy work and careful manipulation and this was fully realised by crew skippers.' The rest of the day was spent going over orders for the attack, before, at 8:30pm, the tanks began to move off to their starting lines, the low rumble of their engines cleverly masked by aeroplanes flying up and down the German front lines. The crews had had little rest for days and progress was difficult over the shell-torn ground with deep mud in places. Up and down the front thirty of forty-two tanks managed to reach their jumping off points, the others ditching in shell holes, dugouts or other weak spots, or breaking down.

Zero hour on 15th September arrived and tanks began to advance in front of the infantry. Seven of these metal beasts had been allotted to 41st Division, including D6 under the command of Reginald Legge. Together they would attempt to help Rawlinson's infantry seize Flers, beyond High and Delville Woods and en route to Gueudecourt and held in the utmost regard when it came to plans to break through the German defences. The division's first objective fell with little resistance at 7am and twenty minutes later the second had been overcome. With relatively easy progress, the tanks were of negligible use early on but as nearby New Zealanders were held up by German resistance, they arrived to turn the tide. As Rawlinson's men made their way towards the village aided by Reginald and his comrades, enemy troops were

for action: 32ft long with their tails, nearly 14ft wide and 7½ft tall. Each weighed 28 tons and it was estimated they would be able to travel 23 miles without needing to be refuelled.

Each tank was manned by one officer and seven men and in charge of one allotted to D Company, HBMGC, was a well-travelled adventurer in his thirties names Reginald Legge. From Linfield in West Sussex, Reginald, an only son, had been educated at Brighton Grammar School. As a teenager he had worked at a wholesale drapery at Cannon Street, but had later gone off to travel the world as a merchant. On the outbreak of war, he sailed from the Gold Coast just before Christmas 1914 and, having arrived running away in front of them. The tanks making for Flers were experiencing mixed fortunes. One had been hit by a shell and the whole crew killed or wounded trying to escape, another had ditched south of the village. A third had made good progress but, hit by enemy fire, had to withdraw later on. Four of the tanks allotted to 41st Division were still in action. Reginald's was still lumbering its way to Flers, 'belching forth yellow flames from her Vickers gun'.

D16 entered the village just before 8:20am, lurching up the main street. In the meantime, Reginald Legge had turned his tank and was rumbling along the eastern edge of the village to aid the infantry making for their objective north-east of Flers. 'This tank was of the greatest material use and the party in charge of it distinguished themselves considerably,' wrote one commanding officer who watched the 28-ton leviathan bump by, trashing strong points and the remains of houses which were filled with machine guns; ambling along wreaking havoc. The four tanks in and around Flers were causing panic to spread among the Germans, who had no idea what they were looking at. Many ran for Gueudecourt, where large numbers of prisoners were passing willingly towards cages at the rear. By 10am on 15th September, Flers had fallen.

Reginald was not finished. He had a reputation for being a hothead and now, deafened by the noise, suffocated by exhaust fumes in the tank and ignoring the German artillery, he pointed his tank towards the last objective, Gueudecourt. Leaving the infantry and any protection they could afford him behind, D6 dodged the fire of the German artillery and made it to Gueudecourt, taking out one enemy field gun with the tank's guns. Unfortunately, there were three more in the vicinity and one scored a direct hit on Reginald's machine, which promptly caught fire. One crewman was burned alive as the inside was destroyed. Reginald managed to get out and help the other six escape the flames, only to find that they were now on enemy ground and fully exposed to German fire.

Rawlinson was receiving conflicting reports as to where his troops were as the 15th wore on. On Reginald Legge's front, Flers had fallen, but although D6 had made it to Gueudecourt, the infantry had never looked like taking it that day. That evening, Rawlinson issued orders for his Fourth Army to push on and take any outstanding objectives the following day. Just before midnight, the 41st Division was told to push forward on the left as per the original plan and join up with the New Zealanders alongside them. Rain poured down on the night of 15th September and made the muddy, shell-shattered ground even

more difficult to negotiate. The following morning at 9:25am the attack continued on past Flers.

The tank had arrived. For a new technology, hurried to the front in its infancy, they had done reasonably well. The beginning of the Battle of Flers-Courcelette had generated varied results. High Wood, with its advantageous view, and Martinpuich next to it had fallen. After the misery of August and early September on the Somme this was something to get excited about, but to the south the attack on the area between Ginchy and Combles was far messier. The creeping barrage had fallen apart and in some areas the infantry were torn down as they made for their objectives. The desired break in the German line, the opportunity to defeat the Germans on the Western Front had not come to pass. Once again Rawlinson had allowed himself to be ordered to bite off more than he could chew. Nonetheless, a large portion of the attacked German front line had fallen and around Flers his men had advanced even further. The cost of Haig's gains was high. His force had suffered 30,000 casualties. The Germans evaluated their prospects and then made a controlled retreat to the ridge running through Le Transloy behind them to dig their heels in.

In April 1917, Reginald Legge's mother was still desperate for news. Reported missing on 16th September, his death had still not been accepted. A fellow D Company man in German hands made a statement to say that he last saw Reginald in a shell hole near the wrecked tank on 15th September and watched him crawl out of it, but he never saw him again. A wounded crew member in hospital in Bristol said that after the crew had escaped, Reginald refused to leave the tank.

There was confusion for some time as to whether Reginald had been captured or not, because the Germans had come into possession of his identity disc. They confirmed in September 1917 that they had no record of him being taken prisoner. The disc had either been removed from Reginald's body and carried into Germany, erroneously suggesting that he might still be alive and a prisoner, or, mortally wounded, Reginald had died quickly in enemy hands and been buried, with no record of his internment having survived. The disc was transmitted by the Red Cross in Munich to the Bavarian War Office and completed its long journey into his widowed mother's hands. Reginald received a fitting epitaph from a fellow tank commander. 'Good old Legge,' he wrote, 'he came so close to being great.' Reginald Legge's body, if recovered, was never identified and he is commemorated on the Thiepval Memorial, Pier & Face 5c & 12c.

17TH SEPTEMBER
2nd Lieutenant Oswald Nixon

70 SQUADRON, ROYAL FLYING CORPS

A Sopwith 1½ Strutter, of the kind used by Oswald Nixon. (Australian War Memorial)

BORN IN CAPE TOWN, 20-YEAR-OLD Oswald Nixon was the youngest of almost a dozen children of an army officer. Educated near the family home at Reigate, Surrey, by 1913 Oswald was at an agricultural college. Enlisting as a private at 18, he was then commissioned in October 1914 and transferred to the Essex Regiment, but soon he was forging a career for himself above the battlefield. A quick way into the Royal Flying Corps for a young officer was to offer to be an observer in two-seater aircraft, because it required far less training than that of a pilot. Oswald did just that and went to France on 25th October 1915. After a long stint at the front he returned home the following May to train as a pilot. Oswald Nixon graduated as a flying officer on 23rd August 1916, re-embarked just over a fortnight later and on 11th September was posted to 70 Squadron. Oswald's unit belonged to GHQ and flew two-seater Sopwiths on some of the RFC's most distant reconnaissance missions, far over enemy lines, counting trains moving enemy troops far behind the battlefield and observing artillery positions.

The air war had progressed since the onset of the Battle of the Somme. At the beginning of July RFC pilots would be hard pressed to find an enemy airman, but now German reinforcements had arrived. British airmen bore the increased numbers of their enemy counterparts, but there were bloody encounters for 70 Squadron. Dawn patrol on 15th September, as the Battle of Flers–Courcelette began, saw the squadron's airmen led out by a veteran pilot who had been flying on the Western Front since 1914. His ambition had been to meet the great German ace Oswald Boelcke in the air, but when this momentous event finally transpired that day he fell to earth with his shattered machine, possibly taken down by the great man himself. Another Sopwith had its petrol tank pierced and the observer was mortally wounded. The pilot was forced to land in enemy territory, while two more aeroplanes were shot up badly and reached Allied lines with dying observers. The squadron's pilots were scattered and forced to fight their way home independently.

Two days later Oswald Nixon vanished on a standard Somme reconnaissance when his engine failed and he was forced to land 15 miles into German territory. His father, a colonel in the Royal Engineers, was away when the news arrived and his mother was naturally frantic. 'What can be done to ascertain what has happened, please, anything. He is our youngest and 20 only,' she pleaded. 'Was he alone? I know the crowd of agonised hearts that fill your every moment with appeals but I cannot help writing and imploring that all possible may be done to trace him.' Sunday 17th September was a sore day for the RFC, most of the victims falling to Boelcke's new fighting squadron, which was one of a number introduced to begin to address Allied superiority in the air. But the RFC was hopeful. Oswald's observer was alive and in German captivity, having been picked up from the wood where they had come to ground. The authorities told his mother that Oswald's name was about to be included on a list to be sent to Germany via the US Embassy and circulated to hospitals and internment corps.

Unbeknown to the British authorities, Oswald's crash had been violent and he was killed instantly. Retrieved by the Germans, they removed his buttons and badges, presumably as souvenirs, before giving him a suitable burial at Hervilly Churchyard to the East of Peronne. Those in charge of German Grave registration erected a cross that read 'Unknown British Officer – Aviator'. In May 1917, having received no further information, the War Office was finally forced to accept Oswald's death as having occurred on 17th September 1916. Oswald Nixon's career as a pilot had lasted just six days on the Western Front. In 1929 the grave at Hervilly was exhumed. Using dental records as part of the identification, the Imperial War Graves Commission was able to identify Oswald. Both his parents had died within weeks of each other in 1924 and never knew that their youngest son had had a grave all along under an anonymous marker. Nearly thirteen years after his death, Oswald Nixon was laid to rest at Serre Road Cemetery No.2, plot XIX.O.10.

18TH SEPTEMBER
The Rev. Rupert Edward Inglis

ARMY CHAPLAINS' DEPARTMENT

The Reverend Rupert Inglis
(Authors' collection)

THE REVEREND RUPERT INGLIS, AGED 53, lived in East Grinstead, West Sussex, with his wife of sixteen years and their children. His father, who died when his mother was barely pregnant, had commanded the British garrison at the Siege of Lucknow. Educated at Rugby and University College, Oxford, where he got his blue for rugby, Rupert was also an England international, having made three appearances in 1886 against Wales, Scotland and Ireland. Ordained in 1889, Rupert had held curacies at Helmsley in North Yorkshire and at Basingstoke before marrying and taking an appointment as rector of Frittenden in Kent. Since the outbreak of war he had been encouraging men from his village to go and felt that he could not very well ignore his own advice. Consequently Rupert had indicated that he would be willing to go to the front. In July 1915, having volunteered as an army chaplain, he was ordered to report for service with the BEF.

Thousands of religious men such as Rupert would journey to the front throughout the Great War, representing about a dozen Christian denominations. Officially there to hold services, in fact it was a flexible role, with men turning their hand to anything that might make life more bearable for their fighting congregations, whether it be burials, helping at field ambulances and dressing stations, visiting hospitals or helping supply men with gifts from home.

Since arriving on the Western Front, Rupert had served at a hospital at Étaples, in the Ypres sector and at a casualty clearing station at Corbie. During the Battle of the Somme he was with 16th Brigade, which comprised men of Kent, Bedford, Shropshire and a battalion of the York & Lancasters. When not conducting funerals or services, or ministering to the men's spiritual needs, he was organising a canteen to keep them supplied with goods. The infantry under the reverend's spiritual care had had a disastrous day on 15th September. On the 17th Rupert wrote home and described for his family his work with stretcher-bearers, helping to get them to dressing stations. Orders were issued to complete the capture of the original objectives, but the attack was put off until the 21st, so the brigade was now biding its time until the main offensive resumed.

On 18th September, the infantry made a small bombing attack to try to set right one of their failures from the 15th. It had been a wet night and the downpour continued as they slipped about on the muddy surface. Their success that day in seizing their objective was a limited one as water swept Rawlinson's front. Rupert was helping a party of stretcher-bearers in no-man's-land as they attempted to round up wounded men when he was hit by a shell fragment. As men of the Royal Army Medical Corps tried to tend to him, dressing his wound, he was hit by a second shell and killed instantly.

'I cannot overstate the sorrow there is today in his brigade. They simply loved him,' wrote a close friend. He was buried near where he died on the battlefield, but the grave was subsequently lost, a cruel irony for the family of a man who had overseen the internment of so many of his charges. Some 179 chaplains died during the war. In recognition of their devoted work since 1914, King George V later conferred the prefix 'Royal' on the Army Chaplains' Department. Rupert Inglis, aged 53 when he died, left behind his wife Mary and their three children Joan, 15, John, 10, and 5-year-old Margaret. His body, if recovered, was never identified and he is commemorated on the Thiepval Memorial, Pier & Face 4c.

19TH SEPTEMBER
Sergeant Frank Reginald Wilson

1ST AUCKLAND REGIMENT

Sergeant Frank Wilson. (Authors' collection)

THE NEW ZEALAND DIVISION HAD played a significant part on 15th September, conquering the Switch Line in between Flers and High Wood. Among their ranks was a school teacher from Ponsonby, Auckland, who enlisted in February 1915. Frank Wilson was, like Rupert Inglis, a stand-out rugby player, having won caps for the All Blacks. With five years' experience as a member of the Public School Cadets, unsurprisingly, Frank was promoted regularly after joining the army, until he was acting as a subaltern in August 1916 when an officer went sick in the battalion.

The 1st Auckland Regiment had been in reserve as their countrymen captured the ground around Flers on 15th September and the men spent the day raiding the Guards' canteen to the rear. The following day they left Mametz Wood in the direction of Flers to take up the line. The enemy was much aggrieved at the loss of the village, and laid down a potent combination of heavy barrages, machine-gun and sniper fire on the New Zealanders in residence.

That evening the weather broke. On 17th September Frank's battalion worked against the elements to fashion trenches ready for another attack, but the rain made every move harder. 'The clayey trenches became ditches, everywhere ankle deep, and many places knee deep, in viscous mud which clogged every step.' The men were soaked through. 'Cases of 'trench feet' caused anxiety. The task of consolidation and drainage became a hundredfold more onerous.' The artillery could not move up either, and so assaults had to be cancelled. The weather had intervened just in time for the Germans to gather themselves after the Fourth Army attack.

On the 18th the rain continued. Wounded, Frank lay out on the battlefield unable to move. The one significant road approaching the New Zealanders' line with rations, water and ammunition was heavily shelled and, while men from the reinforcement camps slaved to keep traffic moving, all other thoroughfares 'became bogs of liquid mire'. There was bombing activity to the west of Flers and the battalion suffered a number of casualties that could not be evacuated until the next day. Frank Wilson was finally picked up and admitted to 45 Casualty Clearing Station on 19th September, but his wounds were too severe and he died later that day. Thirty-one years old, he was laid to rest at Dernancourt Communal Cemetery Extension, II.B.28.

20TH SEPTEMBER
#M2/187784 Private Clarence Thompson Browne

81ST ANTI-AIRCRAFT SECTION, ARMY SERVICE CORPS

BORN AT LAKENHAM IN NORFOLK and raised by his unmarried mother, 21-year-old Clarence Browne lived in Norwich, where his mother's new husband was a publican at The Princess of Wales on Bishopsgate Street. Earlier in the war Clarence had served with a territorial artillery outfit. When his term of service expired, he immediately re-enlisted in June 1916. A chauffeur in peacetime, his route to driver in the army was a logical one and, this time with the Army Service Corps, Clarence embarked for the Western Front again on 9th August 1916.

Along with the explosion of the use of aeroplanes in warfare came the idea of shooting them down from the ground. Anti-aircraft fire did not exist in Britain before the Great War. For the first months of the conflict, the army made do with little pom-pom guns, whose rounds did not even

Anti-aircraft guns in action on the Somme. (Authors' collection)

burst in the air, which meant only a direct hit was any use. Then came the Royal Horse Artillery's 13-pounders, which were mounted on a motor chassis and fired explosives and shrapnel upwards. By January 1915 the authorities were convinced that this was an effective approach to the problem and mobile sections of two guns were implemented on a divisional basis. Shrapnel was good if it went off on top of the machine, but a high explosive shell could send jagged shards of hot metal flying fatally in all directions. It was also far more devastating for morale, for the sound of a shrapnel shell could be drowned out by a noisy aircraft engine, but there was no hiding from a high explosive detonation going off right next to you while you were in a highly flammable aeroplane. Anti-aircraft sections, such as the one Clarence Browne was on his way to join, helped to keep enemy airmen high up and away from its menace, complicating their work. It harassed them as they went about their business and also drew attention to them for the benefit of friendly pilots nearby. But most important of all was the fact that good ground defences reduced the demands made on the aeroplanes for protection of each other, and so released the rest of the RFC's airborne resources to concern themselves with their urgent, primary duties.

There were never enough anti-aircraft sections. Despite the intention of having one per division, by summer 1915 there was not even one for every two. The Germans were proving far better at damaging aircraft from the ground. To rectify this, a new gun was introduced: a field gun bored out. Highly mobile when mounted on the back of lorries and other vehicles, they could fling shells 19,000ft into the air, high enough to hit most aircraft plying their trade on the Western Front. In 1916 this was gradually becoming the standard anti-aircraft gun on the Western Front.

By the beginning of the campaign on the Somme, the number of sections had improved greatly, but was still nowhere near what was needed. Haig calculated that he needed 112 guns. He had sixty-seven. The French also wanted the BEF to take a hand in protecting bases including Calais and Boulogne and this would impose an even greater strain on his anti-aircraft resources. By July he had built his stock to eighty guns plus reserves, plus a dozen of the old pom-poms. To highlight the shortage, on the night of 20th/21st July, several enemy aeroplanes bombed the great ammunition depot at Audruicq near Saint-Omer and destroyed much of what was stored there. At the time it was only protected by two anti-aircraft guns and two searchlights.

Eight guns were based at GHQ and eighty-seven among the four armies in the line, twenty-four of them with Rawlinson's. At the onset of the Battle of Flers-Courcelette, Clarence Browne was driving a lorry bearing one of these guns behind the middle section of the Fourth Army, to the rear of the New Zealanders, as well as Reginald Legge and his tank. The section raced up and down its sector with Clarence at the wheel as enemy air activity built. Each comprised a four-gun battery, grouped together so that they might work tactically side by side and encourage better co-operation. One artillery officer referred to life with an anti-aircraft section as 'disgustingly safe', but they presented an attractive target for the enemy gunners if they could just range their guns correctly. On 20th September the German artillery scored a hit on 81st Section. Clarence Browne was mortally wounded; his body was devastated by shrapnel wounds and, although he was rushed to a dressing station at Dernancourt, he could not be saved. The 21 year old was laid to rest at Dartmoor Cemetery, plot II.A.94.

21ST SEPTEMBER
#6/3601 Private George Anderson
2ND CANTERBURY REGIMENT

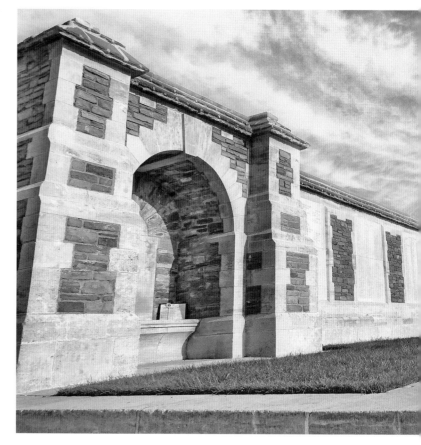

ON 20TH SEPTEMBER THE WEATHER cleared somewhat. Having now been pushed back beyond their original positions of 1st July with their strategic withdrawal to the Le Transloy Ridge in Rawlinson's sector, the Germans had dug in furiously. It had become clear that Haig's grand offensive was not going to blow the Kaiser's army away as planned. The French were losing their enthusiasm for the campaign on the Somme, under tremendous pressure thanks to Verdun and their own significant losses on 15th September. It was decided that new troops must now be brought forward before any more major attacks could be carried out with co-operation between the Allies. This would happen by 25th September, and plans were made to continue the offensive, taking in Gueudecourt, Lesboeufs, Morval and the so-called Meteorological Trenches in between the first two villages: a group with names such as Misty, Storm, Cloudy and Rainbow. In the meantime though, the situation on Rawlinson's front was far from settled.

Forty-year-old miner George Anderson, a single man, had left his Northumberland home and sailed for New Zealand some years before the war. In 1914 George was working for the Stockton Coal Company at Mine Creek on the west coast of the South Island. Having served with a volunteer artillery unit at home in Alnwick, George gave up his job the following year and volunteered for the New Zealand Expeditionary Force, joining the 2nd Battalion of the Canterbury Regiment in Egypt in March 1916.

At 5:30pm on 15th September, George and his cohorts were ordered to relieve New Zealand troops that had made the assault to continue with consolidation, and they also began forming large carrying parties for stores and ammunition. Work continued amidst heavy showers over the following days, under a persistent bombardment of high explosive shells that left the Canterbury men cowering in their sodden shelters. The intensity of their spell in the lines was raised again on the 19th when the battalion relieved those holding the front line, before, on the 20th, the 2nd Canterbury were ordered to attack Goose Alley, a long trench to the north-west of Flers that blocked off the villages of Le Sars and Warlencourt in the distance, without a bombardment to procede them.

George's company was one of three that took part in the assault. They left their trenches and went forward without a barrage, creeping to within 50 yards under cover of darkness before they were detected. The enemy immediately opened up heavy machine-gun and rifle fire when they spotted the New Zealanders. In spite of the casualties, George's battalion rushed the enemy trench and managed to clear it. The artillery promptly began bombarding the area around the captured positions to prevent the Germans bringing up troops to claim back conquered ground.

The New Zealand Memorial at Caterpillar Valley Cemetery. (Andrew Holmes)

Heavy fighting continued all night; first the Germans were on top, then the Brits and the New Zealanders.

Finally, at about 4am, the enemy were driven back from their hard won position. There was no rest for the Canterbury men though as they were forced to dig and then dig some more, furiously trying to steel themselves to defend their ground before the next inevitable counter-attack. The officer in charge rallied anyone that he could find to help, leading his own counter-attack 'with unsurpassable determination'. Just before dawn the German effort slackened and throughout the day George worked with pick and shovel to form a suitable position facing the valley that led off towards Le Sars past Eaucourt l'Abbaye. The battalion also formed bombing posts to man the block that they had put up in the trench they were sharing with the enemy.

George Anderson's ordeal was still not over. Having paused to compose themselves, on the evening of 21st September a determined counter-attack was delivered without any warning by about 200 Germans, who worked up three approaches towards the Canterbury battalion. George and his companions, who had been fighting and working all day and all night, clung on for dear life. Then, utterly exhausted, they began yielding their trench one bay at a time. The New Zealanders climbed out of their saps and, in view of enemy snipers, crept along the parapet and began flinging bombs down at the Germans inside. At the tip of a bayonet, the enemy was driven back down the slope. The 2nd Battalion of the Canterbury Regiment had somehow held on, quite literally in the face of everything that their Bavarian opposition could throw at them. Despite the competency of the Kaiser's bombers, the enemy was routed by a bayonet charge over open ground.

For their efforts, almost half the already seriously depleted Canterbury battalion were now casualties. The ground was littered with dead from both sides. George Anderson was reported variously as both wounded and missing on 21st September until an inquest was held. Witnesses revealed that for some time during the course of the day he had sheltered in a shell hole with members of his company. Their platoon commander was killed while they sat there. The next morning, when the men went back to search for the officer's body they also found George. His remains, if recovered for burial, were never identified and George Anderson is commemorated on the memorial at Caterpillar Valley with more than 1,200 other New Zealand soldiers with no known grave on the Somme.

Nonetheless, at 10pm the enemy launched a strong counter-attack, forcing George and the rest of the Canterbury men back. Hand-to-hand, vicious fighting ensued. The Germans surged at them with little egg-shaped bombs until reinforcements arrived carrying supplies so that George's battalion could counter their efforts. 'No quarter was asked or given. Now a storm of bombs would kill or maim the defenders, now the ride would flow once more up the bloody trenches amid the dead and mutilated and dying.' The enemy seized a trench on the New Zealand left and parts of the lines around Flers. They were coming round on both flanks and threatening to cut off the New Zealanders. The men were exhausted and the Bavarians coming at them smelled blood. George's battalion were fiercely determined to stand their ground.

22ND SEPTEMBER

Lieutenant The Hon. Edward Wyndham Tennant

4TH GRENADIER GUARDS

Lieutenant the Hon. Edward Tennant.
(Authors' collection)

THE SON OF LORD GLENCONNER, Liberal MP, a nephew of the prime minister and therefore a cousin of Raymond Asquith who had fallen on 15th September serving with the same regiment, Edward 'Bim' (or 'Bimbo') Tennant joined the army at just 17. Nicknamed 'Boy Wonder' during his initial training, he had been a keen poet at both prep school and Winchester. Joining the 4th Grenadiers, which counted Harold Macmillan among its officers at the time, the future prime minister recalled Bim as 'a young man of singular charm and attraction'. It was not only the other officers who were struck by him. The men thought their boyish leader was wonderful. 'If any of them showed signs of exhaustion on the march, there was no berating from Edward. Instead [he] would help and, shouldering the rifle and pack himself, he carried on.'

Bim was sent to the front in the latter half of 1915, in time to see the carnage of the Battle of Loos, which inspired him to write his poem 'The Mad Soldier' in 1916. His 19th birthday marked the opening of the Battle of the Somme and on 9th September the Guards arrived to join the fray.

On the day that Edward Cazalet was killed nearby with the Welsh Guards, Bim was also in action, running up and down with messages for the company commanders from headquarters in the mayhem. 'The trenches were full of men, so I had to go over the open. Several people who were in the trench were saying they expected every shell to blow me to bits.' He escaped unharmed. 'We were safely relieved last night,' he told his mother. When they finally made it out of harm's way, the Grenadier officers found that someone had managed to get hold of some champagne. 'That is the time one really does want champagne,' Bim reflected. 'When one comes in at 3am, after no sleep for fifty hours, it gives one the strength to undress.'

Preparations were now fully under way for the resumption of the offensive on 25th September and the Guards were to play a leading role. Strong resistance was anticipated and there was much digging to be done to fashion communication and assembly trenches for the battle. It was an exhausting march up for Bim's battalion through significant congestion and over horrible ground thanks to the recent rain. The only road available to them was stuffed with transports and guns, and the mud was so deep that they could barely wade through it. The guides themselves were lost, the communication trench leading up was blocked by decomposing corpses, and it was 3am before they got into place. The front-line trench that the Grenadiers now manned was too shallow and not at all bulletproof. Enemy snipers were everywhere. Bim was seemingly determined to keep his spirits up. 'I am full of hope and trust,' he wrote to his family. 'The pride of being in such a regiment! ... I have never been prouder of anything, except your love for me, than I am of being a Grenadier.'

Bim's company was placed in the line near Combles, south-east of Guillemont. It was holding a sap that was shared with the Germans, the two groups of combatants separated by a simple block. On the night of 21st/22nd September he was out passing the time with a spot of sniping when there was some movement in the German lines. Bim loosed off his revolver and a moment later he was killed, shot through the head by an enemy sniper. He had told his mother:

I always carry four photos of you when we go into action. And I have kept the little medal of the blessed virgin. Your love for me, and my love for you, have made my whole life one of the happiest there has ever been. Brutus' farewell to Cassius sounds in my heart: 'If not farewell; and if we meet again, we shall smile.' Now all my blessings go with you, and with all we love. God bless you, and give you peace.

'He was loved by everyone,' wrote one of his fellow officers, who had been censoring the men's letters in the aftermath of Edward's death. 'Especially among the men; I think there could be no greater tribute paid than what they wrote home about him, praising him, quite a number asked their relatives to send them his photograph from the picture papers.' One of them, Sydney Adams, wrote to his mother:

> He wasn't only an officer, he was a great friend to all the men … When things were at their worst, he would pass up and down the trench, cheering the men, and it was a treat to see his face always smiling. When danger was greatest his smile was loveliest. All were ready to go anywhere with him, although he was so young. All trusted him … Anything he could do make us happy he did.

They were heartbroken. These fleeting but strong relationships, struck up as men were huddled together in horrible circumstances and then severed by shell or by rifle, were put into words by Bim himself when a friend of his died at Neuve Chapelle in 1915.

> It is the lot of some to keep a friend
> Lifelong, and sharing with him young endeavour,
> Take the last fence 'longside him at the end,
> Well-tried companions, who no fate may sever,
> And though for six short months I knew my friend,
> My heart shall keep his memory forever.

Edward 'Bim' Tennant was laid to rest in the same row as his cousin Raymond Asquith at Guillemont Road Cemetery, plot I.B.18.

23RD SEPTEMBER
#3738 Sowar Husain Muhammad
36TH JACOB'S HORSE

Indian troops made a huge contribution to Britain's war effort. During the course of the war, more than 140,000 men would make the journey to the Western Front alone. Led largely by officers of European descent, Indians had begun arriving in France as early as September 1914 and were involved heavily in the first battle for Ypres a few weeks later. During that battle, Khudadad Khan became the first Indian-born soldier

Indian cavalry on the Somme in 1916. (Authors' collection)

and the first Muslim awarded the Victoria Cross. A native of modern-day Pakistan, he had continued to man his machine gun despite the death of his comrades, enabling reinforcements to arrive. In 1915 Indian soldiers made up a large percentage of the attacking force at Neuve Chapelle, as well as fighting at Festubert and Loos before most were redeployed east in December.

Swathes of cavalrymen and labourers remained on the Western Front, and serving amongst them with Jacob's Horse was a young man named Husain Muhammad, son of Faiz, from Mohib Banda, a small village to the north-east of Peshawar on the Kabul River. In March 1916, Husain and his compatriots had been sent to the Somme. In line with British cavalry units, as the battle began in July Husain joined trench working parties. At the end of August, Jacob's Horse sent a large party of officers and men for a week of assisting with tunnelling work. At the same time another 150 men were riding off to the Forêt de Lucheux to work seven-hour labour-intensive shifts every day.

It was hoped that the cavalry's moment would come during the Battle of Flers-Courcelette in mid-September. After a few days' training, Husain and the rest of his battalion began concentrating with the rest of the cavalry in the area hoping to exploit any breakthrough in the enemy line. On 15th September they remained at Dernancourt awaiting orders, with instructions to be ready to move at an hour's notice. When no such orders came, Husain and the rest of the Indian cavalrymen were allowed to stand down. With the resumption of the offensive planned for 25th September, Husain and elements of Jacob's Horse were employed to carry up tools and explosives to Mametz. Officers reconnoitred the cavalry tracks up to the front line, which had been made by the dismounted men ready for their hoped-for advance. On 23rd September the preliminary bombardment began to pave the way for the infantry assault to come. Jacob's Horse was in billets at Dernancourt, but still providing assistance nearby. During the course of the day Husain was killed by enemy fire after nearly two years in Europe. His body, if recovered, was never identified. Of the troops from countries throughout Britain's Empire, none lost more men than India. The Neuve Chapelle Memorial commemorates Husain Muhammad and 4,656 of his fellow Indian soldiers who fell on the Western Front during the Great War and have no known grave.

24TH SEPTEMBER
#G/5968 Private James Richard Sage
1ST THE BUFFS (EAST KENT REGIMENT)

THE RENEWAL OF THE ADVANCE on the Fourth Army front was imminent, but the enemy would not let Rawlinson's men prepare for their attack unmolested. From New Romney in Kent, James Sage had enlisted as a teenager in Canterbury in the spring of 1915. A milkman, the youngest of five children and the only boy, so far he had come through the war without major physical injury, apart from a week in the drill hall at Chatham with trench foot.

On 19th September, James' battalion, the 1st Buffs, began a long march away from the trenches towards Albert, where the entire battalion, exhausted and rubbing their sore feet, expected to have a rest. This dream of respite lasted less than twenty-four hours for, on the evening of the 20th, orders were received for James and his fellow troops to return to the lines the following day for the renewed offensive. James returned to Ginchy and relieved a battalion of the Coldstream Guards on a narrow front to the north of Morval. Depressingly, they were to take over the front line again. To make things worse, James discovered that he and the rest of The Buffs were sharing a trench with the Germans, who sat 50 yards away.

There were assembly trenches to be dug and, more of a concern for The Buffs and a Bedfordshire battalion alongside them, there was a distinct lack of dumps close to the front line to keep them in ammunition and supplies. James got to work. Reconnaissances were made of German positions nearby and on the night of the 23rd the new trenches were finished and the front line reinforced.

At 5:30am on 24th September the enemy took to the offensive before Rawlinson's men had a chance to attack. An SOS was sent up by James' battalion as a German force emerged from wet mist and drizzle and made a determined effort to break the line. The enemy succeeded in dropping into The Buffs' trenches but was ejected swiftly thanks to a nearby Lewis gun. In the course of protecting the line, the day before going over the top, James Sage was killed. His body, if recovered, was never identified and he is commemorated on the Thiepval Memorial, Pier & Face 5d.

25TH SEPTEMBER
#17469 Sergeant James Phillip Donnelly

1ST EAST YORKSHIRE REGIMENT

IT WAS CLEAR THAT RAWLINSON could no longer entertain the idea of smashing through the German defences on the Somme in one attempt. The British Army would now be paving a new way forward: biting off an objective, then holding it, then repeating their endeavours. The renewed offensive of 25th September was orchestrated to seize objectives that had not been claimed on the 15th. Attempting to take ground in manageable chunks would mean that the field artillery could keep up and support the infantry for starters. It was a more measured approach that would focus on limited objectives and therefore maximise the chance of any success.

Going into action was a 41-year-old coal merchant from Kensington named James Donnelly. Having previously served in the East Yorkshire regiment for twelve years before the war, James re-enlisted in March 1915 and arrived with a draft of men in May 1916. His experience as an NCO was much valued and he was promoted to the rank of sergeant on the Somme. James had been wounded in the head during the Battle of Bazentin Ridge in July, where his unit were used to reinforce Bazentin-le-Petit Wood, but was awarded a Military Medal as he returned to his battalion after a brief convalescence at Boulogne.

In action at Gueudecourt on 15th September, the battalion was relieved from the line having suffered nearly 200 casualties and praised for its 'gallant conduct' before being turned around forty-eight hours later and sent back again. On 21st July, the East Yorkshires began a 6-mile march up to the front via Trônes Wood and Guillemont. Two days later they had advanced to support trenches and were preparing to attack. The plan was relatively straightforward. The 1st East Yorkshire Battalion would be attacking Gird Trenches and Gueudecourt beyond for a second time.

At 11pm on 24th September they set off on a trying march through muddy communication trenches. Forming part of the right flank of the

Grave of Sergeant James Donnelly at Guards' Cemetery Lesboeufs. (Andrew Holmes)

attack on the village, they were to take the Gird Trenches and then wait for a battalion of the Lincolns to pass through to Gueudecourt. Then James and the rest of his battalion would meet the Lincolns and together they would attempt to advance out the other side of the village. The bombardment laid down for them was impressive. It began at 9am on the 25th and each hour would rise to a crescendo to put the Germans on alert until at noon it became a hurricane bombardment that lasted half an hour. Five minutes after it finished James Donnelly went forward in his allocated wave towards Gueudecourt.

Immediately he found himself under heavy shell, rifle and machine-gun fire, but pushed on with the rest of the Yorkshire men. Somehow they reached Gird Trench, only to find that the imposing tangle of wire cutting them off from it had been untouched by the artillery barrage. The waves of men closed up on each other and drew heavy casualties. James' battalion began flinging themselves into shell holes to try to find some protection against the enemy fire. Some tried to put their heads up and fire back, but their position was atrocious. The Lincolns and any other troops coming up from behind to try to pass through to Gueudecourt could not even reach no-man's-land owing to the rate of fire being thrown at them. They simply bedded down in the assembly trenches. The attack on Gueudecourt on 25th September had been a catastrophic failure, but to the south Rawlinson's men ran riot with this new, methodical approach. Lesboeufs and Morval had both fallen as the Fourth Army swept into the German front lines.

The men pinned down in shell holes opposite Gueudecourt had no choice but to wait for nightfall and a chance to get back to their own lines safely. The day's efforts had cost the 1st East Yorkshires more than 120 men, including veteran soldier James Donnelly. He left behind a wife, Mary Ann, and three children: William, 13; Elizabeth, 10; and 1-year-old Florence. He was originally buried to the east of Flers, but in 1919, as the area was cleared, James was finally laid to rest at Guards' Cemetery Lesboeufs, plot VI.F.7.

26TH SEPTEMBER
2nd Lieutenant Patrick Riddle Grey
8TH NORTHUMBERLAND FUSILIERS

2nd Lieutenant Patrick Grey. (Authors' collection)

TWENTY-THREE-YEAR-OLD PATRICK RIDDLE GREY WAS a Northumberland native, the son of a wine merchant and volunteer artillery officer from Berwick-upon-Tweed. Educated at Avenue Academy, by the outbreak of war, both Patrick and his younger brother William were studying engineering at Heriot Watt College in Edinburgh and lodging at Marchmont Crescent near the castle. A member of the Berwick Amateur Rowing Club, with military experience gleaned from the engineer's contingent of the Edinburgh University OTC, Patrick and his brothers enlisted in May 1915. Patrick spent time in Egypt with a Lancashire regiment and, after receiving a commission, he joined the Northumberland Fusiliers and relocated to the Western Front.

Whilst Rawlinson's army went forward on 15th September, Gough's distracted the enemy in their sector with a monstrous artillery bombardment. There was an ulterior motive. After two months of minor 'but sometimes fierce' scraps, there were now plans to attack in force at the northern end of the Somme battlefield. Convinced that the Germans were rocking, Haig believed that it was the right time for Gough to assault with ferocity. His men would strike north along the Thiepval Ridge, finally seizing the village and the ground east of it. As soon as it had been secured, Haig anticipated turning Gough's men about and resuming the eastward advance, like that which had been planned but never really got started in that sector at the onset of the campaign.

In the third week of September, orders were issued for an attack on Thiepval Ridge to begin on the 26th at 12:35pm, the first big offensive effort for Gough's army proper. The front line had barely changed since 1st July at Thiepval and the Germans were dug in securely behind the village. Redoubts with names such as Zollern, Schwaben and Stuff were about to become achingly familiar to the troops ordered to claim them. A British division that included Patrick Grey's battalion was selected to attack in a northerly direction towards Zollern Redoubt, before moving on to Stuff Redoubt on the crest of the ridge beyond. Success would help drive the enemy on to lower ground, cutting off their view towards the British bastion of Albert and opening up observation for Gough's men over the whole valley of the upper Ancre.

The preliminary bombardment, 800 guns bludgeoning Patrick's objectives and the German positions across no-man's-land, began in the Thiepval sector on 23rd September as the Northumberland Fusiliers were advancing up from La Boisselle towards the front lines. By the night of the 25th, with rain cascading down on the battlefield, Patrick's battalion had taken over the front lines in preparation for the attack. They were in position by 3:30am the following morning, having elbowed their way through congested trenches, their progress made even more difficult by the fact the men had their packs on and were forced to shuffle sideways past each other. Then the waiting began, punctuated by desultory shelling and rifle fire. Half an hour before zero hour, rum was issued. Set up at Pozières Cemetery, Patrick's commanders were ready to send their charges into battle.

At zero hour, Patrick Grey and his men attacked with the 9th Lancashire Fusiliers at their side. Almost immediately the enemy barrage took up on the front line, and voluminous machine-gun fire erupted from Mouquet Farm and from the Zollern Redoubt ahead. The battalion had met with heavy resistance and swathes of men were killed within 40 yards of their line. Some had not even managed to scramble over the parapet before they had been cut down. Smoke masked the battlefield and immediately the whole attack became confusing. Troops were pinned down by enemy fire and observers could not decipher what was going on. Reports going back 'tended to be somewhat over-optimistic'. The likes of Patrick Grey were being ordered to consolidate the Zollern Redoubt while it was still brimming with Germans.

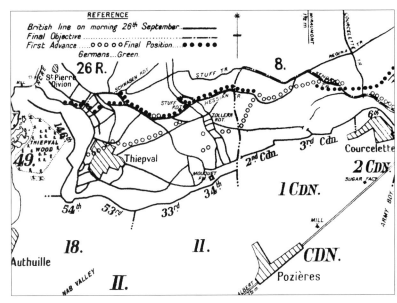

Map showing Mouquet Farm, Courcelette, Thiepval and surrounding areas. (Authors' collection)

Nonetheless, both battalions reached the first objective. The Northumberland men pushed on gallantly and reached the centre of the Zollern Redoubt, sticking their coloured flags in the ground as markers, but this initial success had come at a great cost. One single officer was now alive and fit to continue. Patrick's men were engaged in a desperate struggle around the enemy dugouts. All cohesion was lost, communications were cut. The day had been a partial success, with notable advances made in places, but although the enemy's losses were heavy, the most commanding positions on the Thiepval Ridge remained in German hands and the Kaiser's men still appeared capable of vigorous resistance.

Late that night, two officers of the 8th Northumberland Fusiliers that had remained to the rear were sent out from headquarters to see if they could find out what had happened to their worryingly silent battalion. Six hours later they had reported that there appeared to be no trace of them and that the Germans remained in Zollern Redoubt. One of the officers returned to find the Germans gone later on the 27th and began to collect the men that he could find, who had been cowering in shell holes. The battalion managed to scrape together just 170 men, some of them unarmed members of carrying parties. Nineteen officers and 430 others were gone, including Patrick Grey.

Tributes were paid by the company commander and chaplain, who referred to him as 'a real good fellow and a good soldier'. Another officer wrote that 'his loss is one which will not easily be replaced either in the mess or in the company'. Patrick's body was later recovered and buried by a fatigue party, but the grave was lost during subsequent fighting. If discovered, Patrick's body was never identified and he is commemorated on the Thiepval Memorial, Pier & Face 10b/11b & 12b.

The Battle of the Somme continued to inflict misery on the Grey family for decades to come. Patrick's brother, William, had been given a commission in the 11th Battalion of the Lancashire Fusiliers alongside an officer by the name of John Ronald Reuel Tolkien. He was grievously wounded at the end of August 1916 at the northern end of the battlefield. With shell and gunshot wounds to his chest, back and shoulder he was shipped home at the beginning of September and, at just 19 years old, his health was permanently destroyed, rendering him incapable of continuing with his engineering work. In 1922 William emigrated to Australia to try to fashion a life for himself in a new climate, but he fell ill and returned five years later. 'He returned to his family home but was unable to work and was only able to take an extremely restricted diet.' In the early hours of 12th July 1939, Patrick and William's sister entered his bedroom to find William had attacked his own throat with a razor blade. Unable to stem the flow of blood, by the time she returned with a neighbour he had bled to death. A doctor who had seen him recently, 'found him to be seriously ill and depressed. He had noticed his shrapnel scars and believed him to be suffering from shell shock.' Twenty-three years on from 1916, after more than two decades of misery, 42-year-old William Grey joined his brother as a casualty of war; a chilling testament to the thousands of men who never recovered from their part in the Battle of the Somme.

27TH SEPTEMBER
#429642 Lance Corporal Ewart Gladstone Smith

7TH CANADIAN INFANTRY

TAKING PART IN THE BATTLE for Thiepval near the Northumberland Fusiliers was Gough's Canadian contingent. On 26th September the 5th and 8th Battalions of the Canadian Infantry assaulted in a comparatively small advance on a set of German trenches to the north-west of Courcelette, which had been captured by the Canadians on 15th September. They were almost completely successful. The fact that the crest of the ridge was now almost within reach was considered an adequate day's work. The Canadian commander, an English Old Etonian called General Byng, was of the opinion that he had plenty of troops available to push on. Still under the fog of war after the opening day of the battle, at 8:45pm Gough's Reserve Army HQ announced by telegram that all objectives given for the 26th and not yet achieved stood for the following day.

With the 7th Canadian Infantry, a British Columbian outfit, was a Brit by the name of Ewart Gladstone Smith, named after a four-time Liberal prime minister. Ewart's father was a well-travelled minister and had relocated his family to the United States, where Ewart was born in Ingham County, Michigan, in 1892. Raised in Northampton and East London, at the outbreak of war he was working as a shipping clerk in British Columbia, having emigrated with his brother just before the start of the war. Ewart already belonged to the militia and he volunteered for overseas service in November 1914, arriving back in Europe in June the following year.

Byng was not sure where his forward troops were as 27th September dawned. A heavy bombardment had come down on the Canadian front all night, on both Courcelette and the front line, and continued throughout the morning. In the early hours Ewart's battalion sent out patrols and pushed forward, encountering neither British nor German troops. However, by the time they returned to occupy the position in force, the enemy had got there first. The Canadians attacked the

View from the Canadian front line at Courcelette. (Authors' collection)

Germans and drove them both west and north towards Stuff Redoubt. The enemy was not about to give up though. At about noon the Germans returned and a scrap began, lasting until the Canadians put up a trench barricade. All ground was eventually regained, but machine-gun fire from Stuff Redoubt swept the Canadian trenches all day long as the men attempted to consolidate and evacuate the wounded. Ewart was resting in a trench having spent the night out on listening post duty when he was killed by a shell. In a five-day stint in the trenches the battalion had lost five officers and more than 200 men. Twenty-three-year-old Ewart Smith lay on the battlefield until March 1923, when his body was recovered and identified by the style of his uniform and his identity disc. He was laid to rest at Delville Wood Cemetery, plot II.R.6.

28TH SEPTEMBER
2nd Lieutenant Thomas Percy Wilson

7TH BEDFORDSHIRE REGIMENT

ALTHOUGH FROM HERTFORD, 23-YEAR-OLD THOMAS Wilson had enlisted in Manchester in November 1914 and was originally part of a Lancashire territorial force. Promoted to sergeant, Thomas was then given a commission and sent to Edinburgh for training before being put into the Bedfordshire Regiment later in 1915.

The 7th Bedfordshires were part of the attack on the opposite side of the Thiepval front from Patrick Grey and Ewart Smith. On 26th September British troops were ordered to attack Thiepval from the south and the Schwaben Redoubt beyond. Thomas' battalion was in reserve, subjected to severe shelling, while Middlesex troops and a battalion of the Royal Fusiliers worked up the enemy front-line system that had proved so immovable since the beginning of the Somme campaign. Supported by a battalion of the Northamptons, by 2:30pm the village of Thiepval, reduced to a mass of ruins over the course of the summer, had fallen almost entirely, with only the north-west corner holding out.

On 27th September, supported by men of the West Yorkshires, the 7th Bedfordshires were to attack and clear the remaining part of the village. Their relief had gone so well that two companies were in position and ready to go by 5:45am. 'The finest example of discipline in battle and efficiency in a crisis yet displayed by the division.' Their orders had been altered at short notice. Without guides, their path to battle was lit only by the bursting of shells. Their prompt arrival was some achievement for a battalion unfamiliar with the ground; 'the most awful country that human being ever saw or dreamt of. July 1st was a playground compared to it.' Nonetheless, by 11am Thiepval had been cleared by bomb and by bayonet as this approach was deemed more likely to succeed than a more prolonged preparation including artillery. Having suffered casualties of almost 100 men, the Bedfords consolidated their new positions.

Unusual lying down headstones, including Thomas Wilson's at Mill Road Cemetery. (Andrew Holmes)

On 28th September the rest of the battalion, including Thomas Wilson, was to help take the fearsome Schwaben Redoubt to the north of Thiepval. The men had been out all night. A few were lucky enough to get into dugouts, but most had hidden in shell holes, having either exhausted themselves with bomb throwing or having been engaged with the enemy at close quarters. As they waited in position for the next phase of the assault, the men chatted among themselves and tried to mask their nerves. There was a rotten smell of decomposition coming from nearby corpses in the vicinity. There were no forming up trenches. There had been no time to dig them and they had to settle for far more exposed positions, forming up behind lines of tape that men had started to lay out the day before.

By 1pm the first significant attack on the Schwaben Redoubt since Oswald Webb's Ulster Division had assaulted it at the beginning of July had begun. Thomas and the Bedfords followed the barrage closely, taking grievous fire coming from the redoubt. The Queen's, a battalion of whom were also involved in the attack on this critical objective, were pressing on their left because they had swerved off course. Finding their way across the barren ground was a nightmare. 'It was an extraordinarily difficult battle to fight, owing to every landmark such as a map shows, being obliterated; absolutely and totally.' Recent wet weather and rampant shellfire had also taken its toll. 'The ground was, of course, the limit itself, and progress over it like nothing imaginable.'

By 2:30pm men were approaching the redoubt from the east, but in the confusion, with troops fighting now in a maze of shell holes and broken trenches, it was decided that the best idea would be to push as a coherent force on the Western Face. Danger lurked around every corner. As one participant wrote:

> The ground was made for skulking, and every yard of it afforded opportunity for men to drop down unseen and stay there. If I saw evil and wicked sights in Trônes, I saw more and varied ones in Thiepval.

Thomas' battalion was throwing up bombing stops in trenches to attempt to block the enemy's path. The Germans continued to attempt to counter-attack and, frantically, the Bedfords showered them with explosives thrown by hand. By 4pm they were beginning to run out of bombs and ammunition, and had begun raiding enemy supplies they came upon in dugouts.

An hour later the Queen's battalion had taken the southern face of the Schwaben Redoubt, linking up with a muddle of troops on their left. The Western face of the redoubt and a trench facing north-west on the slope beyond had also been seized. All of the men clustered around the objective were told to consolidate their positions, but the fight was still going on. The Bedfords and West Yorkshires were still attempting to beat down German resistance to the west slope of the redoubt. By the time that it had been secured, Thomas Wilson's battalion had suffered more than 120 more casualties. It was not until nearly midnight that the situation became clearer as to the disposition of the attacking troops and the remnants of the German defenders. Schwaben Redoubt remained in the hands of the enemy and the assault had cost 23-year-old Thomas Wilson his life. He was laid to rest at Mill Road Cemetery, plot I.C.2.

29TH SEPTEMBER
Lieutenant Colonel William Drysdale

COMMANDING 7TH LEICESTERSHIRE REGIMENT

BACK IN RAWLINSON'S FOURTH ARMY sector, the fight for objectives such as Gueudecourt was still continuing as Gough's men attempted to conquer the Thiepval Ridge. Units present that had not yet seen action on the Somme were now rare. Commanding a battalion in the Leicester Tigers Brigade, which had distinguished itself at Bazentin on 14th July, was a career army man with a wealth of experience.

Thirty-nine-year-old William Drysdale had been a regular in the 2nd Royal Scots. Born in Kirkcaldy and educated at the Loretto School, Musselburgh, and Sandhurst, in a twenty-year military career William had served in Burma and India. As well as a long track record of competency in his work, he also had a bronze medal from the Royal Humane Society for 'a plucky endeavour to save Private Weaver', who had sadly drowned in a river near Poona. By 1907 William was at Staff College, where he was a keen cricket, hockey, golf and tennis player. He held a number of staff appointments, before he was appointed a brigade major to 7th Division. This proved to be his first wartime role. Wounded during the First Battle of Ypres, William stayed with his brigade nonetheless and was awarded the DSO before being taken away to recover. He had served at the front again on the staff until he was given command of the 7th Leicesters. William was wounded on 14th July, the day that Luther Cordin was killed under his command, as the battalion was marching up into position in front of Mametz Wood. Ever keen, as soon as he recovered, William took back his command and was now with his battalion at Gueudecourt.

On 25th September, as Rawlinson's army began its assault, the 7th Leicesters were in reserve and did not leave their bivouacs until 5am, sending two companies up towards the front line. Gueudecourt had finally fallen on 26th September and they were to be filing into the line nearby. On 29th September, Lieutenant Colonel Drysdale was killed by a sniper as he carried out an early reconnaissance of the village before his battalion was due to take over the north and north-east parts of the village.

Another officer was passing the regimental aid post laden with rations when he noticed a stretcher holding a covered body on the ground. 'I lifted up the blanket to see who it was and found it was the commanding officer, Lieutenant Colonel Drysdale, who had just been brought in, shot through the head by a sniper.' Throughout the day a number of men approached the body, saluting and paying their respects. One brigadier would miss him sorely. 'Working with him,' he wrote, 'put more life and go into one than I ever thought possible. He had the soundest possible judgement, and it was his spirit that really made the 110th Brigade what it was.' William Drysdale left behind a wife of twelve years, May, and three sons, William, 11, John, 7, and 5-year-old James. He was laid to rest at Caterpillar Valley Cemetery, plot VI.E.11.

30TH SEPTEMBER
#G/16163 Private Frederick Hillard

8TH EAST SURREY REGIMENT

BACK AT THIEPVAL, 32-YEAR-OLD FREDERICK Hillard was serving with a battalion of the East Surrey Regiment. From New Malden, Surrey, the painter and decorator lived with his parents, three unmarried sisters and two brothers. Frederick embarked in July 1916 and joined his battalion to help replace their initial losses at the Battle of the Somme. The 7th Queen's had been in action since the onset of the battle for Thiepval Ridge, had lost almost all of their officers and NCOs and had had no rest since the 26th. The 29th September was dedicated to getting them out of the line. At 2pm Frederick's battalion was ordered to relieve them on the southern face of Schwaben Redoubt and to attack the northern face at 4pm the following afternoon, to try to seize the stronghold once and for all.

Having struggled up without guides, who had gone missing, Frederick and the rest of the men began their subsequently long relief at midnight. The rest of the darkened hours passed fairly quietly, which was a

The scene at Thiepval in 1916. (Authors' collection)

blessing for a battalion largely depleted in numbers. Two platoons had been lent out and were not sent back as promised, meaning that they were to attack as a significantly weakened force. One of their companies was only sixty strong; roughly half strength.

After the fury exacted upon them by men such as Thomas Wilson and the 7th Bedfords in the preceding days, the Germans were determined to regain lost ground at Schwaben Redoubt. Before the Surreys had had time to settle in, at dawn a counter-attack began with a 6am barrage to the south of the redoubt. Then the Germans came at Frederick and his comrades with a strong bombing attack on their exposed left flank. They drove the Surreys from the southern face of the Schwaben Redoubt with their menacing little bombs, pushing them until they were almost 200 yards back from the face of the stronghold.

Their position was fought for hand-to-hand, the men brandishing bayonets, the East Surreys advancing again across the open. Meanwhile though, Kent men were being pushed off the western face of the redoubt. Frederick's battalion regained its position at the southern face, but it was coming under its own barrage in the shared trench, even though the men had let off flares to advise of their position. Gradually the shells whittled away at the British troops until there were only seventy-five Surrey men left. Frederick and his comrades had been hurried into place, some without rations; dispositions were confused owing to the movement, or lack of, of the men around them. The East Surreys were having to communicate back to their headquarters through another brigade, which made messaging far too slow and meant they could not get information to the rear quickly enough.

Enemy shelling continued on the south face of the redoubt all morning. One company of the 8th East Surreys reported that two of its platoons had been reduced to ten and seventeen men respectively before they had even reached zero hour for their attack. At 4pm Frederick assaulted the northern and eastern faces in the open, with some measure of success. But attempts elsewhere on Schwaben Redoubt failed because the attackers simply ran out of men, all of them being cut down by shell and machine gun. Troops were scattered throughout the north face, and to the east and south of the redoubt.

The enemy retaliated by bombarding the strong point for two more hours as the dwindling ranks of the 8th East Surreys clung on. If they had attacked earlier in the day, perhaps they could have taken more advantage of their success, but the Germans just harassed them until after nightfall. In the dark, nobody could get about without being impeded by shell holes everywhere, let alone fashion another attack. The enemy was brave enough to try at 9pm, forcing the East Surreys south again. By this point they were exhausted and, despite trying hard, could not hold on. Despite all their efforts, at the end of September, the Reserve Army's task was not yet completed. The Thiepval Ridge was a formidable obstacle. For the 8th East Surreys, it had been a confusing, endless day of fighting at close quarters and fierce bombardments had cost the battalion 320 men, including Frederick Hillard. His body was laid to rest at Mill Road Cemetery, plot XV.G.5.

1ST OCTOBER
#8/3504 Sergeant Donald Forrester Brown VC

2ND OTAGO REGIMENT

Sergeant Donald Brown VC.
(Authors' collection)

DESPITE THE APPROACH OF WINTER there was no question of abandoning the offensive. With the capture of the Thiepval Ridge almost completed to the north and the villages of Morval, Lesboeufs and Gueudecourt in British hands, as far as Haig was concerned progress was being made and the Germans were consuming vast resources. All of the preceding work might be about to pay off. The enemy was weakened and, in spite of what it may be doing to Haig's own force, he believed they must persist. The British strategy at this point was not complicated. Rawlinson's Fourth Army would continue to press the enemy in the direction of the Le Transloy Ridge and, as the direction of its advance was slightly muddled at this juncture, attempt to swing the line of attack around to a definitive north-easterly or eastern approach.

Among the troops that were to be used in October's endeavours were the New Zealand Division and within its ranks was a farmer who had already shown notable bravery on the Somme. Donald Forrester Brown was from Dunedin, on South Island. Twenty-six years old, in October 1915 he sold his farm at Totara, near Oamaru, and joined his local outfit, the Otago Regiment. Going abroad in January 1916, Donald arrived in Egypt in March and then embarked for France on 9th April.

New Zealanders pose for the camera in their trenches. (Authors' collection)

Donald had attracted attention for his efforts on 15th September as the New Zealanders had gone forward bravely in between Flers and High Wood. His company had suffered heavy casualties at the hands of a particularly menacing machine gun. Together with another soldier, Donald got to within 30 yards of it. They killed four of the crew and seized the weapon. The company continued on until the same scenario developed again. For a second time, Donald and his companion rushed the offending machine gun, killed the crew and silenced the offending weapon. For the rest of the day, the Otago men sat under heavy shellfire, 'and the utter contempt for danger and coolness under fire of this NCO did much to keep up the spirit of his men'.

On 1st October, Donald and his compatriots were to attack to the right of Eaucourt l'Abbaye and towards Le Sars to the north-west of Flers, although the weather threatened to dampen the offensive spirit. Nevertheless, the troops on the Somme were about to embark on two more weeks of relentless, small-scale and largely ineffective attacks. 'The Commander in Chief considered that, in normal autumn weather, the above tasks were well within the capacity of the armies.' By this point though, the New Zealand battalions were many men short. As they prepared for the attack the weather was foggy with drizzle, and on the night before the men were heavily shelled. As the 2nd Otago Regiment lined up in a trench facing north-west towards their objectives, they numbered only 314 men, a scenario of reduced numbers in the aftermath of weeks of bloody fighting that battalions were facing up and down the Somme front. From 7am a deliberate and steady bombardment was flung on to the enemy positions, with no increase in the run up to zero hour that might give away the intentions of the waiting infantry. Suddenly, at 3:14pm forty oil projectors were discharged in the direction of the Germans and a minute later an intense barrage opened up on no-man's-land. Four waves of Otago men launched themselves at the enemy as thirty drums burst 'and enveloped the greater part of the New Zealand objectives in red flame and heavy black smoke'.

Wave followed wave as the New Zealanders struggled forward, many of the men coming under immediate enemy machine-gun fire. Donald's company suffered fewer casualties, but it was a complicated advance. Two companies had a difficult manoeuvre to carry out, changing direction as they went forward, but they managed it and reached the crest of the ridge. By this time though, they had experienced relentless machine-gun fire and a high percentage of officers had become casualties, and many of the men with them. The situation rapidly became confusing. On Donald's front, his company were now advancing north-east and encountered no opposition until they came upon a trench blocking the way to their objective. They were also held up by a machine-gun barrage coming out of another trench next to them, which was still partly filled with Germans. The determined Otago men shot down the enemy troops in their way or watched them flee.

By this time, thick smoke had enveloped the battlefield and, with thinning ranks and no visibility, troops began to lose touch with each other. Donald and his company were hell bent on their objective: a German strong point known as The Circus to the north-east of Eaucourt l'Abbaye. The problem was that the whole area was so smashed up that it was hard to define what piece of mashed terrain this strong point may have been. The Otagos had actually strayed too far north towards Le Barque, and the company commanders began a discussion as to where they might find The Circus.

In the meantime, German machine gunners were still wreaking havoc. It was here that Donald took it upon himself to silence yet another one of them. Singlehandedly he launched himself at it, killed five of the gunners at the point of his bayonet and caused the others to run away. Having put their weapon out of action, Donald was sniping at the fleeing troops when he was killed by an arc of machine-gun fire coming from some distance away.

It took until 10pm for the New Zealanders making the attack to organise themselves and make a solid attempt at consolidating their newfound positions. 'It was regrettable that half my battalion over-stepped the mark,' noted the Otago commander. 'The enemy had abandoned The Circus.' His already much-depleted battalion had suffered 55 per cent casualties. The New Zealand Division had been in action for sixteen consecutive days and when it was relieved on 3rd October, by which time British troops had managed to clear Eaucourt l'Abbaye, it had suffered almost 7,000 losses.

Donald had been recommended for a Distinguished Conduct Medal, but this was upgraded to a Victoria Cross posthumously, New Zealand's first on the Western Front. It was presented to his father at Oamaru in August 1917. Twenty-six-year-old Donald was originally buried where he fell, until 1920 when the area was cleared and he was finally laid to rest at Warlencourt British Cemetery, plot III.F.1.

2ND OCTOBER
#8/1384 Private John Joseph Sweeney
1ST OTAGO REGIMENT

ALSO SERVING IN AN OTAGO battalion was a 37-year-old Australian named John Sweeney. A bushman from Northern Tasmania, John was working for Payne & Sutherland at Pirinoa, near Wellington, when war was declared. He was quick to enlist, and originally joined the Wellington Mounted Rifles in October 1914, but was later transferred to the 1st Otago Regiment. Embarking in December 1914, John had reached Gallipoli by the following May, joining his regiment at Cape Helles. After serving there until the end of August, his service became sporadic. First, John was evacuated and admitted to hospital in Cairo with colitis. Having rejoined the 1st Otago towards the end of October, still on the peninsula, he was only with the battalion for two days before he was admitted to hospital again for another six-week stint away from the front.

The newly formed New Zealand Division arrived in France in April 1916. Much of its early time in the lines was spent acclimatising to the Western Front and mounting trench raids and improving defences. In mid-July the division has reached Armentières, where, after less than a week, John deserted.

It took five weeks for the authorities to apprehend him. On 11th September, pending a court martial, John was sent to the Somme, where his adopted countrymen had relocated in his absence. The court martial took place four days later. The verdict returned was guilty and John was sentenced to death.

Shortly before 6am on 2nd October, in the presence of a medical officer and a chaplain, John was executed by firing squad at 5:44am. In a sad footnote, his brother was killed in 1918. A broken man, shortly before the list of New Zealand wartime executions was made public, John's father walked off into the bush and committed suicide by poisoning himself with strychnine. John Sweeney was laid to rest at Dartmoor Cemetery, plot II.B.1. I.

Grave of Private John Sweeney at Dartmoor Cemetery. (Andrew Holmes)

3RD OCTOBER
Lieutenant Claude Castlemaine Temple

2ND CANADIAN MOUNTED RIFLES

Lieutenant Claude Temple. (Upper Canada College)

IN THE RESERVE ARMY SECTOR, Gough had begun to reorganise his men north of the River Ancre, his wider objective an eastward attack at that end of the battlefield. In the meantime though, his troops south of the river still had plenty to do. At the end of September, Gough was immediately concerned with both driving the enemy out of strong points such as Stuff and Schwaben Redoubts and the capture of Regina Trench, a long German line running from north of Courcelette westwards towards St Pierre Divion. Even by Somme standards, this single trench was destined to become an embittered bone of contention between the Germans and the combination of British and Canadian troops facing them.

Among the Canadians was a 34-year-old bank manager named Claude Temple. Born in Quebec of Irish extraction, Claude's family boasted a rich military history all over the globe. Raised in Toronto, he had attended Upper Canada College, in eastern Ontario, where he was a talented hockey player and athlete. At the outbreak of the war, Claude was the manager of the Granville branch of the Northern Crown Bank in Vancouver, where he had been severely wounded in 1913 when robbers held up the establishment and he refused to hand over the keys. Claude was with the first contingent of Canadians to enlist and arrived in Europe at the end of 1914. Wounded at Langemarck, near Ypres in the spring of 1915, he was transferred to a military hospital in Orpington and then given a commission in the 2nd Canadian Mounted Rifles on recovery.

When the battalion left the line after Robert Killip was killed on 12th September, he was amongst forty casualties. Three days later Claude and the rest of the men played their part in the capture of Mouquet Farm in the advance of 15th September, being detailed to deal with a certain strong point; but this came at a cost of almost 100 men. By dawn on 17th September the mounted rifles had consolidated their position and handed it over to a battalion of the Dorset Regiment. A period of rest and provision of working parties followed before, in the last week of September, the unit was ordered to be ready to move back into the lines at two hours' notice.

Troops had been in and out of Regina Trench already in an attempt to seize it, but it would be a 'baffling stumbling block'. British, Canadians and Germans would simply lose count of how many times they had taken it and then lost this position by the time the matter was settled. The death toll would be appalling for such a small gain. It was a bleak spot.

The whole country over which the Canadians were to battle, before they could claim finally that they had gained their objective, was a barren waste; nothing was to be seen in front but innumerable shell holes – not a tree standing in the immediate vicinity to serve as a landmark. The roads were shelled so incessantly that their appearance changed each day.

On the night of 27th September, Claude and the rest of the 2nd Canadian Mounted Rifles relieved the 8th Canadian Infantry in the front lines to the west of Courcelette. It was a puzzling relief, their guides as clueless as they were about where they were all to go. It was not until after dawn the following day that the Mounted Rifles finished getting into position. No trench stores were taken, neither did they find any in the lines they took over. A number of dead Germans were lying in their trench and also some wounded of multiple nationalities. The dead Germans were thrown over the parapet and the wounded attended to and evacuated as soon as possible. Claude's battalion also managed to get out into no-man's-land and retrieve a number of wounded Canadian and British men from the open, who were also attended to and removed.

Whilst Claude's battalion was sent back into reserve, back up in the lines, the beginning of October saw the first concerted effort to take Regina Trench from the enemy. As part of this, the 5th Canadian Mounted Rifles were ordered to attack from Destremont Farm on the Albert-Bapaume Road, to a point north of Courcelette, on 1st October.

The initial attackers got to within 100 yards of Regina Trench when the enemy opened with machine-gun fire, causing high numbers of casualties. They could, however, see the Germans getting out of their front line and there were very few left in the trench when they got there. They found that section of Regina blown in and work was at once commenced to consolidate the position and make it habitable. To the rear, there was confusion as to how many of their men had made it to Regina Trench as many men had failed, being caught on uncut wire. Those coming up behind them were forced to fall back. Reinforcements were sent up just to ensure that the battalion could hold on to its original line.

Back in Regina Trench there was vicious fighting in the captured section and the men inside found both their flanks in confusion. The scene was frantic. One group managed to get a German machine gun turned on its own men to drive off constant counter-attacks; another had put up trench blocks on either side of them but were surrounded by the enemy. A light mortar was rushed up to join them with as much ammunition as the available men could carry. By 5:30pm the fighting numbers were so low that it was necessary to send up the last of their reinforcements and some men scraped together from headquarters, including officers' servants and usually unarmed men.

Still the Germans attempted to flush out their Canadian attackers. The artillery had been laying a mixed bombardment behind Regina Trench to try to prevent any enemy support coming up, but a gap had opened up between two Canadian battalions along the line and the Germans seized the opportunity to get back in the trench and start bombing their way down it towards the 5th Canadian Mounted Rifles. Blocks were now up at both ends of the captured section of Regina, about 100 yards in length, and the men were already attempting to dig a communication trench back towards their own front line, but numbers were dwindling fast and the counter-attacks continued. The battalion had nobody left to call on and so an officer called for Claude Temple to round up two platoons and rush to their aid.

At about 6:30pm Claude arrived and was ordered into a trench ready to move up into a support line next to Regina as soon as the men that were in it moved forward. Another bombing attack was made on Regina Trench, the Canadians trying to move along with packs of riflemen attacking in the open on either side of the trench to support them. After proceeding 150 yards, the bombers ran into a large force of the enemy and were driven back, but the flanking parties rushed overland into the trench and beat the enemy back with their bayonets. The relentless, hand-to-hand fighting continued into the night.

At about 1:30am, having received reinforcements and reorganised, the Canadians again pushed the enemy back and gained approximately another 500 yards. By 4am they had cleared the Germans out of a sizeable portion of Regina Trench. The piece of the enemy line that they had now seized was deep and the officer in charge considered it a suitable place to put in a block. Casualties were such that it seemed unwise to attempt to take any more. The ground was littered with Canadian and German dead, the latter caught heavily by machine guns as they attempted to retire into their support lines. No more reinforcements had arrived, so the officer in charge went looking for them himself. Claude and his men were called into the support line 'with all possible speed' as the Canadians braced themselves for a German counter-attack, rushing forward parties with a mortar and bombs. Before any of them could get into position, though, the counter-attack came.

The enemy came forward in overwhelming numbers, attempting to outflank the mixed force that included Claude and his men. They held on until two machine guns had been put out of action and the supply of bombs exhausted. At 7am on 2nd October the Canadian position became untenable and the men fell back, bringing the majority of wounded out with them. The reinforcements, including Claude, had arrived just too late to retain the section of Regina Trench that had been so stubbornly held. The Canadians had to be content with consolidating the support line and, as Claude and the rest of the exhausted men worked on tirelessly, they were subjected to heavy intermittent shelling. Every effort was made to bring in as many wounded as possible, but that evening a furious bombing attack started to the right of their sector. SOS signals were sent up but the men could not tell whether the assault was being made by the enemy or the battalion on their right. The bombing and rifle fire seemed to be spreading towards their front and a heavy barrage was requested on the enemy front line and support. As 3rd October dawned, Regina Trench was back in German hands.

The Canadians were exhausted, 'often fighting practically hand-to-hand for thirty-four hours against superior numbers'. In the confusion, Claude Temple had been killed.

Tributes flowed to his family. 'He was utterly fearless and was held in high esteem by the men of his company,' read one; 'Courage, pluck, cheerful endurance of hardship' and 'a soldier and a gentleman,' said another. A stretcher-bearer revealed that he had seen Claude trying to establish communications with another battalion. He said that he had seen Claude jump into a German trench and come out again further up. They thought they had seen him hit by machine-gun fire, but his body was nowhere to be seen. Reported wounded and missing on 3rd October, Claude was later accepted as having died on or around this date. His body, if recovered, was never identified. At the end of the war, Vimy Ridge was selected as the site for a memorial commemorating Canadians on the Western Front. On it are the names of 11,163 men who have no known grave, including Claude Temple.

4TH OCTOBER
2nd Lieutenant Robert Main Graham

10TH DUKE OF WELLINGTON'S (WEST RIDING REGIMENT)

ROBERT GRAHAM WAS THE SON of a Glasgow doctor, born in 1891 in Pollokshields near Govan, but he had since moved out to near the football ground at Hampden Park, which at the time was the largest stadium in the world. Educated at Albert Road Academy and Glasgow University, by the outbreak of war Robert was working as a chartered accountant. He joined the Glasgow University OTC in June 1915 and received a commission a few weeks later. Joining the 10th Battalion of the Duke of Wellington's (West Riding Regiment), by the beginning of October 1916 Robert found himself to the south of Le Sars, which sat north of High Wood and on the approach to Bapaume astride the main road from Albert. Here the Yorkshire battalion was tasked with edging forward towards Le Sars ahead of them, to help bring Rawlinson's line very close to Bapaume, a fair-sized town behind the German lines with good rail links where the enemy had established some of their artillery batteries. The weather was miserable at this juncture and planning was difficult on the Somme because the battlefield had become confused; the enemy had forward posts in front of their main lines, and troop dispositions were baffling to those with responsibility for orchestrating the campaign.

At dawn on 4th October the West Riding Battalion sent several parties on a north-easterly path towards Le Sars with both with rifles and bombs. The lines they advanced along were rough saps, no deeper than 3ft. As they passed through, the enemy suddenly opened a heavy machine-gun barrage on these exposed positions from a nearby trench and also began lobbing bombs towards members of Robert's battalion. The men were forced to retreat again, one group having only made it 10 yards before it was almost entirely wiped out by German fire.

Peeking at the trench that was the source of this resistance through periscopes and binoculars, it was apparent to Robert and the other officers that the position was strongly held. It appeared to have been deepened and every 8–10 yards they spied German sentries manning niches cut into the walls. At the main road there seemed to be a great deal of tangled barbed wire. Ideally, both the wire and the trench needed to be attended to by the artillery before any further attack was made. To cap it all, it was thought that 'undoubtedly' beyond this there was a machine gun covering the approach to Le Sars in the path of their advance and two snipers were also thought to be occupying a well-placed house.

This assessment was made at noon but, nevertheless, just a few hours later, Robert's battalion was ordered to go forward again and attack the problematic trench in front of them, taking on all the obstacles that they had reviewed. The assault was launched at 6:03pm in three waves, spaced out at intervals of 80 yards. Robert went forward in charge of the left flank. The Yorkshire battalion was protected by an artillery barrage, but as it lifted to allow them to advance, they found that the wet, soggy ground sucked them down and slowed their progress dramatically.

Robert and the men made ambling, easy targets for German machine gunners, who enfiladed their ranks as they stumbled on, causing heavy casualties. Only a few men managed to reach their objective and their number was so small that they were compelled to retire almost immediately. It was an outcome that would have been obvious to the officers that had reconnoitred the position earlier in the day. The 10th Duke of Wellington's had been given an impossible and quite futile task and suffered expensive casualties in the case of their officers. Six of the eight who took part were gone from their strength, including Robert Graham. The 25 year old had been trying to see his men through uncut barbed wire towards their objective when the enemy turned bombs and machine guns on them. 'Your son was a splendid officer; steady, cool and brave,' wrote one of his comrades. As the battalion retreated, 25-year-old 2nd Lieutenant Graham was left on the battlefield. His body, if recovered, was never identified and he is commemorated on the Thiepval Memorial, Pier & Face 6a/6b.

5TH OCTOBER

#G/7803 Private Frederick Silsby

7TH ROYAL SUSSEX REGIMENT

IT HAD BEEN ORDAINED THAT the next cohesive push along Rawlinson's line would take place on 7th October and the ground beyond the village of Gueudecourt, to the north-east of Flers, was to be among the objectives. Filing into the lines facing the village to prepare for its intended capture was the 7th Royal Sussex Battalion.

Frederick Silsby had already given the regiment fourteen years before leaving the army, but in August 1915 the 40-year-old labourer left his home in the Caterham Valley in Surrey to travel to Guildford and re-enlist. He arrived in France in the spring of 1916 and joined the 7th Battalion just before the beginning of the Battle of the Somme.

On 1st October his Sussex outfit received orders to go into the trenches near Gueudecourt. By 1am the following morning, Frederick and his companions had taken up residence in the support line behind two battalions of the Royal Fusiliers. As soon as their stint began, the men were heavily shelled throughout the day. It continued on the 3rd, when the Germans also bludgeoned Flers behind the Sussex line with shells. At 6pm, Frederick moved up to switch into the front trenches, during which time the enemy artillery was mercifully quiet, but the

battalion was soon to find out that the German gunners had their weapons ranged perfectly on these trenches.

Although the weather began to improve slowly as the next offensive on the Somme approached, the nights were quiet in terms of small arms fire, so that the men could hear orders being shouted in the distance. But during the day the enemy artillery remained relentless, pouring unceasing shellfire on the front and support trenches. It grew so traumatic that the Sussex men crawled out in front of their trenches into no-man's-land and began digging a new trench to sit in that was not in range of the German guns. Of course, this kind of barrage came at a cost to the men in the front lines and, on 5th October, nineteen men of the 7th Royal Sussex were killed, including Frederick Silsby. He was wounded in the back by a shell fragment and rushed to a casualty clearing station, but died later in the day. He left behind a wife, two step-children, Ellen, 14, and Wilhelmina, 11, and a son, 3-year-old Frederick. His wife, Elizabeth, was a widow for a second time. Frederick Silsby was laid to rest at Longueval Road Cemetery, plot B.15.

6TH OCTOBER

#455315 Private Donald Connor

2ND CANADIAN INFANTRY

BACK IN FRONT OF REGINA Trench, the Canadians still faced being part of a monumental struggle to take it from the enemy. Shortly after Claude Temple was killed, a night reconnaissance was carried out and it showed that the enemy were occupying Regina Trench with large numbers of troops. Then the rain came down and prevented any infantry work, and instead Gough's Reserve Army carried on by way of artillery preparation only. The British and Canadians facing the spot were left to try and work on their front lines in front of their coveted prize.

As the 2nd Canadian Infantry, an Eastern Ontario battalion, moved into the line there was to be a period of comparative quiet. Among their number was a 22-year-old Scottish emigrant named Donald Connor. From Kingussie to the north-east of Fort William in Inverness-shire, Donald's father had decided to start a new life with his children following

Grave of Donald Connor at 2nd Canadian Cemetery. (Andrew Holmes)

the death of their mother. The family left Glasgow on the SS *Numidian* in April 1913 and sailed into Halifax. Moving to Ontario, Donald had been farming by the St Lawrence River when war was declared. He served in the Home Guard before deciding to enlist in August 1915 at Cornwall, some 60 miles south-east of Ottawa.

On the morning of 5th October, Donald and the rest of the men underwent a rifle inspection before moving up into support positions near Courcelette. All were in place by 8:40pm, traipsing up through the mud in showery weather. That night Donald was sent out on listening post duty as the Germans shelled the Canadian positions at a derogatory rate. The following morning the guns increased in ferocity, but it was still comparatively quiet compared to the frantic action of late. The

enemy seemed to be on the alert, nervous, perhaps anticipating a resumption of the assault on Regina Trench. The Canadians, though, were planning nothing more than continued snooping on their front.

Men went out to inspect the enemy's wire in front of Regina. That night on Donald's front, reconnaissances were carried out amid enemy shellfire while the Germans focused particularly on Courcelette and the surrounding area. Donald arrived back from sitting out in front of the lines at dawn and lay down to rest, but during the course of the day a shell struck the spot he had chosen and he was killed outright, a victim of chance based purely on where he chose to relax following his vigil. Twenty-two-year-old Donald Connor was laid to rest at 2nd Canadian Cemetery, plot A.2.

7TH OCTOBER

#L/22756 Bombardier Arthur William Grosvenor

282ND BRIGADE, ROYAL FIELD ARTILLERY

THE 7TH OCTOBER ARRIVED AND with it a delayed new offensive on the Somme. On the morning of the 4th, Rawlinson had informed his generals that, on account of the weather, this would be the case. 'The troops might as well have been in the middle of a pond. No one could move.' The 56th Division, London Territorials, had come into the line at the end of September ready to play their part in this new effort. In their sector the plan was to press north-east from Lesboeufs and seize positions suitably close and tactically sensible for an attack on the defences around Le Transloy at a later date. The infantry would be going forward in tandem with the French, and the general bombardment leading up to the battle would begin on the 6th.

Manning guns behind the 56th Division was a pair of brothers, sons of a Prudential agent from Norwood in South London. Educated locally, the eldest, Arthur, was then employed as a steward at the Dulwich and Sydenham Golf Club. He had enlisted on 21st April 1915 and arrived in France in December, where he now served in the 282nd Brigade with his 18-year-old brother, Thomas.

Arthur and Thomas Grosvenor were suffering side by side as the weather began to deteriorate towards winter. The gunners were in a sorry state. While divisions rotated in an out of the line, to keep up the rate of fire often the artillery remained, exhausted, working and constantly enduring German fire power. To avoid it they were forced to dig holes and sit in them. They rapidly filled with water. Guns were packed in tightly, often firing wheel-to-wheel, so that there was no break from the din.

The guns were as exhausted as the men were. Barrels were worn out as they had fired too many shells without proper attention or maintenance. Mechanisms were also in need of repair and replacement.

All of this combined to make fire inaccurate as it caused shells to burst at the wrong time. They also had to live with patchy support from the RFC, as the bad weather kept pilots on the ground and unable to help range the guns or observe their fire. Living in this squalor and enduring the reality that they were not performing their job to the best of their ability was grinding, but it was unavoidable, and through no fault of their own. Nevertheless, Arthur had a positive outlook on things, performing his duty 'cheerfully and efficiently', and surprising his officers '[with] his good temper under all conditions, which have often been most trying'.

As soon as the brigade began its preliminary bombardment on the 6th October the enemy began to respond vigorously. The division's infantry went forward at 1:45pm the following day next to the French. On the far left they were fairly successful, but to the right the attack was held up by heavy machine-gun fire. The brigade attacking on the right fared worse, the remnants of one battalion coming under a heavy barrage and diving for cover in shell holes, where they cowered until dusk and then crawled back to their original line. At 8:30pm the German counter-attack developed. Although the London Scottish did their best to withstand it, more troops had to withdraw to their starting positions. Throughout the course of the day, a telephone wire keeping Arthur's brigade in touch with the forward positions was broken and, as it was essential to help them fire accurately where their shells were needed most, the Grosvenor brothers went forward to help repair it. For his trouble, as he mended the wire, Arthur was hit in both arms and the spine. He called out at once to the man who was with him, but he quickly lost consciousness and died about half an hour later with his teenage brother by his side.

Thomas was utterly distraught. Completely unable to put into words the awful news in a letter to his parents, he asked his commanding officer to do it for him. The 28 year old had lost his own brother at La Boisselle on 3rd July. 'I and all his comrades wish to express our deep sympathy with you in your bereavement,' he began. 'He was a man whom, equally, with his brother, I had personally the greatest liking for, and both of them have always been most popular with all ranks of the battery.' He assured them that their 23-year-old son would receive a fitting service. 'He will be buried beside [another man of this battery] this afternoon and I hope to obtain the services of a chaplain and will

Guards' Cemetery, Lesboeufs. (Andrew Holmes)

do my best to have his grave as you would wish it left.' There was much concern about Thomas' state of mind. 'I have done what I can to comfort his brother, who is heartbroken about it, but it is hard for outsiders to help him as I fear it is to help you.' He would have known from his own personal experience. It was the intention of the officer to give Thomas a break from the front lines. 'I hope to send his brother to the wagon line, in a place of safety for a few days' rest and a chance to recover himself'.' Arthur Grosvenor and his deceased companion were originally laid to rest to the east of Ginchy. In 1919, the area was cleared and both were reinterred at Guards Cemetery, Lesboeufs, plot IX.S.5.

8TH OCTOBER

#452396 Private Thomas Carson

58TH CANADIAN INFANTRY

BACK AT REGINA TRENCH, GOUGH'S men were preparing to make a second attempt at seizing it from German hands once and for all. Among the thousands of emigrants serving in the Canadian force was 26-year-old Thomas Carson, originally from Omagh, Co. Tyrone. He left for Canada in June 1913 with his brother, sailing from Londonderry for Quebec and Montreal. They were heading for rural Watford, near the shores of Lake Huron, where Thomas settled, like Donald Connor, as a farmer in Ontario. He joined the army in July 1915 and arrived in France in January the following year, before finding his way to the Somme with his battalion.

Early on 6th October, Thomas and the rest of the men waded back to Tara Hill, behind La Boisselle on the road to Albert, and into reserve after a forty-eight-hour stint in the trenches. The journey was slow, taking most of the night, and caused nearly twenty casualties, two of whom finally reached the end of mental endurance in the miserable conditions and had to be sent away. Despite the slog back, Thomas and the rest of the men were, of course, enthused to be away from the cold, wet misery of the trenches. But it was not to last. The following day they were ordered to relieve a front line battalion. After just a short respite, they had arrived by 11:30pm on 7th October to join the latest attempt on Regina Trench. No less than eight battalions were to attack in an attempt to wrench the objective from the Kaiser's men and withstand the inevitable counter-attacks. Thomas' battalion was to be towards the left of the line. Soaked to the skin from lingering in wet trenches awaiting zero hour, the 58th Battalion advanced shortly before 5am. Long lines of Canadians went forward supported by bombing parties and Lewis guns. The artillery had failed to knock out the German machine guns beforehand and their inevitable torrent of fire began, cutting through the ranks of Thomas' battalion. One company commander was shot in the stomach at the onset, and there he lay, cheering on his men before he found his way into a shell hole, where he died of his wound.

All three companies then ran into uncut wire on the approach to Regina Trench. The entanglements were barbed up to 4ft high and 5ft deep, having seemingly been missed by the British artillery. As Thomas' battalion attempted to cut through it, they were subjected to more heavy fire. One company managed to slice through it, another to find a gap big enough to edge through, at which point they began to file into Regina Trench. Working methodically along it, these men managed to hold on to 100 yards of the trench for half an hour until they reached a strong bombing post. More men were fashioning breaks in the wire to begin crawling into the

Canadian soldiers fix bayonets. (Authors' collection)

out of bombs and were annihilated almost to a man. One officer was last seen fighting hand-to-hand, surrounded by the enemy. One NCO, finding himself without a leader, rallied the men and helped the wounded into shell holes. Then, under fire, when it became clear the attack could not continue, he dodged from hole to hole, helping his comrades to dress their wounds. Then he found his own shell hole, and with three other men spent the rest of the day sniping at nearby Germans, before they managed to drive off a small bombing attack coming towards them.

Men worked from shell hole to shell hole, crawling across no-man's-land to get back to their own lines, although most of them resolved to lay out until nightfall when they stood a better chance of getting back unharmed. One single officer was still capable of finding his own way back. After an exhausting effort, the Canadians were back where they had started. Regina Trench remained in German hands. That week the Canadian contingent on the Somme lost nearly 3,000 more men, including Thomas Carson. His brother Joseph had also enlisted in the Canadian Infantry and he died aged twenty-six with the 47th Battalion on 29th September 1918, just a few weeks before the end of the war. Buried where he fell, Thomas Carson's body, if recovered, was never identified and he is commemorated on the Vimy Memorial.

Right: Sculpture on the Canadian National Memorial, Vimy Ridge. (Alexandra Churchill)

enemy trench. The Germans bombed them viciously from a position further to their rear to enhance the effects of their machine guns and not long after their arrival the enemy also ranged their artillery on to the captured trenches.

In the meantime, the battalion to the right had failed to capture its allocated portion of Regina Trench. Seeing that the 58th was isolated, the Germans began to target the battalion even more. A fierce fight ensued. Once again, the fighting for Regina Trench had become desperate and took place at close quarters. Inside, the Canadians ran

9TH OCTOBER
#36044 Private Merrill Price

10TH CHESHIRE REGIMENT

WHILE THE BRITISH AND CANADIAN troops at Regina Trench suffered repeated misery at the hands of stubborn German resistance, more of Gough's men fought on in the Thiepval sector. Among them was Merrill Price, a painter and decorator from Ellesmere Port in Cheshire. Enlisting in Chester in December 1915, he received minimal training before being sent to the front. Having been wounded, he returned to France again and was posted to the 10th Battalion in August 1916.

On Gough's front, the latest attacks were designed to press the German line eastward from positions such as Beaumont Hamel and Thiepval, towards objectives like Grandcourt and Miraumont. But all of these plans were being held up by the weather at the beginning of October. 'The weather seems dead against us,' wrote the colonel of Merrill Price's battalion, knowing that as soon as it cleared he and his men were expected to move on Stuff Redoubt, still in German hands after September's efforts to the north-east of Thiepval. Whilst they awaited dry weather, new orders were received, expanding their objectives.

After more setbacks owing to the weather, by 10am on 9th October Merrill and the rest of his battalion had returned to the lines ready to make their attack on Stuff Redoubt. As they waited they were served a hot meal while the heavy artillery pummelled their objectives. At dawn, another battalion had been sent forward, but found itself forced back by enemy fire. The Cheshires were told that they would make a second attack at 12:35pm.

At zero hour field batteries opened an intense barrage, but the shells flew long and overshot the enemy positions. Merrill Price formed up alongside his comrades in no-man's-land and went forward 'in excellent style, keeping good direction'. Germans began sniping at the advancing line, 'their shooting, however, was wild and our advance so rapid that our men were in the trench before the enemy could man it in strength and fortunately before they could bring a machine gun into action'. A bombing party also met with little resistance. At one end of the attack, a watchful officer noted that the artillery had barely touched the German front line and, fearing for the leading waves of his men, he ordered them to close up on those in front as quickly as possible, so that they could all rush the enemy line together 'with great dash'. Many Germans simply gave themselves up, glad to be out of the mud and out of the way of flying bullets and shells. Others poured out of dugouts. 'A melee ensued,' resulting in dugouts being bombed, more men surrendering and others being killed at close quarters.

Throughout the afternoon the fighting continued. Dugouts were set on fire, trench blocks were put up and beaten down, double blocks put up in their place, and prisoners were taken and sent down the line. All communication with the artillery was cut, wires 'torn to shreds' and Cheshire posts came under fire from British guns. At one point, the Germans made a concerted effort to bomb Merrill and his battalion away from the redoubt, attempting to push through their trench blocks. But using stick grenades the Cheshires, although they had to cede ground and casualties, eventually managed to fend them off. Reinforcements were thrown in and all the while the Germans targeted the southern side of Stuff Redoubt with their guns along with the trench running into it, preventing bombs and other material from getting up to the battalion.

As evening came on, the Germans sent a weighty counter-attack up a trench towards the redoubt, but the Cheshires beat them back with a Lewis gun and their rifles. A Wiltshire battalion had been sent up to reinforce the British position and to help carry up supplies of bombs. But as the Cheshire battalion clung on, the Germans refused to give in. At about 6pm they put down another heavy barrage and tried to advance, but were checked by the British artillery. An hour later activity at Stuff Redoubt had died away to intermittent shelling and the odd mortar round. Engineers came up to help deepen the trench and put up sturdy barricades. Stuff Redoubt had fallen, and the Cheshires' commanding officer was immensely proud. 'It was a treat to see the men coming with a grin from ear to ear, with German helmets and other [stuff] hanging all over them.'

It was almost inexplicable why some attacks on the Somme should succeed, and others should fail, but one thing was clear: in terms of the two armies' wider objectives, they were not progressing nearly as quickly as would be required to achieve what they wanted before operations were suspended for winter. Men were repeatedly attacking

Grandcourt Road Cemetery. (Andrew Holmes)

the same objectives. And, of course, there was a price to pay. The 10th Cheshires lost 143 men in the capture of Stuff Redoubt, twenty-six of them missing in action, which more often than not meant dead. Merrill Price was among their number. In November, the War Office accepted he had been killed in action on 9th October. The 25 year old's body was later retrieved from the battlefield and he was laid to rest at Grandcourt Road Cemetery, plot D.49.

10TH OCTOBER
#26263 Private George Lee

16TH SHERWOOD FORESTERS
(NOTTS & DERBY REGIMENT)

ALMOST DUE WEST OF MERRILL Price and his Cheshire Battalion was a 30-year-old Nottingham local named George Lee. Prior to the war, George worked at a local lace factory where he was a bobbin and carriage hand. Enlisting in his home town in May 1915, he left three children at home: Winnie, 6, George, 4, and 3-year-old Doris. His wife, Mary, was also heavily pregnant with a fourth, Hilda. George arrived in France in 1916. Just two weeks after reaching the Western Front, baby Hilda died at the age of six months suffering from convulsions and enteritis, but there would be no chance of him returning home because the 16th Sherwood Foresters had already begun their journey towards the Somme.

British troops had managed to get part way into Schwaben Redoubt, north of Thiepval. On 4th October George Lee's battalion took over the sector of the line that included it during daylight, the men coming in for heavy shelling and losing twenty-eight of their number. The Germans were of no mind to simply let Gough's men hold on to their gains at this strong point. Three days later, they attacked using *flammenwerfer* in an attempt to push the British out of it, but George's battalion, along with a neighbouring Sherwood Foresters outfit, drove them back, the enemy leaving a trail of casualties and prisoners as they retreated. The Notts and Derby men's efforts were enough to draw letters of congratulation from generals: 'units supported each other; liaison with

artillery was very complete and satisfactory, and all units showed much spirit and dash.' Likewise though, sharing the position with the enemy was not ideal for the British, and on the same day that Stuff Redoubt was attacked by the 10th Cheshires, Merrill Price among them, the Reserve Army also made a play for Schwaben in its entirety.

There was no preliminary bombardment. The Sherwood Foresters went forward at 4:30am on 9th October, attempting to surprise the enemy in the dark. The weather had begun its permanent decline towards the end of the year now, with conditions enough 'to make mere existence a severe trial of body and spirit'. The mud in the trenches was so thick and cumbersome that the men moved over the open on their way to the crest of the redoubt and its north side. But the Germans were waiting. They opened up on George Lee's battalion with machine guns and rifles before the men had got halfway across no-man's-land. Three minutes into the attack they also began an artillery bombardment. The Notts and Derby men ran into wire as they approached their objective, if they could get through the storm of enemy fire. Only one flank managed to get into the enemy trenches, but were promptly pushed out again and driven back. There was to be no success to mirror that at Stuff Redoubt to the east. The Germans kept their hold on Schwaben Redoubt as the 16th Sherwood Foresters suffered almost 240 casualties. George Lee was among the dead. It was known he had been wounded, but he was never brought in by a stretcher party. In 1917 it was accepted that he had died of his wounds on 10th October. George had, in fact, been buried quickly on the battlefield and in 1919, as the area was cleared, he was finally laid to rest at Connaught Cemetery, plot X.H.6.

11TH OCTOBER
2nd Lieutenant Arthur Frederick Taverner

1ST KING'S (SHROPSHIRE LIGHT INFANTRY)

2nd Lieutenant Arthur Taverner.
(Rutland Remembers)

TO THE SOUTH-EAST OF GUEUDECOURT was a teenage officer who had just turned 19 on the Somme. The eldest of a rural clergyman's four children, Arthur Taverner had been born in Leicester and raised in Rutland, in between Leicester and Peterborough. Educated at Oakham School, where he got his football and cricket colours, he also spent four years in the OTC. Having reached an age where he could get a commission in the army, Arthur did not return to school in autumn 1915, instead joining The King's (Shropshire Light Infantry). After his training the young subaltern was sent to join his battalion at the front in the summer of 1916.

Since the attack of 7th October the rain had been pitiless on Rawlinson's front as well as Gough's. The lines were full of under-strength battalions, and the mud was sticky, making it difficult even to walk. The area was dominated by craters filled with water, hundreds of them as far as the eye could see in some places. And worst of all was the sight of wounded men trying to drag themselves through the mud to safety. Evacuating injured men in these conditions was a nightmare, but orders for an immediate resumption on all the original objectives came with just a few days' notice. Rawlinson wanted his men to take the objectives that they had missed as soon as was possible, though it was clear that time would be needed to move new troops into the line and bring up supplies.

Arthur Taverner's was one of the battalions being moved up to take part in the renewed assault, now set for 12th October. Bolstered by a draft of men joining from the Derbyshire Yeomanry, The King's marched up to Trônes Wood on 8th October before accepting more drafts and taking up their positions in support lines to the south-east of Gueudecourt.

The rain finally stopped, which at least meant that the mud did not get any worse. Throughout the 9th Arthur and his charges were shelled heavily as they sat in it, causing twenty-five casualties. However, the counter-attack that they were tentatively expecting did not materialise. Nonetheless, their own attack was approaching. Moving anywhere in the muddy conditions was a trial, as was trying to dig assembly trenches, and The King's were unfamiliar with their surroundings. On 10th October the battalion struggled in the boggy conditions to dig a new communication trench and spent some time erecting a memorial plaque to their friends killed nearby during an attack in mid-September. Hostile fire continued throughout the day. Twelve men were wounded on the evening of the attack,

The ruins of the village of Morval at the southern end of the battlefield. (Authors' collection)

including Arthur. The 19 year old's injuries were critical. Hit in the mouth, he had suffered a compound fracture to both his upper and lower jaw. He was taken to a casualty clearing station, but they could do nothing for him. Arthur Taverner died the following day. At home in Rutland, his father had a memorial plaque put up in his church by the pulpit and preached next to it for the next thirty years. His teenage son was laid to rest at Grove Town Cemetery, plot I.B.1.

12TH OCTOBER
Lieutenant Eustace Emil Hyde

1ST ROYAL IRISH FUSILIERS

Lieutenant Eustace Hyde. (Private collection)

TO THE SOUTH-EAST OF THE King's Shropshire Light Infantry, the 1st Royal Irish Fusiliers were ready to attack on 12th October. Among their officers was the 24-year-old son of another clergyman, from Dudley Hill, near Bradford. Educated locally at Bradford Grammar School, Eustace Hyde worked for the Hunsworth branch of the Bradford Dyers' Association. He and his brother joined the local pals battalion together at the height of the recruitment boom in September 1914 but both later received commissions. Eustace, the younger of the two, was gazetted to the Royal Irish Fusiliers in April 1915. He was present for the Easter Rising in Dublin in the spring of 1916, and then travelled to the Western Front in July.

Eustace's brother Charles had remained with the Bradford Pals. While Eustace had yet to set foot on the Somme, the Pals had been shattered on 1st July, almost completely wiped out on the northern reaches of the battlefield. Among the dead on that day was Eustace's brother, who fell aged 27.

By now divisions being pulled on to the Somme to participate in the autumn advances knew exactly what they were getting into. Many had already been there. Before Eustace's arrival, the Irish Fusiliers' division had been bludgeoned at the northern end of the battlefield on day one. Now the 1st Royal Irish Fusiliers, Eustace included, were to attack in a north-easterly direction towards Le Transloy on 12th October.

By 9:30pm on the 11th, Eustace's battalion, which numbered just over 450 men, had cleared everything away in its trenches and orders had been received for the following day. The Irish Fusiliers' advance was to take place in two stages, one to mop up small trenches in their path and the second to move on to their objectives proper. Zero hour was to be 2:05pm the following afternoon.

The 12th October brought heavy showers. An artillery bombardment started promptly at zero hour and Eustace's battalion rushed forward, hugging the creeping barrage so closely that some of the men were tragically hit by their own shells. Taking a moment to regroup on account of the confusion that this caused, the advancing troops were then caught by fire from a machine gun, which began spraying through the artillery barrage. The men stopped. This was all the time that the German machine gunners needed to swing their weapons around. 'The Regiment then had no chance at all.' All the officers in the leading two waves were hit bar one or two. Reports were sketchy as to what then transpired. Coming up in support, Eustace and his men could make no inroads into the trenches north-east of Lesboeufs. A witness in a company moving up behind saw the 24 year old heading for an enemy machine gun just after 3pm when, some 30 yards away from it, Eustace was caught by the German fire. His men were forced to retire and had to leave his body behind. It took until midnight for the Royal Irish Fusiliers' staff to ascertain that the regiment was holding its original lines. Eustace Hyde's remains were eventually retrieved and identified. He was finally laid to rest at A.I.F Burial Ground, plot III.H.1.

13TH OCTOBER
#1581 Private William Morris
1ST NEWFOUNDLAND REGIMENT

FOUR DAYS AFTER THE OUTBREAK of war in 1914, the Governor of Newfoundland communicated with London to say that the colony would be able to find 500 men to serve in the army. Within a month there were more than 700 attempting to join the war effort, from a tiny population that was equivalent to just one thirtieth of London's at the time. A training camp was set up and at the beginning of October the First Five Hundred left for Europe. But more men needed to be recruited as reinforcements and so the colony got to work. The vast majority of the Newfoundland recruits came from St Johns, but a special team was recruited to travel to more remote communities and find able-bodied young men.

One of those who was moved to enlist was William Morris, whose large family lived in isolation some 3 miles away from the local community in Robinson's Head, a tiny hamlet named after an Irishman who had lived in a cave nearby. William's was one of the long-settled families in the Outer Bay area. His father, a farmer and a fisherman, was a widower, his mother having died after having her tenth baby at the age of 39. William was the eldest boy, and in May 1915 he enlisted while still a teenager and began training at St John's. Embarking for England at the beginning of 1916, he had arrived at Marseilles in April just in time to join his battalion for the Battle of the Somme.

The Newfoundlanders were the only Dominion troops present on 1st July. Ordered to attack in the Beaumont Hamel sector, William was lucky to survive. The battalion went into action with about 780 men. At 9:30am the Newfoundlanders moved up to support the faltering attack on their front. By now the communication trenches were full of wounded from the first wave returning for treatment and so the battalion stepped out from the trenches and headed towards the British front line in the open. Without cover, they had immediately started incurring heavy casualties. Many of those Newfoundlanders who made it to the British front line were picked off by German machine guns, who had already pinpointed the gap in the British wire through which the troops were advancing. The few soldiers that made it into no-man's-land were caught up in a maelstrom of artillery and a hail of bullets, unable to advance much further. In less than an hour the Newfoundlanders had almost been wiped out. Fewer than seventy answered roll call the following morning, including William Morris. Every other man, including all of the officers, was dead, wounded or unaccounted for. Understandably the battalion was completely unable to function following its losses, and was sent away to the Ypres area in July.

Private William Morris. (Private collection)

By the time William Morris was recalled to the Somme at the beginning of October, the Newfoundlanders had built their complement back up to almost 600 men. On the 8th they boarded trains south and two days later left the rear area in twenty-one motor buses to return to the battle, sent to man the lines north of Gueudecourt. Once troops were left with the transports to the rear, including a nucleus of officers to prevent the entire battalion being wiped out if the worst occurred, the 1st Newfoundland Regiment found itself just over 385 strong, hugely under strength, as was the case for battalions throughout the battlefield by the autumn of 1916.

More than 100 of these men had already become casualties by midday on 12th October, two hours before zero hour, thanks to heavy shelling. As Eustace Hyde's battalion went forward next to Lesboeufs, at 2:05pm William Morris and the rest of the Newfoundlanders also swept forward in waves. Keeping as close to the barrage as they could, the men seized the enemy trenches as planned. Company commanders were cut down, but the battalion kept its cohesion and prepared for its second objective. The plan was for William and his companions to go out in front of their captured trench and dig a new forward line. The first party led out to do it was obliterated. In the meantime, the rest of the men carried on consolidating the captured trench: digging in, throwing bombs down into dugouts and clearing them. Any Germans that they found were rounded up and sent back to cages at the rear as prisoners.

As the afternoon wore on, it transpired that the Essex battalion that should have been on the left of William and the other Newfoundlanders had retired as their position was untenable. They had fallen back to their original trenches, leaving the Newfoundland flank without direction. The battalion immediately fanned out and occupied the empty space, putting up a trench barricade as the Germans emerged into the open and counter-attacked. Frantically, they were beaten back and the Germans retreated again. Darkness fell. At about 9pm a group of Hampshire men were sent up to help reinforce the Newfoundlanders' dwindling numbers, which were now, despite their partial success, almost too low for them to hold their position. In the early hours, more men of the Hampshire Regiment arrived to relieve them. Once again, the 1st Newfoundland Regiment had been decimated on the Somme. The attack on 12th October cost them another 230 men, 40 per cent of their strength.

Caribou Memorial on the battlefield near Gueudecourt in tribute to soldiers from Newfoundland. (Alexandra Churchill)

Apart from some small gains, across the board the day was a failure and very little progress was made anywhere along Rawlinson's line. If the Germans were close to crumbling, as Haig believed, it had transpired that it was simply not close enough. Nevertheless, the British Army would keep trying. More objectives were given out to prepare for another general advance, provisionally set for 18th October. Nobody seriously believed any more that the Germans could now be defeated in 1916, but still the battle went on.

William's body, if recovered, was never identified. Witnesses appear to have confirmed that he died of wounds on 13th October. In the aftermath of the war, the scene of his battalion's horrific loss on 1st July at Beaumont Hamel was selected as a site for a memorial. Included are panels that bear the names of 814 Newfoundlanders, including 21-year-old William Morris, who died on land or at sea in the Great War and have no known grave. More than 8,000 Newfoundlanders fought in the war. Of those, as many as 1,500 never returned home. For a colony whose largest city boasted about the same population as Guildford's at the time, it was a crushing loss.

14TH OCTOBER
2nd Lieutenant Frank Lloyd Sharpin

8TH BEDFORDSHIRE REGIMENT

2nd Lieutenant Frank Sharpin.
(Authors' collection)

THE 8TH BEDFORDSHIRE REGIMENT HAD been present at the advances of both 15th and 25th September, and so was spared the action of 12th October. To the rear of the fighting was Frank Sharpin, a 33 year old born in Bombay, where his father was an archdeacon. Educated at Bedford Grammar School, Frank went into a career in banking. He was with the London Company & Westminster Bank at St James' in August 1914 when war was declared and he volunteered for the Honourable Artillery Company. Frank spent the winter of 1914 in the trenches and remained on the Western Front until he was wounded in the face at St Eloi in March 1915.

While at home, Frank was given a commission in the Bedfordshire Regiment and underwent training at Ampthill Park and Oxted, then joined his battalion in France on 2nd October. His fledgling career as an officer was somewhat threatened while on leave in the spring of 1916. After what appeared to be a particularly good night out in London, he was caught out by a military policeman, rather drunk in Leicester Square. Cunningly, when asked to identify himself, Frank gave the name of another officer in the regiment. Unfortunately for him, the authorities saw through his ruse quickly and after a court martial, during which he sheepishly pleaded guilty, Frank was severely reprimanded and then released without prejudice.

Frank and his men had spent October so far receiving plaudits for their involvement in the September offensives, attempting to get clean and training. There were lectures by the divisional gas officer and another on physical training and bayonet fighting. Lewis gunners and bombers went off on their own to rehearse their part in a future attack. On the 8th the Bedfords marched to Trônes Wood in pouring rain and took over shelters from another battalion behind the lines. From there, as Rawlinson's army prepared to go forward again on the 12th, Frank Sharpin's men formed large working parties to go forward and work on the lines or help prepare for the upcoming attack.

At zero hour on 12th October the 8th Bedfordshires were in support behind Gueudecourt. As the battle played out in front of them they awaited orders. They came at nightfall. Frank and his men were ordered to cross to the east of Gueudecourt and relieve two exhausted battalions that had taken part in the day's action: Arthur Taverner's and the 2nd York & Lancasters. Within hours, Frank Sharpin had been mortally wounded: shot in the stomach. He was evacuated to a casualty clearing station, but succumbed to his wounds on 14th October.

'Need I say how deeply we mourn his loss?' His colonel wrote to Frank's parents. One of his old comrades from the HAC was more effusive:

Having been companions under conditions in which men get to know one another very well indeed, I can only say he was the very best of a grand type of Englishman, To know him was a privilege in itself ... the most marked trait was that of a simply grand unselfishness. He had no thought for himself, so long as there was something he could do for a comrade.

Second Lieutenant Sharpin was laid to rest at Grove Town Cemetery, plot I.B.4, three graves away from Arthur Taverner.

15TH OCTOBER

#151639 Lance Corporal Charles Richard Leach

179TH TUNNELLING COMPANY, ROYAL ENGINEERS

CHARLES LEACH WAS A 30-YEAR-OLD married sawyer when he enlisted into the 3rd Battalion of the Manchester Regiment shortly after war was declared. He remained at home until April 1915, when he was sent to France. In February 1916, Charles applied for a transfer away from the infantry and into the Royal Engineers, not an illogical step given his occupation in peacetime. In August 1915 Charles was moved into the 179th Tunnelling Company, which was responsible for mining and other operations from Thiepval down to La Boisselle. Tunnelling here had been started by the French in December 1914 and by the time the 179th took over operations both the French and the Germans had already detonated several mines.

Tunnelling was dark, dangerous work. Men worked eight-hour shifts in almost pitch-dark conditions, in a fetid atmosphere, in cramped spaces and in almost complete silence. Tunnels were dug approaching and underneath German front-line positions. Defensive networks were also constructed that protruded out under no-man's-land with a view to intercepting enemy tunnelling operations. The need for silence was paramount, for if the enemy got any indication of threatening tunnelling activity they would aim to detonate a small charge alongside the offending tunnel, killing the occupants or breaking in, where fierce hand-to-hand fighting took place in confined spaces.

In October 1915, the 179th Tunnelling Company started work to deepen the shafts at La Boisselle. On 22nd November the Germans blew a charge alongside the British tunnels, killing six tunnellers of the company, the bodies of two of whom were never recovered. Rescue attempts were hampered by the amount of gas caused by the explosion that remained in the tunnels. Whether resulting from enemy explosions

Tunnel at The Glory Hole, La Boisselle. Courtesy of the La Boisselle Study Group. (Andrew Holmes)

or otherwise, gas was another worry for those working under the battlefield; like miners beforehand, tunnellers used mice and canaries to alert them of its presence.

In preparation for the attack on 1st July, two large mines were prepared at La Boisselle. One, just to the north of the Albert–Bapaume Road, was known as Y-Sap mine. The other was further south and known as the Lochnagar Mine. Y-Sap mine was completed at the end of June 1916. At the end of a tunnel that traversed across no-man's-land, it was charged with 40,000lb of explosives. The 179th Tunnelling Company took over construction of Lochnagar in March 1916. Progress for Charles' company was slow due to the need to work in almost absolute silence. The tunnellers worked barefoot on a carpet of sandbags, using a bayonet to prise chalk out of the face of the tunnel. Any noise at this stage would compromise the existence of the mine. Eventually, the tunnel was completed and an aggregate of 60,000lb of explosives was placed in two separate chambers at the end. The two mines were successfully detonated at 7:28am on 1st July along with two additional smaller ones, causing a huge explosion just to the side of Billy Disbrey's front. 'All these mines did considerable damage to the enemy field works … All mines caused casualties.'

Although further mines were fired during the Battle of the Somme after 1st July, the 179th Tunnelling Company was not involved directly in their construction. After the detonation of the Y-Sap and Lochnagar mines, Charles Leach and the company were involved throughout September in the construction of tunnels at Thiepval, and dugouts and shelters in Mametz Wood and High Wood, throughout September. At the end of September, Charles was promoted to the rank of temporary lance corporal. The work undertaken by Charles and the company at this time was not without risk as being out in the open increased the possibility of being hit by the enemy. On 15th October 1916, Charles was killed after he was hit by shrapnel near Thiepval. After his death his only surviving possession was one wooden charm, which was sent to his wife, Sarah, in Bradford. Charles Leach was laid to rest at Albert Communal Cemetery Extension, plot I.J.31.

16TH OCTOBER
Captain Oliver John Sykes
23RD SIEGE BATTERY, ROYAL GARRISON ARTILLERY

THE SOMME WAS STILL GETTING progressively worse for the artillery. Airmen were finding it increasingly difficult to get up and over the lines in deteriorating weather to feed through information on targets. 'Little could be seen from the air through rain and mist, so counter-battery work suffered and it was often impossible to locate with accuracy the new German trenches and shell hole positions.' Barrages were fired too short or too long. Added to that, the maintenance of the guns was so neglected owing to their relentless work, or they were simply worn out, so that they may not have been able to fire accurately enough anyway. The ground was so soft that they sank on their platforms, and crews had to try to restore their stability using any battle debris they could find. 'Bursts of high explosive were smothered in the ooze' and the mud was so deep that to move one field gun, ten or twelve horses were often needed. 'Ammunition had to be dragged up on sledges improvised of sheets of corrugated iron.'

Amidst this grime and squalor was a 41-year-old officer named Oliver Sykes. Born in India, where his father was the late principal of La Martiniere College, Oliver had been educated at Brasenose College, Oxford, in the 1890s before joining the Indian Civil Service. He had been an officer in the ICS Finance Department for fifteen years and had progressed to a high level, also acting as a financial adviser at one stage to the Siamese Government and officials in Kashmir.

Oliver had also been a captain in a volunteer artillery unit at Madras since 1912. In 1915 he volunteered for Imperial Service and obtained a month's leave from his post to join a gunnery class in the Punjab to get his knowledge of heavy artillery up to date. Then he applied for a year's leave from the Government of India and arrived in England in April 1916. He was commissioned as a captain in the Royal Garrison Artillery two weeks later and joined his battery in June, overseeing the firing of

howitzers from positions in the Ancre Valley, Ovillers-la-Boisselle and Martinpuich in the opening weeks of the campaign on the Somme.

On 16th October, from near Pozières, Oliver had written to his family. 'The shelling has slowed down a bit,' he explained. 'We have to do some walking in the open above ground; we have had a lot of casualties and shall probably have more.' He elaborated on the conditions of being under constant enemy fire. 'The last few days have been very active; we had high-explosive shell and tear gas shell mixed for one and a half hours on end two evenings ago; my eyes are still feeling the effects.'

A howitzer undergoing cleaning on the Somme. (Authors' collection)

That night Oliver and another officer were up to the battery approaching midnight. It had been hit by enemy shelling and a dugout blown in with men inside. Three were dead and the other six were being pulled out wounded. The shelling began again. 'I heard [him] speaking to me from the road close by,' his companion recalled, 'suggesting how to get the wounded out of the battery and away to the dressing station, and as he spoke a shell arrived almost on top of him.' Those in a fit state rushed to Oliver's side. 'We got him into a dugout, where the medical orderly dressed his wounds, two very severe ones, one through the thigh and another across the back, and some smaller ones.' Oliver Sykes' prognosis did not look good. 'The shock must have been terrific and he was practically unconscious from the first.' He was taken back to a field ambulance at Albert, where he died during the night. 'I am miserable about his death,' his fellow officer admitted to Oliver's family. 'A more gallant fellow never breathed.'

Oliver became number fifty-seven in the Brasenose College Roll of those who had fallen in the war so far. He left behind a wife, Dulcie, and three sons: Hugh, 8, John, 7, and 3-year-old Charles. Captain Sykes was laid to rest at Bouzincourt Communal Cemetery Extension, plot I.1.17.

17TH OCTOBER
#S/11390 Lance Corporal John MacDonald

7TH SEAFORTH HIGHLANDERS

LE SARS HAD BEEN CAPTURED on 7th October, three days after Robert Graham's death. Rawlinson's men were one small step closer to Bapaume, further down the main road to the north-east. But the weather was becoming even worse now; damp, cold and wet threatening to take all of the impetus out of the British advance. The 9th (Scottish) Division arrived in the area and took up a position north of Eaucourt l'Abbaye and to the East of Le Sars. Almost three months had elapsed since their hideous experiences inside Delville Wood in mid-July and the Scotsmen and their South African contingent returned to the fighting on the Somme in the autumn to find that the Germans in front of them had now been pushed back to a fourth set of defences.

Among their number was a 22 year old from Partick named John MacDonald. Educated at Thornwood Public School on the west side of Glasgow, John had worked for optical engineers Barr & Stroud until his enlistment at the end of 1915. The scene in front of him on the Somme was one of total devastation, a 'vast waste of wilderness created by three months of savage warfare. Its general colour scheme was a dull uniform grey which changed to a dingy yellow when the sun shone.' There were no landmarks, no features to break the grey monotony:

> Here and there a body arrested attention by the peculiar contortion of its attitude and served as a landmark to guide runners on their way. The air was rank with the odour of death. To eye, ear and nose the whole place was repellent …

The whole area was blanketed in debris from the fighting, 'but worst of all from Mametz Wood to the front line were scattered corpses and a heavy, fetid odour pervaded the atmosphere'. There was simply not the manpower available to concentrate on clearing them away. Even inside Mametz Wood, which had been in British hands for months now, there were still both British and German bodies everywhere:

> The entire area was intersected by rutted roads, which even in fine weather could barely stand the stupendous amount of traffic that passed over them in a never ending stream.

Men not manning the trenches worked daily to repair them, 'but all the labour served only to keep them passably decent, and when the weather broke down, almost superhuman efforts were required to keep them from collapsing altogether'.

Nonetheless, despite the conditions, the undermanned state of battalions and the men and material being expended for limited gains, it was still believed at this point, with fair weather and tenacity perhaps, that before winter came Rawlinson's Fourth Army could get beyond Warlencourt and Le Sars and take Bapaume to establish themselves upon advantageous ground. Now that Le Sars had fallen, as was the nature of the fighting on the Somme, attention was drawn to the next stubborn obstacle that lay in the path of the British Army. In this case, it was the Butte de Warlencourt, an ancient burial mound which was a pile of chalk some 50ft high alongside the straight road running to Bapaume that had been skinned of all vegetation by shelling. Protected by a network of trenches, it was rife with dugouts and tunnels sheltering the enemy, while they enjoyed a clear view all the way back across the barren countryside to Flers in one direction and up to Bapaume in the other.

On 12th October John MacDonald and his battalion were sent into action to try to storm the Butte, first taking possession of Snag Trench, which lay in their path, before they reached the Butte itself. John and his fellow Highlanders had suffered machine-gun fire as soon as they left the trenches, and although another battalion was sent forward to reinforce them, their advance was minimal. Under cover of darkness they dug in, confused, with South African troops on their left.

The resumption of the attack would again see the Scottish division heading for Snag Trench and the Butte beyond. The 7th Seaforth Highlanders were relieved on 13th October, but would be coming back up before the assault began. In the meantime, they pooled their resources to form companies of as few as thirty men. There was gruesome work for John and his comrades to do. They formed burial parties, and went up to find any lingering wounded in the area. There was also the rather morbid job of removing valuable greatcoats and other material from fallen men out in the open who no longer had use for it. All the while, they had to operate under enemy shellfire and wade through clay-like mud. The preliminary bombardment was already under way, with intense bursts of fire and a fierce response being belted out by the enemy guns opposite. As work continued on 17th October, John was killed just hours before his battalion marched up to prepare for its advance the following day. It was customary for an officer to write to the man's family, but by this point on the Somme, battalions had been decimated, filled with drafts and then torn apart again so that often men barely knew each other. 'I did not know him very well,' a young subaltern wrote to John's parents, 'but he was without doubt very popular with his companions.' John MacDonald's body, if recovered, was never identified and he is commemorated on the Thiepval Memorial, Pier & Face 15c.

18TH OCTOBER

#20540 Lance Corporal David Trons Blacklaw

5TH CAMERON HIGHLANDERS

Lance Corporal David Blacklaw.
(Authors' collection)

THE ADVANCE ON THE BUTTE de Warlencourt went forward on 18th October. On the previous night, the 5th Cameron Highlanders had lined up along taped markers, among their ranks a 25-year-old mill worker from Lochee, Dundee, who had enlisted in the summer of 1915. David Blacklaw waited to advance while officers took compass bearings to make sure they did not veer off in the wrong direction among the maze of shell holes and trenches on the featureless landscape.

At 3:40am David and his comrades attacked in the dark as rain hammered down. Officers and men stumbled and fell in the slippery ooze, rifles and Lewis guns became clogged with it so that bomb and bayonet were soon the only weapons. Smoke had been discharged to try to obscure the battlefield and reduce the fire from the direction of the Butte and Warlencourt line. The Scotsmen kept close to the barrage and stormed the German trenches as soon as it lifted. Capturing the front line with slight casualties, David's battalion began throwing up blocks to stop the enemy from bombing their way towards them, but within fifteen minutes they had done just that on the Highlanders' right flank, driving out the Wiltshire men next to them and getting a foothold back in the trench. On their left, the Scotsmen had no idea what was occurring with the South African troops at the end of their line.

The Cameron Highlanders surged forward in a counter-attack, frantically flinging bombs and driving the Germans back 200 yards. This put an end to enemy resistance in that direction. By 9:30am, David's battalion had linked up with the South Africans. They had progressed forwards, but there was no chance of claiming the Butte. The day passed quietly with the exception of a threatened counter-attack, which came at about 2pm. Some 300 Germans grouped together as if they were about to charge. David's battalion at once sent up an SOS 'and the men in field grey, peppered with bullets and shellfire broke up in disorder and scrambled for shelter'.

David Blacklaw fell in attempting to seize the enemy trench. Just before he was hit he had singlehandedly captured an enemy machine gun. The 25 year old left behind a widow, Maggie, and a 4-year-old son, David Jr. Maggie placed the following memorial in the local newspaper on behalf of her little boy:

I'll always pray for you dear daddy
For your country you nobly fell;
Although of you I cannot remember
My mother can always tell

David Blacklaw was buried on the battlefield where he fell. His body, if subsequently recovered, was never identified and he is commemorated on the Thiepval Memorial, Pier & Face 15b.

19TH OCTOBER
#S/17722 Rifleman William Lesurf

1ST RIFLE BRIGADE

THE ATTACK OF THE 18TH had fared little better to the south-east, almost at the end of the British line. At Lesboeufs Rawlinson's men were attempting yet again to push north-east towards the Le Transloy line. Serving with a regular battalion of the Rifle Brigade was a 27-year-old dock labourer from Duckett Street in Stepney, East London. William Lesurf enlisted in December 1915 and was not mobilised until April the following year. He stepped off a transport and on to French soil on 14th September 1916. Having joined the battalion two weeks later, he was only in his third week of active service when the 1st Rifle Brigade was ordered to seize a collection of trenches to the east of Lesboeufs.

Here, as at the Butte, the conditions were deplorable. 'All movement was painfully slow through the flooded trenches and water filled craters ... The only possible way for the infantry to take its objectives was to get to close grips with the enemy and fight with bomb and bayonet.' William's battalion went into battle with just over 500 men. In the pouring rain he and his comrades rushed forward, narrowly avoiding a sweeping barrage laid down by the enemy that came in on no-man's-land just as they cleared it on their way forward. One company could not get within 20 yards of the Germans thanks to a machine gun that opened as soon as it started its attack. Another got lost as soon as it set off, and was only spared annihilation by the fact that the Germans opposite appeared to do the same.

Scrapping went on from shell hole to shell hole and the situation became utterly confusing in the dark. On the front of another company, the enemy had begun sending up flares. Here the riflemen were caught by the quick barrage laid down and, as they crested the top of a small ridge to advance, they were mown down by machine-gun fire. Parties of the battalion began reaching their objectives, but had to withdraw. The failed attempt towards Le Transloy had cost the 1st Rifle Brigade more than 260 men.

Across the board the day had been a disaster. No-man's-land was littered with wounded and dying men, including William Lesurf. The men of the battalion that remained unscathed after their ordeal collected them one by one as the rain continued to tip down. As the battalion was relieved the following night, William was not among those collected and was later deemed to have died on 19th October. William left behind a widow named Margaret and four children: Lily, 7, Mary, 5, Violet, 3, and 2-year-old William. He never met his fifth child, a daughter, also named Margaret, born just nine days before her father's death. William Lesurf lay on the battlefield until his remains were discovered in 1923. He was identified by his clothing and a serial number on his boot and finally laid to rest at Bienvillers Military Cemetery, plot XVIII.H.2.

20TH OCTOBER
2nd Lieutenant Cuthbert John Creery

21 SQUADRON, ROYAL FLYING CORPS

THE RFC WAS HAVING A miserable time trying to stay in the air in the midst of the appalling weather, battling, 'rain, high winds, mist and cold in their exposed cockpits'. Observing the ground was growing ever more difficult 'but full advantage was taken of every bright interval to direct artillery fire and to photograph new work in the German defences'. Among those doing his best to stay airborne was a 21 year old born in England but raised in Vancouver. Cuthbert Creery originally enlisted as a trooper in a battalion of the Canadian Mounted Rifles, but towards the end of 1915 he had obtained a pilot's certificate and on arrival in London was immediately nominated for a commission in the RFC. Cuthbert had a sense of fun while training at Netheravon. Given a dud aeroplane with an engine too weak to get off the ground one afternoon, he and a friend made the most of a chance for mischief. 'Creery got in the observer's seat and I got in the pilot's seat, and we taxied all over the aerodrome doing figure 8s, etc., all over the ground. The engine was so weak it wouldn't leave the ground, but we had a good time tearing around and amusing the rustics grouped along

Five Brothers, Vancouver Boys, Enlist for Fight Against Huns

Newspaper headline in tribute to Cuthbert Creery (far left) and his four brothers. (Authors' collection)

a fence.' Cuthbert qualified as a flying officer in April 1916 and was sent to 21 Squadron two weeks later. He was wounded after just a few days. Accidents were frequent in the life of an airman and Cuthbert suffered a cut lip and a graze to his face.

However, he had been working solidly since before the infantry campaign on the Somme had officially begun on bombing and reconnaissance missions. The latter in particular was critical in the build-up to 1st July, and squadrons were busy gathering all the information possible to help the men on the ground progress when zero hour came. Cuthbert had a close shave on 17th June. At 4:30pm, he was one of four pilots to take off on a reconnaissance flight. Three of the aeroplanes suffered major mechanical difficulties and Cuthbert managed to make sure he was over British lines before he was forced to bring his 'bus' to ground.

On the opening day of the Battle of the Somme, Cuthbert was diverted to bombing raids, targeting a German strong point. The squadron flew from aerodromes near Saint-Omer and Beaumont Hamel throughout the month and dropped nearly 30 tons of explosives on Bapaume alone. Airmen made repeated flights on 1st July, and in the afternoon Cuthbert took off on a flight with a large 336lb bomb dangling from his machine. He dropped it from a height of 9,000ft, while skirting the range of German anti-aircraft guns.

As July wore on, Cuthbert's targets were the village of Le Transloy and Cambrai Station as the attack on Bazentin Ridge commenced, in order to slow the progress of any German attempts to reinforce their

divisions and hopefully disrupt their supply chain. On 21st July, Cuthbert and his observer were part of a flight that took off in the direction of Ephey, another German-held town to the rear of their lines. This time Cuthbert was armed with smaller bombs and they registered five bursts: two on Ephey Station, far across the line behind Combles and Maurepas and on the important rail line running up to Cambrai. One bomb hit the ground in the station and another a large stone building. German anti-aircraft fire that day was accurate. While in the air it made sense for either of the RE's occupants to note anything of interested and they spotted a train steaming to the east of Ephey and another in the station facing south-east for intelligence men on the ground to ponder. They also spotted an enemy aerodrome and, if that wasn't enough work for one outing, Cuthbert and his observer, who manned a gun from his seat, would now have to fight their way home.

Cuthbert turned to the left and followed a fellow squadron member who had got himself separated from the others. He spied a German machine circling around his comrade and watched as it swept down and opened fire from behind. Cuthbert could see tracer bullets from the other RE pouring out towards the enemy airman as his fellow pilot attempted to fight him off. Arriving on the scene, Cuthbert dived at the back of the hostile machine, but his observer was unable to open fire, the German turning sharply to the right and firing upwards at them as he went down. As he did so, Cuthbert's observer managed to fire a drum of ammunition at him. Meanwhile, two more enemy machines had overhauled Cuthbert and now began firing at him from above.

The observer returned the fire, and the two enemy machines turned to their left in the direction of the other REs, apparently not too interested in the fight. Such was the frantic chaos of air combat over the Somme, but on this occasion Cuthbert was lucky enough to get home.

In August, 21 Squadron gravitated more towards offensive patrols, flying over enemy lines and seeking out German airmen. They had also switched to flying B.E.12s, a single-seat version of the RFC's workhorse, the B.E.2c. During the attack of 15th September, Cuthbert flew over Vélu aerodrome, taking off at 7am, and dropped six 20lb bombs from 5,500ft on to the German machines. He reported that he thought he saw four bombs explode, dropping close together, although there was very low, thick cloud obstructing his view. The other two went off among machines near a hangar.

As the Battle of the Somme wore on, the daily toil of offensive patrols, raids and scrapping with German airmen took its toll on Britain's airmen. It was a different type of stress to the infantryman, who endured endless hours of non-activity in the trenches, stretched out over days. When the pilots were on the ground, they were relatively safe to the rear, but for those few hours a day in the air, the much higher chance that they might meet their end was enough to quickly fray the nerves of the often very young men employed to fight the battle from above.

Cuthbert had been on leave at the beginning of October and shortly after he returned the weather broke, grounding the squadron. On the 20th, however, it was clear enough to get up and a flight promptly set off over enemy lines and encountered hostile aircraft. Cuthbert did not return. His friends in the mess were deeply concerned. Often an airman would telephone in from up the lines and request a transport, having come to ground somewhere in the British lines, but in Cuthbert's case this was unlikely. 'It is feared he was done in as he was last seen diving at a hun.' The following day was foggy and his best friend in the squadron sat glumly in the mess writing letters. News filtered in throughout the day. 'Latest news of Creery is that he fell in a Hun front line trench which we captured later ... He had been shot through the head and the heart. The huns had pinched his buttons, etc., and rifled his pockets.'

Cuthbert's body was recovered and entrusted to another squadron, in which his brother was serving, for burial. Another of the Creery boys was not to return home. Ronald was 20 when he died from 'severe wounds' during the spring advance of 1917. Two days later, a third of the brothers, Kenneth, was involved in an air crash that ended his war,

allegedly coming to with his left leg dangling over his right shoulder. He pointedly refused to have it amputated and subsequently recovered from his wounds. After a year's convalescence in Britain, Kenneth returned home to Canada. His brother, 2nd Lieutenant Cuthbert Creery, was laid to rest at Heilly Station Cemetery, plot V.A.9.

21ST OCTOBER
#704076 Corporal Arthur Gerald Leeson

102ND CANADIAN INFANTRY

IN GOUGH'S SECTOR, REGINA TRENCH was still in German hands, and on 21st October his men were to carry out a third attack to attempt to seize it. There had been a period of comparative quiet on the northern part of the battlefield after the events of 8th October, but on the 14th, Schwaben Redoubt finally fell. Despite the German use of *flammenwerfer* to try to claim the ground back, the attackers held on. Plans then had to be postponed during the rainfall of the next few days. In both of the previous attacks on Regina, the trench had been reached, but the Germans had unceremoniously dumped Gough's British and Canadian troops out of it again. Now the Reserve Army was determined to capture and this time hold on.

Forty-six-year-old Gerald Leeson had been born in south-east London, the only son of a doctor and educated at the Merchant Taylor's School. In adult life he had been imbued with a spirit of adventure, travelling the globe. In 1895 he emigrated to Canada and spent eight years in the North-West Mounted Police. Subsequently Gerald became a mining engineer and moved to the United States, settling in California long enough to meet an artist named Adelaide Hanscom. They married in Alaska in 1908, while Gerald was employed at the Treadwell Gold Mine for three years. At the end of that tenure they returned to California and settled in Danville, in the San Ramon Valley, where for another three years Gerald farmed locally. There was a brief spell in Kellogg, Idaho, near the border with Montana, for work on another mining project

Canadian troops receive a lecture from an officer before going into battle. (Authors' collection)

that lasted well into 1915 before Gerald abruptly left home, crossed into Canadian territory and enlisted at Rossland, British Columbia, some 200 miles away.

By mid-August 1916, he had arrived in France and had been ensconced in pleasant country south of Calais until the new arrivals swapped their rifles for Lee Enfields, picked up box respirators to protect them from gas and began the journey south to the Somme. Gerald Leeson was at Tara Hill, to the north-east of Albert, by the second week of October. The Canadian Corps was now being removed from the line and Gerald was among the last left, moving into a British Corps. The view was something to behold for men completely new to the field of battle. 'The Albert–Bapaume Road was literally alive by day and night with a never-ending stream of vehicles of all kinds travelling east or west.' The traffic encompassed a multitude of different types: 'lorries laden with ammunition going east, or crowded with weary soldiers coming west, ambulances, ration wagons, motor cycles, all the traffic of an army actively engaged poured ceaselessly back and forth along this main highway which miraculously escaped complete destruction by the enemy's artillery.'

After practice sessions, on the night of 18th October, the 102nd Battalion went into trenches as rain cascaded down. The ground was a morass, 'making the trenches almost impassable'. No sooner had Gerald arrived than word came down the support line that the men next to them were being bombed by a German attack and calling for help. In silence the men flitted past headquarters; 'jumping over trenches and shell holes they looked like phantoms in the dark, illumined by the light of German flares and leaping to the crash of bursting shells'. Rain continued all night along with constant shelling. The artillery were desperately focusing on smashing the German wire entanglements, in the hope that this time the men would not be left lingering in no-man's-land trying to get into Regina Trench, they sought out machine-gun spots and any gatherings of enemy troops spotted. Patrols were reporting that their efforts were successful.

Owing to the weather the infantry attack was put back until the 21st, so Gerald, 'a most efficient Non Commissioned Officer', and his battalion were sent back out of the line to rest until they were needed. Back they waded in hip-high mud. 'Men had to be literally dug out by their comrades as they sank exhausted in the liquid, glue-like substance.' The following day they made the same journey in reverse and arrived exhausted in the front line trenches. Overnight they had more work to do, digging assembly trenches in which to form up and establishing dumps of ammunition for the following afternoon. At dawn all was ready and then there was nothing to do but wait in the mud.

Zero hour was at 12:06am on the 21st, a fine, chilly day. The first wave went over, followed by two smaller ones. Gerald kept up behind a creeping barrage, 'lying down until it again lifted and advancing as it moved, all in perfect uniformity'. Aided by an intense overhead machine-gun barrage arced up towards the German lines, Gough's men got into Regina Trench 'with practically no opposition'. It was all over in half an hour. A defensive flank was formed with outposts well forward of Regina. The first wave had poured out 150 yards in front of the captured trench ready to defend it and the enemy appeared to be in disarray. The Canadians found the macabre spectacle of Regina Trench brimming with fallen Germans and their wounded comrades. The enemy initially limited their response to laying down a barrage as the third wave of British and Canadians went out to help secure the forward position in front of the trench. The second did the same in Regina, rounding up prisoners, and more men began restocking the dumps and bringing up supplies ready to mount any defence necessary. Just like that Regina Trench had finally been conquered and the capture of Thiepval Ridge was complete. Inexplicably considering all that had passed before, the 102nd Canadian Infantry had only lost five men killed and ten wounded in taking it.

Throughout the afternoon though, the German bombardment increased in ferocity. Then came the counter-attacks. Three times the enemy attempted to repeat the success of ejecting Gough's troops from Regina Trench, but this time they failed. By the end of the day, in doggedly clinging to their prize, the 102nd Battalion had suffered almost 100 casualties, including Gerald Leeson. As well as his widow, Adelaide, he left behind two children, Gerald Jr., 6, and Constance, 4. Adelaide broke down and her husband's death contributed to spells in mental institutions later on. She moved to England for a time to be nearer to his relatives, but eventually returned to California. She was killed in a hit-and-run incident in Pasadena in 1931. Buried where he fell, the location of 46-year-old Gerald Leeson's grave was subsequently lost and his body, if recovered, was never identified. He is commemorated on the Vimy Memorial. Canada's contribution to the Battle of the Somme had been bloody to say the least. By the time the last of her countrymen departed the field of battle, it was to the tune of some 24,000 casualties in just a few weeks.

22ND OCTOBER

#60513 Gunner Albert James Langford

Y BATTERY, ROYAL HORSE ARTILLERY

SERVING WITH THE ROYAL HORSE Artillery approaching the end of October was a 24-year-old gunner named Albert Langford. From London, Albert had joined the artillery in 1910, but left the army after three years' service. He had been working as a driver and as soon as war was declared, as a reservist he was called back up and initially served with a battery of the Royal Field Artillery. After being wounded at the end of the 1st Battle of Ypres in November 1914, Albert served in the Mediterranean before being routed into Y Battery on the Western Front.

The Royal Horse Artillery operated light guns that could be moved about quickly in support of the cavalry. Albert had played his part in the preliminary bombardment on the Somme at the end of June by joining in his battery's efforts at cutting the enemy barbed wire. They had then been moved back up to the Ypres Salient, but by 22nd October Albert was back on the Somme and just to the north of Delville Wood.

So hard was it now to move guns in the shambolic conditions on the Somme, that gunners were known to just go up and assume command of the ones that were there as opposed to try and moving their own across the saturated ground. Mud made even basic work vastly more difficult. With the German air services on the ascendancy too, the effectiveness of aeroplanes sent to help range the enemy artillery made life even harder. Among the benefits of this improvement on the German's part was better results in counter-battery work at this point, and so the likes of Albert Langford would likely be under a deafening barrage of enemy shells as they tried to work themselves. Albert and the rest of Y Battery moved into action and took over gun positions in mid-October, covering the 12th Division's infantry in front of them.

There they were when rain began cascading down on the 18th and all their efforts to support the troops in front of them were in vain. As the gun pits and the men's shelters filled up with water and the

gunners slid about in deep mud trying to keep up their rate of fire the following day, their German counterparts tortured them with shellfire all afternoon and into the night. The downpour finally ceased on the 20th and Albert and his fellow gunners spent two days on their normal work in fine, but chilly weather, shelling targets by zone as a frost began setting in.

On the 22nd the intensity of the enemy's counter-battery work increased again. The whole valley was shelled by heavy artillery, although the Germans managed to miss anything of consequence aside from a pile of ammunition to the rear, which promptly exploded. As late afternoon approached though, Y Battery was attempting to clear away from its position when a single shell landed in among the men and went off. Eight were killed by the blast, including Albert Langford, and ten more were wounded. The devastated remains of all of those killed were collected, including Albert, and laid to rest in one grave at Bernafay Wood British Cemetery, plot E.30.

Artillerymen attempt to move their gun in muddy conditions. (Authors' collection)

23RD OCTOBER

#S/19841 Rifleman William Dexter

2ND RIFLE BRIGADE

Rifleman William Dexter. (Private collection)

WHEN HE WASN'T AT WAR, William Dexter lived almost on the doorstep of London Zoo where he worked, as had his father before him. Originally a painter and decorator until he followed his father into the job, he had since risen to the position of Junior Keeper of Ostriches. Enlisting at the end of 1915, William arrived in France on exactly the same day as William Lesurf, but was routed to the 2nd Battalion of the Rifle Brigade while the latter went to the 1st and subsequently to his death on 19th October. William had been with his battalion for precisely three weeks as the end of October approached.

On the 23rd, Rawlinson's troops were going to make what was being termed as a preliminary attack on the Le Transloy Line to the north-east of them in conjunction with the French, the object of which was to establish a good starting point for a proper attack at a later date. A bombardment was already in place when William's division came into the line. Their objectives for the day were to advance from in between Gueudecourt and Lesboeufs towards Le Transloy, first taking a strong point at the junction of two trenches. There would be a halt of half an hour and then the battalion would push on past the trenches in question and establish a new line out in front. The weather held as William and his companions began to make their preparations, trudging back and forth over boards sinking into their muddy trenches. But the lines were in a filthy state due to all the recent rain. Rations and stores needed to be dragged 5 miles to reach the 2nd Rifle Brigade on the back of pack animals and it was a similar scenario for their water supplies. It could take an officer nearly two hours to cover 1,000 yards in doing his rounds to check on his men.

As the weather improved on 20th October, the artillery on both sides picked up the pace of their gunnery. Nights now were frosty as a rule and the men struggled to keep warm. At 10pm on the 22nd William and the rest of his battalion began making their way to their new assembly trenches. Here the men would have to spend the night. There were no dugouts for shelter and no fires were allowed. At dawn the prospective battlefield was so misty that the attack was put back until later in the day in the hopes that visibility might improve. The fog duly cleared as the heavy artillery continued to bombard Le Transloy in the distance.

By now, numbers were so low in battalions that most attacks would be made on the Somme with them using two weak companies. After what seemed like endless hours sitting in cold, damp trenches, the 2nd Rifle Brigade launched itself forward at 2:30pm. The leading waves bunched up close behind the creeping barrage in good order, but seizing the strong point allocated to the battalion proved an insurmountable task. In the meantime, the battalion on the right was being systematically pushed back by machine-gun fire. The other waves of William's battalion had more luck, seizing a line of shell holes further left that stretched for more than 100 yards. Behind it, the remaining men of the battalion had flooded into the now vacated assembly trenches ready to go forward in turn. At 2:55pm they advanced. Some of the men were beaten back from their objective, but eventually the remainder managed to reach the original attackers and help them join up the shell holes they had occupied to make a trench and form a strong point at one end.

It had been a confusing attack, with companies becoming intermingled. The battalion suffered not only heavy casualties in going forward, but more so in their consolidation work. The surviving riflemen were also busy in dealing with a number of German prisoners, some of whom deserted and simply turned themselves over to get out of the place and others that turned out to be a ration party who had become lost and wandered into the path of the riflemen. There was also the work of collecting the wounded, both friend and foe, so it was unsurprising that in such disarray, casualties were overlooked.

The 2nd Rifle Brigade initially calculated their losses at almost 240, a huge percentage of their available men. William was not reported missing until six days after the battle, but for his wife at home in Regent's Park, there was then an agonising wait to find out if he was in German captivity. It was ten months before the War Office, having heard nothing of him, confirmed that the 31 year old must have died on 23rd October 1916.

William left behind four children: Ena, 6, Dora, 4, Edward, 2, and 1-year-old Joan. His widow, Sarah, was forced to go and live with his parents when her husband died after little more than three weeks with his battalion. Edward, like his father and grandfather before him, would become a keeper at London Zoo, in the reptile house. For seven years William lay on the battlefield, but in 1923 his remains were discovered to the west of Le Transloy and he was identified by his clothing and by a serial number on one of his boots. William Dexter was finally laid to rest at Bienvillers Military Cemetery, plot XVIII.J.5.

24TH OCTOBER
2nd Lieutenant William Clifford Hales

2ND ROYAL BERKSHIRE REGIMENT

2nd Lieutenant William Hales.
(Authors' collection)

DESPITE THE EFFORTS OF WILLIAM Dexter and the 2nd Rifle Brigade on 23rd October, the main objective, Zenith Trench, north of Lesboeufs, that had been allocated to their division remained outstanding. On the 24th it was decided that the 2nd Royal Berkshire Regiment and an Irish battalion would make another attempt on it. Needless to say, attacking the same objective in the same manner a few hours later, the battalion stood little chance of success.

One of the officers who would be sent into action with his men regardless was William Hales, the only son of a solicitor from Wimbledon. Educated at King's College Wimbledon and subsequently at the University of London, William followed his father into a law career, articled to a firm of solicitors and passing his final exams just as war was declared. He enlisted within three weeks at St Paul's Churchyard and was sent to one of the New Army battalions of the Norfolk Regiment before being given a commission in the Royal Berkshires in March 1915.

At 8:30pm on 22nd October, William's Battalion vacated the front line and went into support trenches at 11pm ready for the attack the following day. As the likes of William Dexter advanced on the 23rd, William Hales and his men moved up to occupy assembly trenches that they had vacated on their way towards Le Transloy. On their way up they were harassed by enemy artillery fire and then forced to sit still and await orders while the bombardment continued around them. Just after 3pm instructions finally arrived to go and support a battalion of the Lincolns, who were trying to seize its first objective, Zenith, and the Rifle Brigade, who were similarly still poised to try to storm its first target.

When the advance broke down, William Hales and his men were instructed to attack again on 24th October. At 8pm verbal orders arrived to send two companies forward in the early hours of the morning. Zero hour was set for 3:50am, but the weather had now turned again. A deluge of freezing cold rain had been drenching the Royal Berkshires since the onset of darkness. With commanding officers realising that it meant the troops were going to be slower, they left early, William was ordered to lead his company out before zero hour to attempt to make sure they were close behind their barrage. It made no difference. Wading through the mud they lost the protective artillery fire because they could not keep up with it. The mud was so thick that the bursting shells crept away from them as they attempted to drag themselves through it. Targeted by heavy rifle and machine-gun fire, they got no further than 70 yards as William was cut down leading his men. In less than an hour, the battalion had been ordered to withdraw to its original positions in the British support trenches.

Their failed attacks on Zenith Trench had cost the 2nd Royal Berkshires more than 200 men as they attempted to attack through a quagmire towards a heavily reinforced German position. William's commanding officer was stung by the loss of the 25 year old. 'He was an excellent officer in every way and I could ill afford to lose him.' Second Lieutenant Hales was originally buried at Sunken Road Cemetery No.1 near Le Transloy. In the aftermath of the war, the graves in the area were concentrated and with forty-nine other servicemen who were killed in October 1916, William was exhumed for reburial at another site. He was finally laid to rest at Bancourt British Cemetery. His headstone is a special memorial, plot C5, as the exact site of his reinterment within is unknown.

25TH OCTOBER
#40832 Private William Thomas Low

1ST ROYAL SCOTS FUSILIERS

Private William Low. (Authors' collection)

AT THE OPPOSITE END OF the battlefield, right on the northern fringes of Gough's sector, the 1st Royal Scots Fusiliers faced Beaumont Hamel on the north side of the River Ancre. Among their number was 32-year-old William Low. Born in Dunkeld, on the banks of the River Tay north of Perth, he had gone to school at Pitlochry before moving south to Edinburgh. A coach painter by trade, in his spare time he was also second in command of the 31st Edinburgh Boy's Brigade. William's brother, George, had been serving in a motor ambulance at the front, but William, although a former Black Watch Territorial, was a family man and refrained from enlisting until the advent of conscription. Joining the Royal Scots, he had only been serving in his current regiment a matter of days, having transferred on 20th October.

The battalion was out of the lines, supplying carrying parties and groups for labour and returning to flooded huts at the end of the day. When the downpour stopped, the day after William's arrival, there was a full brigade exercise and an even more elaborate divisional one the following day in biting cold weather. Then the relentless rain started again and the men were confined to their damp huts, their move back up into the trenches delayed. Instead they helped carry up supplies to the unfortunate men manning the lines. Any thoughts of attacking were being shelved until there was respite from the wet conditions.

On 25th October the Royal Scots Fusiliers could delay the relief of the battalions in the trenches no longer. William and his company waded off into the mire towards the front lines. It was a torrid exchange; thirteen men of the battalion were wounded and two vanished in a communication trench just in the act of moving along. Seven were killed, including William Low. It was not clear whether or not their deaths were as a result of enemy fire or the murderous, clinging mud that pulled at them as they struggled towards their posts. William left behind a wife, Bessie, and two daughters: Alison, 2, and Isabella, 9 months. He was laid to rest at Euston Road Cemetery, plot I.C.4.

26TH OCTOBER

#21447 Lance Corporal Albert Ernest Deakin

1ST WORCESTERSHIRE REGIMENT

BACK DOWN AT GUEUDECOURT, TO the north-east of the ruined village, operations to press towards Le Transloy were also being postponed on account of the constant bad weather. From Worcester, Albert Deakin was the son of a boot finisher and at the onset of the war was working in the goods depot of the Great Western Railway. His wife was heavily pregnant and their daughter, Nellie Frances Mons Deakin, was born at the end of September 1914 and named partly in patriotic honour of the battle waged just a few weeks earlier. Four months later, Albert enlisted and joined his local regiment before heading off to the Western Front.

His battalion was not part of the attack on 23rd October; Albert and his comrades were manning a support line should they be needed by the battalion ahead who were attacking directly north-east of Gueudecourt. Over the course of the assault, niggling casualties were suffered while the Worcesters stayed put in thick mist, their injuries caused mainly by enemy shellfire. Eight men were wounded on the

23rd, another four on the 24th. The following day, Albert's battalion went forward to take over the newly captured line from men of the East Lancashires who had seized it. One man was killed and another two wounded before they had even arrived. The trenches afforded little cover, if any. 'The greatest difficulty was found in the matter of supply as all rations and water had to be brought up by pack animal and man handling 5 or 6 miles over a roadless waste of shell holes, which in conjunction with the wet weather, became a sticky mess of wet mud.'

On the 26th the German artillery fire became more intense as the men suffered horribly while trying to consolidate the new position. Yet more of them were accounted for by the enemy, including Albert Deakin, as he became yet another victim of the wasteful, ceaseless attrition on the battlefield. He was simply bringing up rations to the men manning the front line. He left behind his wife, Frances, and Nellie, who had just turned 2. Albert Deakin's body, if recovered, was never identified and he is commemorated on the Thiepval Memorial, Pier & Face 5a/6c.

27TH OCTOBER

#3057 Private Henry Palmer

1/5TH NORTHUMBERLAND FUSILIERS

TWENTY-ONE-YEAR-OLD HENRY PALMER KNEW HE was going to die on 27th October 1916. From Wallsend, North Tyneside, Henry, among the eldest of nine children and working for a coal merchant at the onset of war, still lived with his mother, Phyllis, who was now a widow. Enlisting in the Northumberland Fusiliers, he arrived in France at the beginning of November 1915 and joined the 1/5th Battalion, a territorial outfit.

The Northumbrian Division, to which Henry now belonged, had not been engaged in any offensive warfare since his arrival on the Western Front. On 9th September though, his battalion moved north-east from Contalmaison and went into support lines. Their contribution to the Battle of the Somme had begun. That night, Henry listened as the troops on their right attacked High Wood.

Grave of Private Henry Palmer at Albert Communal Cemetery Extension. (Andrew Holmes)

The Northumberland battalion's proximity to the assault led to a stream of constant shellfire coming down nearby. The following day, Henry went into the front line, which was being regularly and fiercely shelled by the enemy. Casualties began to mount. Then there was the fierce noise and the surrounding chaos as the attack of 15th September went forward; Henry and his battalion remained to the rear manning trenches. The weather turned and showers swept the battlefield as they were relieved for a spell, but evidently there had been a mounting problem with Henry's state of mind after these opening experiences near High Wood. He and his company went back into the line on the 20th and found it in a disgusting state. The following evening, orders came for some of the men to support an operation on a German trench and that appears to have been the final straw for Henry. At about 9:30pm, as he and his company were proceeding up to the front line, he fell out and disappeared, remaining absent for about twelve hours. He simply appeared the next morning, emerging out of the fog and saying that he had brought with him the ammunition that he had been asked to carry up. He arrived six hours behind his comrades with no coherent explanation.

On that day, Henry was attached to a team operating a Lewis gun in the battalion. As the men were going out and occupying German lines that had been vacated in front of them, at 9:15am Henry guided another member of the team further to the rear. They picked up spare parts for the gun and when the other man went to return, he could not find Henry anywhere. He looked for him up and down the trench and asked around, but Henry had vanished. Once again, a few hours later, the 21 year old simply reappeared.

All of this happened whilst the battalion was in the lines, but not imminently about to go into battle. A week later, however, Henry's battalion of the Northumberland Fusiliers received orders to participate in the same action in which Donald Forrester Brown had been killed near Eaucourt l'Abbaye. Henry was given orders to go forward and help seize 300 yards of trench in front of them in conjunction with the rest of the company. The assembly trenches were shallow and in several places simply did not exist, forcing some of the company to lie out in the open as they waited for zero hour.

It came at 3:15pm. The men on either side of Henry climbed up and moved off. He didn't move. 'We walked over, and halted twice, lying down before we reached the objective.' By this time Henry had disappeared. At the time that John Sweeney was being executed a few miles away, Henry was again absent from his battalion. He wasn't seen again until 2pm on 2nd October when he was spotted making his way up a communication trench towards the firing line. Henry was arrested pending a court martial.

It took place nine days later at Millencourt, just to the West of Albert, and all of his absences were rolled together for a charge of constructive desertion. The man in charge of the Lewis gun gave a damning testimony. 'There are six in the team besides myself. It was impossible for the accused to have advanced without my seeing him.' It was clear to those present that Henry was not capable of mounting a vigorous defence for himself, although he declined to have one made for him. Neither did Henry cross-examine or question any of the witnesses brought forward, which again was his right.

Of his disappearance on 21st September he said, 'It was very dark and I was helping a stretcher bearer with bad feet and got left behind. There were a lot of shell holes and I could not find the company so I went back.' He said of his wandering the following morning that he had gone off to ask for a cup of tea and that when he returned he couldn't find his companion. 'On the way back they were shelling so heavily that I could not go over the open.' He then claimed to have got lost again moving about in the trenches near High Wood before finding his way back to the beginning of his journey again.

His explanation for his actions on 1st October was painfully simplistic and transparent. Henry falsely claimed to have started the attack with the rest of the gun team. Then he said he had been hit in the knee by something, he knew not what, when halfway over no-man's-land and near the German wire. 'I went back and stopped in the communication trench to rest myself,' he explained. The trench was apparently full of men, but when he was asked if he sought medical attention about his injury, Henry said he hadn't, that it hadn't swelled up at all, it had just hurt the bone and made his leg numb for twenty minutes. To account for that time he said, 'I sat in the trench rubbing my knee.' There was not a mark on him to substantiate the claim that he had been wounded and a witness had claimed he had never advanced at all. Henry called no witnesses to defend him, although he did add that he had nothing marked against him since arriving in France. But there was the problem of Henry's having been prone to wandering during

his initial training in England. He was by no means unique in having been absent before embarking for war, missing parades or not arriving back from leave on time, but the eighteen instances he had marked against his name were hugely excessive. Henry was not a bright boy and had made no real attempt to mount a serious defence. He was found guilty of desertion only for 1st October and, on noting this, the officers overseeing proceedings added a notation to the sentence. 'To suffer death by being shot. Strongly recommended for mercy on the grounds of the man's intellect.'

A guilty verdict and a death sentence only actually meant death less than 10 per cent of the time. Most of such sentences were commuted. The brigade's commander agreed with this sentiment in Henry's case. 'I am of opinion that state of discipline of the 5th ... Northumberland Fusiliers is "good". Therefore, no example need be set.' In the battalion a man had recently also been tried for desertion and sentenced to death, a sentence that was afterwards commuted to penal servitude for ten years. 'The behaviour of the battalion on the 1st October 1916 ... was very good and their general behaviour in billets is quite satisfactory.'

Unfortunately the brigadier found opposition. Of Henry, the commanding officer of the battalion, probably going on information provided to him rather than a personal perspective, stated that: 'Private Palmer's character from a fighting point of view is poor, and as far as I can ascertain he has shown no instances of bravery. His general conduct is unsatisfactory ... In my opinion he deliberately absented himself to avoid going into action.' He was advocating the sternest punishment. As the case passed up the chain of command, General Pulteney, in charge of the entire corps, did not see the need. The battalion had a good record and he supported the court's recommendation for leniency. However, the decision was ultimately passed to the divisional commander of the 53rd Division, who wrote, 'I can find no mitigating circumstances in this case, and can only recommend that the extreme penalty be carried out.' The brigadier appeared to have made an about turn. 'I consider that in view of the gravity of the offence of which this man has been found guilty, and after carefully considering the facts of the case, that he should suffer the extreme penalty.'

So Henry's Palmer's fate was sealed. The 21 year old was executed by firing squad on 27th October at 6:20am and was laid to rest at Albert Communal Cemetery Extension, plot I.P.65. In 2006, under Section 359 of the Armed Forces Act, Henry Palmer was pardoned.

28TH OCTOBER

Miss Edith Fanny Rowe

YOUNG MEN'S CHRISTIAN ASSOCIATION

Edith Rowe. (Authors' collection)

EDITH ROWE WAS THE ELDEST daughter of a former Mayor of Exeter. At 44 years old, she was well known in the city as a Sunday school teacher at the Mint Chapel, a representative on the local Board of Guardians and Education Committee, as well as a member of Exeter Women's Liberal Association and the National Union of Women Workers. She had also carried out the duties of mayoress for her widowed father while he was in office and was even a member of the Ladies Sewing Movement.

As soon as war was declared in 1914, the Young Men's Christian Association went to work. In less than two weeks, 250 recreation centres had sprung up across Britain, many of them near transport hubs where they would see plenty of military traffic. From these centres mostly volunteers, whether it be women or men too old to serve, handed out sandwiches and food, even something for men to read on their journeys. As early as November 1914, the first YMCA contingent also arrived in France and began setting up a similar operation at Le Havre. By 1916 they had gone on to establish them in other base towns such as Étaples, Rouen, Boulogne and even the likes of Paris and Marseilles.

In mid-1915, the YMCA gained permission to establish one of their respite centres for troops closer to the front line. By the end of that year they had hundreds of them on the Western Front, located in villages, towns, dugouts and close to dressing and casualty clearing stations: anywhere where tired and hungry men may come by. Here they offered hot drinks, biscuits and cigarettes. The YMCA huts were a familiar sight to all and were hugely appreciated by the soldiers. One location by a railway siding at Étaples gave out nearly a quarter of a million cups of cocoa every month.

The YMCA huts were just the tip of the iceberg as far as the organisation's contribution to the war effort was concerned. All sorts of personal touches and niceties were provided to make life a little easier for those fighting the Great War: religious services, mobilising hundreds of entertainers to go overseas and entertain the men, operating canteens and postal exchanges for the army, looking after the interests of prisoners of war on both sides of the lines, sending photos of loved ones to men at the front and providing writing paper so they could send letters. They even escorted families to hospitals to visit dying loved ones and made sure they had a safe place to stay.

A YMCA concert in progress at the front. (Authors' collection)

On the outbreak of war, Edith Rowe and her sister Katie began by helping at local soldiers' clubs in Exeter, before moving up to London to help with the YMCA canteens at Woolwich, which was experiencing a huge boom thanks to the munitions industry. In mid-October 1916 the two sisters sailed for France and arrived on the Somme. They based themselves at Abbeville, an important junction behind the front line and close to where their brother was serving as a subaltern, although their work carried them out in motor cars to a much wider area.

On Thursday 26th October, Edith complained of a headache and went to bed, telling her sister not to worry and to go on working. She suffered frequently from such headaches and Katie thought no more of it, going about her duties and assuming that, having rested, Edith would be fine by the evening when they were due to help with a concert for some troops. When she returned to their lodgings, however, Edith was much worse and she called for help. Her elder sister's condition continued to deteriorate. A second brother rushed to France but arrived a day too late. Edith fell unconscious and early on the morning of 28th October she passed away. The cause of death was cerebral meningitis. One branch of the YMCA gave a figure of 286 casualties, including six men and two women killed in action while working for them. It also claimed more than 300 awards, citations and decorations, including the French Legion d'honneur, Orders of the British Empire, Distinguished Service Crosses and the Distinguished Service Medals. Edith Rowe, whose life had been defined by her selfless work for the benefit of others, was buried with military honours at Abbeville Communal Cemetery Extension, plot I.H.25.

29TH OCTOBER
#65680 Private George Ambrose Julier

101ST FIELD AMBULANCE, ROYAL ARMY MEDICAL CORPS

FROM NORFOLK, 21-YEAR-OLD GEORGE JULIER was an engine driver when war was declared in 1914. Married just after the onset, the newlywed remained at home in Great Yarmouth until September 1915, when he enlisted and was posted to the Royal Army Medical Corps. George arrived in France at the beginning of 1916 and was sent to work with a field ambulance attached to the 33rd Division. This meant that since the onset of the Battle of the Somme he had tended the wounded men of the division through the opening stages of the offensive, then at Bazentin Ridge and High Wood.

At the end of October the division was at the far end of Rawlinson's sector, near the southern part of Lesboeufs. East of the village were a number of troublesome trenches and the infantry had been ordered to seize them. On the 28th they poured forward. To the rear, George and the other members of the field ambulance were busy operating a relay post out of Ginchy for stretcher-bearers, bringing in the wounded from the battle and treating them at various stations, all in torrential rain.

In front of them, gains had been made, but the Germans had counter-attacked and claimed some of them back. On 29th October the division was ordered to assault the Germans again, this time to claim the rest of a trench named Boritska, east of Lesboeufs, which was at that moment shared with the enemy. Bursting forth at dawn, the assaulting troops were stopped in their tracks and mown down by German troops manning machine guns in fortified shell holes. The bloody bayonet battle that followed was to no avail either. That morning a captain of the field ambulance had taken eleven stretcher-bearers, including George Julier, all the way forward to Lesboeufs to operate during the attack. As rain cascaded down again, they would wade through the mud towards the front line, collecting immobile men from where they were sheltering

The wounded in rows at a field ambulance behind the lines. (Authors' collection)

within trenches or climbing out into no-man's-land to hunt for them out in the open, or in half-filled shell holes as the artillery pounded the ground around them. It was dangerous work and on 29th October two of the twelve-man team were wounded and two were killed in action, including George Julier. The 21 year old was believed to have been laid to rest at Guards' Cemetery Lesboeufs, but no accurate record was made to indicate where within the cemetery. He is commemorated there on Special Memorial 11.

30TH OCTOBER

#PO/16735 Private Harold Haines

2ND ROYAL MARINE LIGHT INFANTRY

BACK WITH THE RESERVE ARMY, which was about to be redesignated the Fifth, General Gough was waiting for a break in the weather that would finally allow him to make a much anticipated attempt, a large-scale effort on either side of the Ancre, where progress had been either well behind the gains made by Rawlinson's men to the south, if not non-existent since 1st July. Originally slated for 23rd October, it was clear this timescale was a fantasy once autumn weather intervened and turned the Somme battlefield into a morass.

And so the men waited it out in abject misery while preparations continued. These included the introduction of yet more troops on to the Somme to bolster Gough's chance of success, and north of the Ancre was a unique division that had yet to do battle on the Western Front. On the outbreak of war, in excess of 20,000 reservists were available to report for duty with the Royal Navy. They provided much more manpower than was required and so it was decided by the Admiralty that some of this excess would be siphoned off and used to create a land force. These men were divided into two brigades of four battalions, which would be named after famous naval heroes: Nelson, Drake, Hood and the like. The War Office was stretched to breaking point already so the Royal Naval Division, as it would be called, would be administered by the Admiralty and overseen by the First Sea Lord, Winston Churchill.

At the beginning of October 1914, with the BEF still to complete its journey north from where it had settled on the Aisne, this mostly untrained, incomplete contingent of men was launched into Belgium to help the tiny native army cling to Antwerp and prevent the Germans from crashing towards the Channel coast. Unsurprisingly, the venture did not end well. Huge numbers of men became prisoners of war. There was public outcry when the wasteful losses at Antwerp became known. Following their Belgian nightmare, the RND needed to replace Hawke, Benbow and Collingwood battalions almost in their entirety

as they were sitting in neutral Dutch captivity. Churchill stood behind them and wrote to the division:

> The Belgian people will never forget that the men of the Royal Navy and Royal Marines were with them in their darkest hour of misery, as, please God, they may also be with them when Belgium is restored to her own by the Armies of the Allies.

Although much reformatting had since been done, the last of the three brigades making up the Royal Naval Division at its conception consisted of the Royal Marine Light Infantry, at the time the only regular soldiers present. One of these was a 23 year old who had left his landlocked home near Warminster in Wiltshire and his job as a mason's labourer to enlist in Southampton at the beginning of 1913. Harold Haines, an only child, had been raised by his mother alone. She worked as a laundress to support them after falling pregnant in her early 20s. Until April 1915, Harold was stationed ashore, at Kingstown to the south of Dublin. With a new campaign in the east looming, he was then sent to join the Portsmouth Battalion, as it was then known, in time to embark for Gallipoli the following month. In its entire lifetime, the Royal Naval Division would only be in one place together while it was being shot at. Gallipoli was to be its first proper campaign. Harold arrived during a lull in the fighting, but was destined to see plenty of action as well as enduring the misery of life in the Dardanelles for the duration of that offensive. Battalions of the Royal Naval Division arrived just after the original landings and their commanding officer was one of the last to step off the peninsula.

Harold Haines' division arrived on the Western Front and concentrated near Abbeville in May 1916 to take in stores and equipment. Here they were fully equipped for the first time, so haphazard had their formation and the cramped conditions at Gallipoli been. They had never seen the likes of a Lewis gun or a Stokes mortar among their ranks. As yet they did not even have machine-gun companies. By July the naval men had reached the area between Lens and Vimy Ridge for preliminary tours of the trenches. The conditions they were about to experience were completely new to them and they took full advantage of schools and courses that had been established.

Harold and his comrades scoffed at first at how flimsily the trenches seemed to be laid out; they never would have got away with that at Gallipoli. But they had a lot to learn about the Western Front. Men in trenches were not the last line of defence in France and Belgium, nor the first on the wide expanse that was defended in comparatively great depth when measured against their own experience in the Dardanelles. They also found there was a lot more work to do on a daily basis in terms of labour. Meanwhile 'the orgy of instruction' continued as the authorities attempted to pump them full of all the information that had been gleaned from two years in France and Belgium. When the Naval Division left the Vimy sector it was to move at almost full strength for the first time. It was given three weeks' rest to the rear before it was sent to participate in the Battle of the Somme.

Harold Haines joined Gough's army at the beginning of October and his battalion was put into the line in between Serre and Beaumont Hamel, where it began rotating in and out of the Hamel sector. 'The trenches had been planned by a short-sighted fool and destroyed by a watchful enemy,' observed one naval man:

> There were virtually no dugouts; the communication trenches, which ran across a conspicuous ridge, were under constant and aimed fire; in the firing and support lines men could only stand and freeze in the mud; there was no room to walk or lie down, and digging, in the face of the enemy, was nearly impossible.

Nonetheless, assembly trenches needed to be fashioned on the slopes leading down to the valley of the Ancre. Raids and patrols to gather information were also stepped up, 'the men finding these operations tiresome in the muddy and often foggy conditions'.

Their plight was barely improved when Harold and his companions were relieved and sent back to Englebelmer, west of Thiepval:

> When battalions were out of the line their lot was no better … for they would go back no further than Mesnil or Englebelmer, from where they would go up nightly to the trenches, engaged in the most exhausting working parties.

By the time the likes of the Royal Marines got around to making an attack, it was questionable as to whether or not they would be in a fit state to fight anybody:

> To get around a battalion front at this time was hours' walk, with mud often above the knees. Yet in these trenches half the battalions detailed for the intended assault had to live, while the other half had to carry up them and across them stores and ammunition for the innumerable dumps which would feed the advancing line of battle.

The fact that a day of attack kept being set and then revoked on account of the weather made their situation even more dire:

> The constant issue and re-issue of battle equipment and stores added to the confusion. These stores had to be counted in and counted out, carried up and counted down, till men would have volunteered, almost, to go out unarmed, if they could be spared the perpetual juggling with bombs and sandbags, and flares and wire-cutters and compasses …

Since 20th October Harold's battalion had been furnishing working parties out of Englebelmer. They went out every day and dug, carried and watched aircraft duelling above them. As the month wore on the conditions had become so bad that it was forcing those in command to scale down the scope of their intended operations either side of the Ancre. On the 28th, Haig stopped by to inspect Harold and his comrades as they were forced to shift their bivouacs to a drier spot; the men turned out in sections so that he could get a look at them. Then the working parties resumed. On 30th October, 23-year-old Harold Haines was killed as his battalion continued to battle the weather rather than the enemy, before he got the chance to participate in an assault on the Western Front. He was laid to rest at Hamel Military Cemetery, plot II.C.28.

31ST OCTOBER
Captain Christopher Mellor Ridley

10TH ESSEX REGIMENT

Captain Christopher Ridley. (Authors' collection)

FOR EVERY OBJECTIVE THAT WAS seized on the Somme, no matter how fierce the struggle, how much it bled the manpower of the British Army, there was always another in front of it waiting to do the same. In front of part of Regina Trench, the next target was another named Desire. The 10th Essex had already seen enough of the sector, but it now rotated in and out of Regina with its eye on this prize. Among the officers of the battalion was a 25 year old from Chelmsford in Essex named Christopher Ridley. His housemaster at Rugby had been Rupert Brooke's father, and when he left school in 1908, after a period of special training he entered the family business: T.D. Ridley and Sons, Steam Mills. In his spare time, Christopher was active in the fledgling Boy Scout movement, running the 3rd Chelmsford Troop. Prior to the war, Christopher had also served in a territorial battalion of his regiment for nearly five years. In November 1914 he volunteered and was granted a commission a few weeks later. By June 1915 he had been promoted to captain and arrived in France the following month.

Christopher had been wounded at Mametz on 1st July when a bullet entered just under his left shoulder blade and stuck there, but he was comparatively lucky. It was a clean wound and it healed quickly. He had returned to his battalion in September in time to play a part in the capture of Regina Trench on the left of the Canadian contingent. On the front of the 10th Essex Regiment, at least 250 Germans were killed and 315 were taken prisoner along with five machine guns. The entire brigade suffered less than 300 casualties.

The Essex men had become closely acquainted with their sector beforehand and seized their objectives comfortably:

In twenty minutes they had possessed themselves of Regina Trench, supported by the excellent barrage ... When the attack was launched the enemy shelled the assembly trenches and did not pay attention to Regina Trench until an hour later, which gave the battalions an excellent chance to dig in.

The conditions in Regina Trench had since grown distinctly unpleasant. 'The tracks up had not yet been properly organised and laid. More often than not, therefore, we arrived already wet, after several miles march, to hold a very wet and muddy trench ... for the most part, if you had tried to lie down, you would have drowned.' The mud all the way back at Albert itself was up to 9in deep. In the trenches it was worse, as Christopher Ridley and his battalion well knew. 'On one occasion two men of the battalion sank up to their shoulders and were found by a passing lieutenant colonel.'

In spite of all of this, preparations were being made to take Desire Trench, although the 10th Essex would not have to make the attack this time. Its part would be to man the lines sufficiently beforehand to ensure that those troops were as fresh as possible when they went into action. Christopher and his battalion took over a support line from the East Surreys on 29th October in yet more pouring rain and found their spot 'very sticky'. They worked through the clinging mud all morning, only to see their efforts fall apart when the rain began again, causing the walls of the trench to begin falling in.

On the 31st, Christopher and his men moved up to the front line to relieve a battalion of Berkshire men in Regina Trench. It was a fine morning, for once, but the trenches were practically impassable with mud and water. As the battalion was moving up, the Germans had spied the activity and began shelling Regina. Christopher had retreated into a dugout to sit down when an enemy field gun scored a direct hit on the flimsy structure. The 25 year old was killed instantly. The month of October had cost the 10th Essex 200 casualties in all, a percentage of which were men who simply could not stand to go on in the misery of the front lines and broke down.

Christopher's fellow officers were wounded deeply by his death. 'He was a splendid fellow,' wrote one. 'I myself, feel his loss very much, as we both served in the same company for so long, and I shall miss him greatly.' But Christopher himself might have been more touched by the sentiment of his men. 'He was my company commander, and he was one of the best officers we have had,' wrote one. 'He was a friend, as well as an officer to the boys and they would follow him anywhere.' It was a fitting epitaph to a young man, who always thought of them before himself and who once said, 'I had rather be spoken well of by the men than by the officers.' Christopher's younger brother, Herbert, was killed less than a year later near Ypres with a battalion of the Royal Dublin Fusiliers. Christopher was buried near his battalion's headquarters just west of Courcelette. His grave was subsequently lost and his body, if recovered, was never identified. He is commemorated on the Thiepval Memorial, Pier & Face 10d.

1ST NOVEMBER
#8967 Private Alfred Spooner
2ND WORCESTERSHIRE REGIMENT

WINTER HAD ARRIVED ON THE SOMME. 'The battlefield, under torrents of rain, had already assumed that forlorn and desolate appearance which ever after remained, burnt in upon one's brain – a vision of living torture.' The havoc wrought by duelling artillery pieces and endless lines of infantry, and all who supported them, had devastated the entire region:

> Every village wrested from the enemy since the 1st July was now but a mass of tumbled or tottering masonry, each day and night witnessing further ruination; every road had been wrecked by mines or was pock marked by shell holes; every wood had been so torn, disfigured and disintegrated that wood was but a misnomer.

It did not end there. 'Farms, quarries, windmills, had gone the way of the villages and the woods – wrecked and ruined by the awful holocaust of high explosive and shrapnel.' Then there was the smell of the battlefield. 'The very earth stank of gas and was discoloured by the fumes from the bursting of gas shells.' Thousands upon thousands of overlapping shell holes were brimming with filthy water:

> ... putrid from the dead bodies of friend or foe to whom no burial had been given. The fetid stench from the rotting carcasses of horses, or the poor remains of Briton or German torn from their hastily dug graves by shellfire and tossed here and there to await the mercy of fresh internment, filled the nostrils as one passed to or from the front line.

But as November dawned on the Somme, conditions had not reached their worst. The mud on the battlefield now became an enemy in itself, sucking men to their deaths. 'The full horrors ... had not been experienced; towards the end of October the mud in many places was only some two feet in depth.' Those conditions, however turgid, were to deteriorate further before the battle came to an end:

> Men and horses and mules had not been yet drowned in mud and shell holes as some were later; and troops coming out of the line still had the appearance of soldiers, not erstwhile Robinson Crusoes, who, burrowing the earth, had become sodden through and covered in mud from tip to toe.

Ensconced in abject misery with thousands of others on the battlefield was 21-year-old Alfred Spooner, an enameller from Aston, Birmingham. Alfred had been a territorial since leaving school. Mobilised as soon as war broke out, he had served at the front since December 1914.

Towards the end of October, Alfred and his battalion were in a muddy camp behind Flers, sending out working parties carrying material for the Royal Engineers from Trônes Wood to forward dumps in the rain, or cutting wood for the sappers to use. As they struggled to drain and improve their camp and get clean after a day's labour, the men were given rations of rum to ease their plight. On the 30th the Worcesters' commanding officer went up and reconnoitred the front lines and, as darkness fell, Alfred and the rest of the battalion embarked on a torrid relief past the ruins of Ginchy, dragging themselves through the mud.

They were finally in place the following morning at 2am. Exhausted on arrival, 31st October was reasonably quiet in terms of enemy activity, but Alfred and his cohorts found themselves sitting in trenches only 4ft deep and full almost to the brim with water. Carrying up rations and supplies to the front companies was nigh on impossible.

But it was not just with mere survival that the likes of Alfred were concerned on the Somme at the beginning of November. Despite the miserable conditions, those in command were still hell bent on taking more favourable positions for future large-scale operations, including the troublesome knot of trenches to the east of Lesboeufs. At 5:45am two Scottish battalions attacked. Some of the men got into Boritska Trench but they were forced out. To their right, Alfred's battalion was ordered to make its own assault on a trench named Hazy. Dutifully men began moving up to their assembly positions. Some of them were forced to lie out in the open as they awaited zero hour, 3:30pm. Punctually, the 2nd Worcesters went forward with the Glasgow Highlanders and attempted to link up with French troops, who were in Boritska Trench just along the way. 'Up to the waist in slime' they were shelled before they even got under way. 'The gunfire had beaten the ground to a pulp' and though their objectives were termed as 'trenches' they were in reality little more than irregular lines of shell holes that had been linked together, 'more or less connected, but extremely difficult to locate and to observe'.

Any kind of physical exertion was exhausting in the swamp-like conditions. 'Never had the battalion struggled through a worse morass. The laden soldiers sank up to their knees in the mud, hauling each other out with the utmost difficulty and in many cases losing their boots and putties.' Alfred Spooner battled on with the rest of the Worcester men. 'Slowly the attacking line waded forward up the slight slope.' As soon as they reached the crest of the little rise that hid the enemy from view they were showered with a hail of bullets from Hazy Trench in front of them, from another German position on their left flank and from the cemetery on the crest of the ridge beyond. Under such determined machine-gun fire the attack could not gain ground. Officers and men fell on every side. When darkness came, the survivors could do nothing more than wade back to their original line. Alfred was not among them. In all his battalion had suffered some eighty casualties. After his death, Alfred's father would serve in the newly formed Tank Corps. Unsurprisingly, given the conditions, Alfred Spooner's body, if recovered, was never identified. The 21 year old is commemorated on the Thiepval Memorial, Pier & Face 5a/6c.

2ND NOVEMBER
#8241 Gunner George Frederick Eley

6TH BRIGADE, AUSTRALIAN FIELD ARTILLERY

Gunner George Eley. (Authors' collection)

SINCE THEIR RELIEF BY THE Canadians, the Australian contingent that had been so bludgeoned around Pozières had been further north, their main purpose a series of trench raids and improving defences. They had heard rumours of the appalling conditions on the Somme in which men were being ordered to attack and the Australians felt the first pangs of apprehension when a British division nearby that had been present at the beginning of the Battle of the Somme was sent back there. Then in early October another, familiar to them from their Gallipoli days, followed. It was still a shock to the men though, when on 9th October it was revealed that certain Australians were going back to the scene of their utter devastation.

Heading south with a brigade of the Australian Field Artillery was a 24 year old from Ross, Tasmania. George Eley, a clerk, had enlisted in September 1915. With two years' gunnery experience with a volunteer outfit at home, the artillery was a logical choice. He had first joined his unit during its defence of the Suez Canal at the end of 1915, before sailing for France in the spring. On board the transport *Arcadia*, George steamed into Marseilles on 23rd March. A cheeky character,

AIF Burial Ground, Flers. (Andrew Holmes)

he was prone to wandering, the odd bit of scrapping and even a spot of drunkenness, but had never been in serious trouble.

Attention might have been shifting to the northern part of the battlefield and Gough's expected attack on the Ancre, but that did not mean that Rawlinson's men were done with the campaign on the Somme, even if their assaults were to be smaller in scale. Australian divisions began replacing British in the centre of the Fourth Army line in preparation for their next series of attacks, which were awaiting an upturn in the weather. George and his battery took their place at Dernancourt, just to the south-west of Albert, on 30th October as Australian infantry also began taking over the line in disgusting conditions. George was immediately introduced to the reality of getting guns going in appalling winter weather. During the following night George and his fellow gunners fired a standard night barrage: 100 rounds each towards the enemy to keep them on their toes. There was no response from the Germans on their front, although the enemy fired a few large calibre shells at Flers. Two shells came slightly near their guns and that was it.

Throughout the following afternoon the batteries took it in turns to register their guns. George's fired fifteen rounds just before 3pm and then rested until they fired their normal night barrage. In exchange, the enemy showed fair activity during the day on the ridges on both sides of the Flers-Longueval Road and between 12:55pm and 2pm the Germans shelled fairly heavily around Flers. Part of setting up operations on arrival in a new sector was the necessity of officers going forward to observe the effect of their fire in the front lines and to co-operate with the infantry. A forward liaison officer dutifully went forward on 2nd November, taking with him two runners to take messages back to the batteries. George Eley was chosen and he spent the day trudging back and forth through the mud, telling the gun teams that everything was more or less satisfactory, just a few rounds were bursting high and a few too long. Throughout the course of the day, George was killed while going to and fro in between the front lines and the guns. The 24 year old was originally buried to the east of Flers, until the area was cleared and he was finally laid to rest at A.I.F Burial Ground, plot I.C.21.

3RD NOVEMBER

#24130 Sergeant Cuthbert Godfrey Baldwin

18 SQUADRON, ROYAL FLYING CORPS

Sergeant Cuthbert Baldwin. (Authors' collection)

TWENTY-EIGHT-YEAR-OLD PILOT CUTHBERT BALDWIN HAD been flying on the Somme with 18 Squadron for a little over six weeks. Born in Byers Green, a village in County Durham some 4 miles north of Bishop Auckland, he was the son of a local clergyman with links to Berwick too. Educated in Shotley and at Newcastle Grammar School, Cuthbert had trained as a solicitor, passed his final exams in 1912 and moved to London. Originally enlisting as an air mechanic in the Royal Flying Corps, he then underwent a pilot's course at Hendon and obtained his licence on a somewhat ancient biplane in February 1916.

The German air services had, as the Battle of the Somme progressed, made wholesale changes to their operations to try to address their overall inferiority above the battlefield. One important introduction was that of the *Jagdstafflen*, nicknamed *Jastas*. Specifically, they were intended to be mobile units that were to spring up in key locations close to the fighting and hunt Allied airmen out of the sky. One particular German pilot was instrumental in bringing about the introduction of these groups of fighters. Oswald Boelcke was a national hero and instigator of a doctrine of how to fight in the air that dominated German thinking. His record was astounding. One of his charges pointed out that the rest of them were merely 'satisfied when we did not get a hiding'. The young pilot in question was Manfred von Richthofen, a relative novice at the time by comparison who revelled in serving with his idol. 'We had a delightful time with our chasing squadron. The spirit of our leader animated all his pupils.'

Boelcke was killed tragically in a mid-air collision with another German airman on 28th October. It was harrowing for his nation to lose this amiable young man, who had shaped the style of its air fighting and led by example. His 'cubs' in Jasta 2 were devastated. 'We could scarcely realise it,' wrote von Richthofen. 'Nothing happens without God's will. That is the only consolation which any of us can put to our souls during this war.' On the day he died, Boelcke's outfit had already amassed 40 victories, be it forcing an enemy aircraft to land, or shooting it down. This was no mean feat given that its first aeroplane had not arrived until the beginning of September. At the time, Manfred's score was quite a good one: six since Jasta 2 began work on the Western Front, the first coming on the very first day that the new unit ran into Royal Flying Corps men in the air.

In the meantime, Cuthbert Baldwin and his squadron had been transferred with several others down to work in conjunction with Gough's army in October, coming from further north in anticipation of his offensive. For weeks British airmen had continued battling the weather. 'In the teeth of the westerly gales, they flew perilously low, registering the guns, reconnoitring the trenches and villages, and attacking infantry and transport with bombs and machine-gun fire, or calling up the guns to get on to them.' It was unsurprising, then, when operations were rained off so often that when a fine day arrived pilots and observers on both sides of the lines ran for their machines.

Such a day dawned on 3rd November. Cuthbert's flight took off from its aerodrome to the west of Albert at 11:35am to look for German aircraft on Gough's front. Patrols generally lasted around two hours, and Cuthbert was nearing the end of his trip when he and the other pilots of 18 Squadron were set upon by Jasta 2. The patrol leader was led off to do battle to the north, twisting and turning to outmanoeuvre von Richthofen and his comrades. The British airmen counted as many as ten machines at varying heights gunning for them. Air battles were confusing. One moment a pilot would be chasing an enemy machine, then a few turns, a change in altitude and he may be dived upon by a German and find himself in mortal danger. As Cuthbert found himself

looking down on Bapaume from the west, he was suddenly set upon by a number of enemy aircraft. Puffs of smoke about his plane revealed that he was also under anti-aircraft fire; their shells bursting close by. 'Accompanied by two machines of the staffel,' reported von Richthofen, 'I attacked a low flying plane.' Training his gun on Cuthbert's machine, he fired 400 shots into it and then watched as it fell to ground. 'The plane was smashed to pieces, inmates killed.'

Manfred von Richthofen – The Red Baron. (Authors' collection)

Cuthbert had become the seventh of Manfred von Richthofen's victims, the first shot down since the death of his mentor Boelcke. By the time he was killed in 1918, Manfred would have amassed eighty victories and earned a nickname: The Red Baron. Cuthbert's death was not recorded immediately, for he had crashed in an area that was difficult to reach. At home the local community was hoping he was safe and a prisoner, but in September 1917 the War Office confirmed Cuthbert Baldwin as having been killed in action. His body, if recovered, was never identified and he is commemorated on the Arras Flying Services Memorial with 990 other airmen of the Royal Naval Air Service, the Royal Flying Corps and, afterwards, the Royal Air Force who were killed on the Western Front in the Great War and who have no known grave.

From above, the airmen had a unique view of the Battle of the Somme:

Pilots and observers flew without rest ... From the air they saw the battlefield robbed of its hideous intimacy. Water-filled craters and trenches and shell-churned communications, stark realities to the man on the ground, added only a different shade of colour to the patchwork view outspread below the aeroplane.

In the last half of 1916, the Royal Flying Corps suffered 583 casualties on the Western Front, most of them over the Somme. It was a harrowing proportion of the men involved. Their success had not come easily; by November squadrons were depleted and exhausted. British airmen would claim victory on the Somme. Across the entire battle they had taken the fight over the enemy's lines despite the reorganisation of the German air services and the reinforcement of their numbers. But already, in charge of the RFC, General Trenchard was anxious: 'He knew, long before the battle ended, that the situation could not last.' The Germans surely wouldn't stand for it. The threat that the pendulum of aerial superiority would once again swing the other way was very real, but for now, the aerial battle on the Somme had been the most coherent air campaign ever seen, and the Allied squadrons had used all aspects of their developing role in warfare to come out on top.

4TH NOVEMBER
Major Harold Smithers

170TH SIEGE BATTERY, ROYAL GARRISON ARTILLERY

Major Harold Smithers. (Private collection)

BORN IN BROOKLYN, NY, THE eldest son of a wealthy accountant and educated at Weymouth College, 35-year-old Harold Smithers had been gazetted as a second lieutenant in the Royal Garrison Artillery in May 1902. He had served in Burma, India and Aden before the war, until finally being attached to a depot in Plymouth. Here he settled with a wife and daughter, to whom he wrote letters from the front sending, 'all my love and kisses to you and mummy, my two precious ones'. From there, Harold was destined to serve with the British Expeditionary Force from October 1914, when he was sent to Antwerp as part of the failed attempt to relieve the Belgian Capital. Returning to England in August 1915, with his wealth of experience, Harold was employed to train new recruits as the ranks of the artillery swelled. A further spell in France followed, before he returned home in August 1916 to take command of his own battery. His unit, the 170th Siege Battery, was ready to proceed to the Western Front the following month and by the end of October was situated at the northern end of the battlefield on the Somme. From there he wrote home to his daughter, Daphne, who was now 2, 'I hope you are being a good little girl and are taking care of mummy whilst daddy is away. It will be very nice when we can be together again.'

Targets for 170th Siege Battery as November approached revolved around the Redan Ridge between Serre and Beaumont Hamel. The wire in front of the enemy's main trenches up on the high ground received 126 rounds from Harold's men on one day, 133 on another. These targets became familiar to them, as in heavy rain the battery continued to bludgeon barbed wire to pave the way for the infantry. They even tried a new type of shell, although one of Harold's officers reported that when they went forward to evaluate its performance, 'the bursts did not appear at all extraordinary'.

The German response to Harold's battery's shelling had been desultory. As November dawned, their heavy artillery battered enemy trenches and wire entanglements. On the 4th, Harold left their gun positions with an orderly and went up towards Fricourt to observe their fire in the distance. At 3:15pm both were killed as they watched their own shells fall on the enemy. 'He was always most gallant,' wrote a general who knew Harold well. He recalled an incident from early in the war when they were in a field being shelled by some German heavy artillery. 'He heard there was an old man in a farm close to where many of the shells were falling. He at once ran up alone and got the old man out and into a dugout.' His subordinate in the battery penned a letter to Harold's family. 'The Major had only been with us a short time, but he had endeared himself to us all in a way it is given unto few men to achieve. Kindly, just, and always cheery, he made an ideal commanding officer.' Harold left behind his wife Nora and his little girl. On her 80th birthday in 1994, Daphne was at her father's graveside in France. Harold Smithers was laid to rest at Bertrancourt Military Cemetery, plot I.J.8. His orderly, 32-year-old William Tasker, was buried alongside him.

Harold Smithers on the beach at Plymouth with his daughter Daphne. (Private collection)

5TH NOVEMBER

#1341 Corporal James Edward Hodgson

1/9TH DURHAM LIGHT INFANTRY

BACK TO THE EAST OF Le Sars, Rawlinson's men were still facing the Butte de Warlencourt. No attack had taken place since John MacDonald and David Blacklaw were killed in mid-October, but on the 30th it was ordained that, whenever the weather permitted another assault, the Butte should be seized from the enemy, part of a series of smaller scale attacks still being sanctioned on the Fourth Army front. At the beginning of November, it just so happened that the men of the Northumbrian Division would be to hand to carry out these orders.

From Whickham, County Durham, James Hodgson was working as a miner for the Priestman Colliery Company at the outbreak of war. As a 17 year old, he had also joined a territorial battalion of the Durham Light Infantry and so when the declaration came, he was ordered to report to Gateshead immediately. Since arriving at the front, James had been wounded in the head by a shell fragment, but his lengthy time away had mostly been due to horrific dental problems that had seen him hospitalised at the front throughout 1915 and 1916. He had rejoined his unit for good in May and had since been twice promoted.

After a few torrid days of cleaning out trenches next to Mametz Wood, as night fell on 3rd November, James marched off with his company to take over the front line just to the south of the Butte from a battalion of the Yorkshire Regiment. It was an uncomfortable position. 'The front line … was very irregular, [one] trench … zig-zagged a good deal.' Communication trenches to the rear were incomplete and dubious looking lines shot off in all different directions and joined up to other random trenches running all over the place.

On the 4th, James and his companions made the last preparations for the following day's attack, with the Butte looming in the distance, visible from wherever they went in the front line. Officers studied the ground through their binoculars and observed the enemy's trenches as best they could. The little figures flitting about in front of them were identified as Saxons. The heavy artillery were busy with practice barrages, conducting two separate rehearsals and even having the front line cleared temporarily mid-morning while they bombarded two positions close by that ran right up to the Butte itself. The Germans clearly knew something was afoot. James and his company spent a restless night awaiting their attack the following morning as twice the enemy put heavy barrages on them. Their misery was compounded by yet another downpour, rendering the night 'a horror. Heavy rain fell and a gale of wind howled about the trenches.' The assault on the Butte was not called off. 'Staggering under their equipment and usual heavy loads, the troops detailed for the attack floundered through mud and water to their assembly positions.' It was remarkable that the likes of James were even able to reach their starting points. 'In some parts of the line the mud was now thigh deep; it is impossible to describe the physical and mental agony of waiting hours on end, drenched through, caked with dirt, shivering with cold and with clothes rain-sodden for zero hour.' There were rumours that men in the next battalion along had even drowned on their way up. Somehow, James' company was in position by 6am on 5th November. The rain had finally stopped, but in exchange, the wind across the battlefield had whipped up into a gale that chilled the soaking wet men as they awaited zero hour. Three companies were to attack in waves, formed up into columns and paced 30 yards apart.

At 9:10am they advanced, in a manner of speaking. 'Crawl is an apt description, for the greatest difficulty was experienced in getting over the top owing to deep mud. The men who were first out pulled and dragged their comrades over the parapet.' As the artillery bludgeoned the German trenches that they were approaching, all the way up to the Butte and an adjacent quarry, James fought the fierce wind to get across no-man's-land. It was cold and wet, the mud 'sticky and plentiful'. No-man's-land was a morass, cloying and pervasive, 'a death trap for advancing troops … [a] ghastly waste'.

Somehow James and his cohorts broke through two lines of German trenches, reached the Butte and established a post past it, on the Bapaume Road. By 9:40am the Durham Light Infantry was reporting that the trench in front of the Butte had been taken without much resistance. 'Independent witnesses stated that our assault was very finely carried out and that our men could be seen advancing very steadily.' Telephone lines were set up back to headquarters, and they held; some of the men had even got into the trenches that protected Warlencourt beyond the

The Butte de Warlencourt looms over the battlefield. (Authors' collection)

Butte, laying out discs as indicators for the artillery. Unfortunately, it was a very different story for other battalions of the regiment attacking next to them. Almost to a man, they were held up by machine-gun fire before they could reach the German front line.

The enemy was not about to settle for being thrown off of the Butte de Warlencourt. Although at first their barrage came on slowly, British rear positions were then heavily shelled. German infantry began by delivering determined little counter-attacks on the Durham troops who had got furthest forward, although for now they managed to repulse them. On the north side of the Butte, a fortified dugout still held out, refusing to fully cede the high ground to the Durham advance. Fierce fighting went on at close quarters as James' regiment tried to seize this last stronghold.

In the middle of the afternoon, the enemy organised themselves sufficiently to deliver a strongly reinforced counter-attack. Hauling themselves through the mud, they pushed the Durham men back south of the Bapaume Road and into the trench that ran around the front of the Butte. Desperately, requests went back to the artillery to shell the northern side of the road to try and break up the determined German force. Isolated men still held posts around the Butte, cowering in shell holes. The situation deteriorated into scrappy fighting which went on all day: hand-to-hand, with bomb and bayonet. Desperately, James' battalion was trying to establish forward posts and dig a new communication trench back to its original positions to ease the path of reinforcements and equipment, but the Germans would not budge.

At 7:15pm another enemy counter-attack came bursting out of their trenches in front of Warlencourt and from the stronghold on the northern slopes of the Butte, enemy troops flinging bombs into the Durham lines. 'The enemy was in great strength. This attack was perfectly organised and was [pushed] with great energy and determination.' The line was faltering. At 10pm the Durham men still clung to a position next to the Butte, but it was not to last. 'Our men resisted heroically, but after a desperate stand they were driven back.' At midnight they were overrun a last time and found themselves falling back, leaving the ground that had been traversed littered with bodies. The remnants of James' battalion were right back where they had started, although the fact that they had got as far as they had in such disgusting conditions was a miracle in itself. Casualties were horrific; almost 1,000 in James Hodgson's brigade alone, and they were not the only Durham battalions that had been sent forward. Several battalions of the regiment had been decimated.

James was reported wounded on 5th November 1916. A fellow soldier claimed that he had seen him hit, but he was never retrieved from the battlefield by stretcher-bearers, nor did he manage to get himself to a dressing station. He lost his life as part of a limited attack that would have made negligible difference to the outcome of the campaign on the Somme. His family were finally notified that he had been officially accepted as killed in June 1917. James had received a burial on the field of battle, a crude wooden cross marking the spot. The 21 year old was exhumed in 1920 and reinterred during a concentration of isolated graves in the area. James Hodgson was finally laid to rest at Warlencourt British Cemetery, plot VII.K.46.

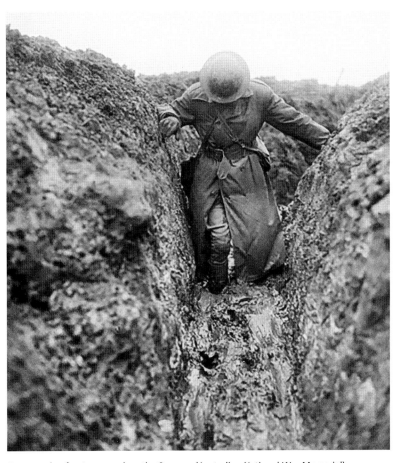

An example of autumn mud on the Somme. (Australian National War Memorial)

6TH NOVEMBER

#2434 Sapper William Arthur Stirling

14TH FIELD COMPANY, AUSTRALIAN ENGINEERS

Sapper William Stirling. (Australian National War Memorial)

TWENTY-FIVE-YEAR-OLD WILLIAM STIRLING WAS A carpenter from Waverley, a suburb of Sydney. He had enlisted in September 1915 and, unsurprisingly given his skill-set, was sent to join a company of the Australian Engineers. Having initially served in Egypt, William embarked for Marseilles with his company in June 1916 and made his way towards the Somme as the summer progressed.

Given the condition of the trenches and the deterioration of the battlefield by November, William's work was never done. At the beginning of the month he and his fellow sappers had been sent to 'rest' at the transport lines, but had in reality been working with parties of infantry sent to them to construct assembly trenches and making general preparations to give the attacking troops at least a chance of success when they went forward on 5th November. Their own infantry were relieved from the lines mid-morning on the 3rd, but there was to be no such release for the sappers. William and his companions were to remain where they were, supporting the new Australian arrivals through the battle.

The night before the battle, in the wind and rain, William was sent out to peg overland tracks, so that anyone making their way up to the front line would not lose their way. The attack duly went off at 9:10am on the 5th, the sappers waiting in a sunken road as their countrymen advanced

The Australian Memorial at Villers-Brettoneux. (Andrew Holmes)

on the right of the Durham Light Infantry. While they fought forward north of Flers, William remained near brigade headquarters in case he was needed. As the light began to fade, the four sections of William's company were ordered up to the flanks of the Australian line to help form a trench back to the original positions. It had been reported that the centre of the line was firm, held by the Australian troops, but this was not the case and the sections became confused. On one flank they simply returned, on the other they found some Australian bombers in an outpost partially linked back to the front line. By the time the sections

7TH NOVEMBER
#1416 Lance Corporal John Clark Scrowther

1/7TH DURHAM LIGHT INFANTRY

BACK IN FRONT OF THE Butte de Warlencourt, to the west of the Australians, battalions of the Durham Light Infantry were still suffering in the line. With them was a bootmaker's assistant from Hylton, Sunderland, named John Scrowther. John's parents had had seven children, but the 21 year old was the eldest of only three who had survived into adulthood. Like James Hodgson, John had been a territorial before the war and was also called straight to Gateshead in August 1914. Here John signed the necessary paperwork to say he was willing to go overseas and embarked at Folkestone in April 1915. Within a month he was wounded: shot in the knee and left out on the battlefield. Classed as missing, the worst was feared until he was finally picked up and evacuated back to England to recover. Fully healed, John returned in September and, aside from annoying recurrences of scabies owing to the rank conditions at the front, had managed to remain physically unharmed thus far during 1916.

John's battalion, the 7th Durham Light Infantry, was one of pioneers. With so much labour necessary to keep the war going at the front, these battalions were formed early in the war and one was attached to each division. They comprised a mixture of men, some of whom had specialities thanks to their jobs at home, such as road builders, carpenters, bricklayers. There is a chance that John's occupation back in Sunderland made him a candidate for such a role, but the pioneer battalions also contained men who were not quite fit to serve elsewhere, such as those with poor eyesight.

In the build-up to the battle on 5th November, John was working to the rear to clear trenches of mud and water so they could be used to move equipment and wounded men under cover. The relevant lines were in such a state that it was thankless work and more rain filled them back up again almost immediately. After three days of backbreaking labour, rendered pointless by the rain, John was given a day off to rest on 4th November.

returned to headquarters at lunchtime the following day and the sector handed over to a new company of sappers, William had been killed in action. In just sixteen days the 14th Field Company of the Australian Engineers had suffered twenty-nine casualties.

William was buried in one of a number of scattered graves throughout the area south of the road between Flers and Eaucourt l'Abbaye. These graves were later lost and 25-year-old William Stirling's body, if rediscovered, was never identified. He is commemorated on the Villers-Bretonneux Memorial.

Troops work at road repairs in muddy conditions on the Somme. (Authors' collection)

The 5th November was a significant date for the Durham regiment. Formerly known as the 68th Light Infantry, it was the date in 1854 it had fought the Battle of Inkerman in the Crimean War and, despite being outnumbered, it helped to break the will of the Russian Army. While the likes of James Hodgson attacked the Butte, John was held in a rearward trench in readiness to start frantically digging new trenches, coming under heavy shellfire and suffering casualties. Any movement at all was a struggle. John and his companions were weighed down by picks and shovels, slipping and sliding all over the place. One company had to settle for just clearing Pioneer Alley, which had been smashed by German shellfire, and then withdrew to Flers Line. Another tried to dig up to the fellow Durham men holding the Butte, but had to give up when the German counter-attack came on. As 6th November dawned, in the rain the pioneers began the monumental task of clearing and rebuilding trenches smashed to pieces in the failed assault on the Butte. Throughout the course of the day, John was wounded and evacuated to a casualty clearing station to the rear; but it could not save him. He passed away on 7th November. His family filled the local press with loving remembrances of their 21 year old. 'He gave up his life for his country and died a hero,' read one. John Scrowther was laid to rest at Dernancourt Communal Cemetery Extension, plot IV.B.16.

8TH NOVEMBER
#144716 Lance Corporal Percy John Lee

ARMY SERVICE CORPS

FIGHTING THE GREAT WAR WAS not just about manning trenches and assaulting German positions. A huge effort was needed to be able to supply the attacking troops with everything they needed to be able to function in battle. By the latter part of 1916, labour employed on the Lines of Communication topped more than 45,000 men.

Key in providing for these soldiers was the Army Service Corps. Formed in 1888 it was a corps trained for combat, not a mere logistical department, and was capable for defending its own convoys in attack. In 1914, the ASC consisted of seventy-one companies. The fact that this number was to expand to more than 1,100 throughout the course of the Great War was indicative of how vital they were to the army in a multitude of different roles and how significant would be their contribution. At one point, there were more than 325,000 men serving in the corps. Transport companies accounted for hundreds, motorised, horse-drawn and even led by donkeys in some theatres. The ASC provided men to work in supply parks, ammunition depots, ambulance convoys, labour, water and petrol supply companies, motor boats, workshops, and mobile repair units. Men worked as labourers, mechanics, bakers, drivers, postmen, even cinema projectionists. The list was almost endless.

In the latter part of 1916, almost 320 men of the Army Service Corps were killed in France alone. Serving on the southern fringes of

Horse transport attempting to move supplies through the mud on the battlefield in autumn 1916. (Authors' collection)

Rawlinson's sector, where it met the French front, was a 19-year-old orphan from Northampton named Percy Lee, a labourer when he enlisted in November 1915. After just three weeks of training he embarked for France with the ASC. Percy was experienced with horses and so moved around various companies working as a driver on their wagons. Since June 1916 he had been placed with a reserve supply park with one of the Indian Cavalry divisions, but at the beginning of November had been attached to another unit nearer to the front lines. On 8th November, Percy was mortally wounded by a shell, with severe injuries to his head and right hand. His left leg was also severed. The 20 year old died later in the day at a casualty clearing station. His brother, Edward, serving in the Northamptonshire Regiment, died at home in October 1918 while working at a depot. Percy Lee was laid to rest at Grove Town Cemetery, plot II.C.13.

9TH NOVEMBER
#72136 Private Sidney Vinall

134TH FIELD AMBULANCE, ROYAL ARMY MEDICAL CORPS

WITH WINTER CONSUMING THE BATTLEFIELD, the question now became when it would be prudent to abandon the offensive and call a halt to the Battle of the Somme. On the one hand, it was almost impossible to effect any meaningful attack through the mud and slime, but on the other, Gough's army was approaching a decisive attack. Beaumont Hamel, Redan Ridge, a stretch of raised ground blown sky high by mines and shells, and Serre had not been the subject of a large-scale offensive since 1st July. For now, at least, the battle would go on.

As the weather deteriorated further, sickness on the Somme increased. It was no wonder that the men grew ill. The battlefield was, quite simply, disgusting. Some areas were actually covered in bodies and the stink was overwhelming: decay mixed with substances such as chloride of lime thrown around to stave off disease, and worsened by bad sanitation and overflowing latrines. Men had not bathed in weeks and the smell of unwashed bodies mingled with that of cordite, gas, food and cigarettes. It was not a healthy environment, nor was it one that the men had to themselves. They shared their trenches with millions of rats, bloated on the endless supply of food they found on the battlefield. It didn't matter how many vermin the troops shot. One single rat could give birth to hundreds of offspring a year, all of whom then scampered about the battlefield spreading germs and contaminating supplies. Then there were lice breeding in the seams of the men's clothing. Not even washing them helped because the eggs remained and as soon as the troops' body heat warmed garments up they hatched and the cycle began again.

There were obvious medical connotations of constantly being in proximity to piles of corpses, walking on them and sleeping with them. One Canadian soldier described them as, 'inky black with a greenish tinge … [they] lay in rows on the parapet at the level of one's heads, stuck into walls, buried in the floor, and felt like a cushion to walk on'. Body parts stuck out the walls of trenches, the floors were carpeted with them in some places, 'several deep or a face with grinning teeth looked up at you from the soft mud'. There was also the odd limb or severed head with which to contend. The men simply had to learn to live with them and tried not to tread on them if at all possible.

The whole environment caused a multitude of ailments. Trench Fever was common, with more than half a million men affected during the war, causing high fevers and pain. Recovery could take months and some troops were struck down repeatedly. It was unknown for most of the war that lice caused this disease, which some 6,000 men still claimed as the source of their disability in the aftermath of the conflict. Nits were common, and many men simply shaved their heads to avoid them. Trench foot was a constant concern, a fungal infection caused by sitting in wet muddy trenches that at its worst could turn gangrenous and require amputation. Studies have even shown that many men might have also suffered from intestinal parasites due to a combination of dirty conditions and poor sanitation, or caused by living with and even eating rats.

One man who was to suffer the consequences of the battlefield's dire environment was Sidney Vinall, a 25-year-old compositor from Merrow, near Guildford. Enlisting in October 1915, Sidney embarked five months later and was serving with a field ambulance in the Thiepval sector. The conditions in which he was suffering in November were clearly unimaginable, when one considered the nonsense being sent out to supposedly help the medical ranks do their work. On the subject of trench foot, one officer on the Somme received a ridiculous letter from a deputy director of medical services lecturing him on hygiene, when in reality the men were sitting in waist-high mud and had been living in inclement weather conditions for a month or more. It prompted 'veritable apoplexy' on the part of the reader and ended with an order to convey the inane drivel to the commanding officers of units that they deal with. The medical officer did just that, word for word: 'We needed something to laugh at just then.'

Near Thiepval, Sidney Vinall's outfit was operating out of an advanced dressing station called Cabstand. In November 1916, as well as all the illnesses and diseases a man could contract in the trenches, men on the

French soldiers relax in close proximity to bodies on the battlefield. Men simply learned to live with them. (Authors' collection)

Royal Army Medical Corps men drag stretchers on sleds through the mud as the weather deteriorates on the battlefield. (Authors' collection)

Somme were susceptible to all the consequences of living in continual wet and cold. For days, Sidney had been part of stretcher-bearing teams hunting the battlefield for wounded and evacuating them back for further treatment. Some of the men the likes of Sidney were bringing in on a daily basis were in an awful state. One group of bearers found a young German who smelled 'like a badger' with somewhat superficial wounds, who had nonetheless been stuck in no-man's-land for days 'forced to eat biscuits and drunk his own urine'.

By 4th November Sidney was feeling distinctly unwell. Later that day he arrived at a casualty clearing station to the west of Thiepval with a temperature of 102 degrees. He grew progressively worse. By the 6th he was running a fever of 104, which the medical staff could not bring under control. His heart began to fail on 8th November and the following day, of all the things that could kill a man on the Somme, the 25 year old died of pneumonia. Sidney Vinall was laid to rest at Puchevillers British Cemetery, plot V.E.46.

10TH NOVEMBER
2nd Lieutenant Walter Gordon Ainslie

33RD TRENCH MORTAR BATTERY, ROYAL FIELD ARTILLERY

RIGHT AT THE NORTHERN END of the Somme battlefield was a young officer working in a type of unit that did not even exist at the outbreak of war. Twenty-one-year-old Walter Ainslie was from Purley. Educated at Eastbourne College, where he was an active member of the OTC, Walter left school in 1914 and became a clerk. He joined the army in line with conscription, registering for service in January 1916 as a gunner for the artillery. Mobilised in April, Walter applied for a commission and was given one a few weeks later. His first posting at the front was the 156th Brigade of the Royal Field Artillery, arriving a few days after father and son George and Robert Lee were killed at the beginning of September. Just three weeks later, Walter was undergoing special training in the use of trench mortars.

At the beginning of the war, the BEF did not have a single trench mortar, nor a round to fire from one. Designed to send ordnance up and back down again at a high trajectory from trench to trench, at relatively short range, they evolved steadily, but rather haphazardly depending on the division they were in. There were three types, light, medium and heavy, and by the end of 1915 it had been ordained that the first would be manned by the relevant infantry and the latter two by the Royal Field Artillery. Walter Ainslie would join a medium battery, and in doing so was part of the divisional artillery.

A working trench mortar attracted enemy fire, so their crews were far from popular when they appeared in any given length of trench, but they were immensely useful. Walter Ainslie's had many uses in the line, including targeting machine-gun positions or sniper posts, with their ability to destroy a fair amount of trench in one hit. They could also

Australian troops load a heavy trench mortar. (Authors' collection)

take on bigger jobs, such as cutting wire in locations where it was too dangerous to see in friendly troops to range a field gun.

By 1916 each division had three medium batteries, designated X, Y and Z. Walter had completed his training and by the beginning of November had joined X battery in his original division, the 33rd. One week later he was in front of Hébuterne, to the west of Bapaume. At 2pm on 10th November Walter met an orderly and the two set off in the direction of the front line. They were never seen again. When Walter's father pressed the issue, he received an unusually callous response from the authorities. 'The body of the orderly was found almost blown to pieces, but no trace of the officer's body could be found.' His 21-year-old eldest son was presumed to have been killed by shellfire while making his way forward. Walter Ainslie's remains, if recovered, were never identified and he is commemorated on the Thiepval Memorial, Pier & Face 1a/8a.

11TH NOVEMBER
#68124 Gunner William Arthur Lawry

110TH SIEGE BATTERY, ROYAL GARRISON ARTILLERY

THIRTY-ONE-YEAR-OLD 'ARTHUR' LAWRY WAS A surveyor and land valuer from St Dominick in Cornwall. The son of a farmer and J.P., he was educated at the Wesleyan College at Truro and applied for leave to join the army as soon as the war began. However, he could not be spared from his employment and was not released until September 1915. By then he had valued the whole of the Penzance, Land's End and East Cornwall districts. Now free to join the army, he promptly enlisted in the Royal Garrison Artillery and arrived in France in May 1916. Arthur impressed straight away and his work had made him meticulous and

painstaking in his attention to detail, so much so that he was to be offered a commission.

In the appalling weather that now afflicted the battlefield, it could take ten to twelve exhausting hours to move an 18-pounder into a new position, let alone the heavy artillery pieces that Arthur was charged with firing. Mud reduced the impact of high explosive shells as they hit soft ground. It also reduced accuracy of guns because of a lack of stability of the gun in question, and it affected the ability to observe their fire and thus correct it properly. But the artillery could not just cease firing. They had to keep going, however awful the conditions and however compromised they were in terms of being able to perform their role effectively.

Arthur's battery was based near the southern part of Delville Wood at the end of October. From here its targets ranged between Leuze Wood to the south-east and Le Transloy to the east. Its work was fairly routine until, on 3rd November, it received a heavy shelling from the enemy that caused half a dozen casualties. As the infantry went forward on the 5th, Arthur and his fellow gunners concentrated their fire on trenches forming a line in front of Le Transloy. When the rain came down in the following days, enemy gunfire died down, but there was to be no respite

As the battle wore on and the ground grew worse, it took great efforts to move guns across the battlefield. (Authors' collection)

for Arthur. He helped to shell roads and fire hundreds of rounds at enemy batteries in the atrocious weather. On the 11th the battery was silent, but the Germans targeted Arthur's guns relentlessly. As the day wore on, the enemy gunners successfully ranged the battery and shells began dropping in among the guns. Arthur had retreated into a wireless dugout, where he was sat with two operators and another man when an enemy shell struck their shelter. Three men were killed instantly, including Arthur. The last was severely wounded. Arthur left behind a widow, Lena, whom he had married shortly after enlisting at the end of 1915. He was originally buried to the north-west of Leuze Wood, but when the area was cleared in 1920 his body was exhumed and William Arthur Lawry was finally laid to rest at Delville Wood Cemetery, plot XXVI.A.2.

12TH NOVEMBER

Lieutenant Colonel Frederick John Saunders

ANSON BATTALION, ROYAL NAVAL VOLUNTEER RESERVE

IN THE FIFTH ARMY SECTOR, Gough had reached the point where he needed to either proceed with his attack or stand his men down for the winter. They had been anticipating launching their offensive since the third week in October. The attack was to be delivered not only eastwards from north of the Ancre, but also northwards from south of the river. However, the operation was repeatedly postponed, General Gough being given full discretion to do so by GHQ. On 27th October the provisional date was altered to 5th November, but the weather had wrought such havoc on preparations that on 3rd November Haig authorised Gough to postpone his offensive indefinitely, 'with the proviso that arrangements are made to bring on the attack without delay as soon as the weather shows signs of being more settled'. More delays followed, until, on 8th November, following a visit from a member of Haig's staff, General Gough conferred with his corps commanders and decided that, provided no more heavy rain fell, the attack should be launched on 13th November.

Headstone for Lieutenant-Colonel Frederick Saunders at Hamel Military Cemetery. (Andrew Holmes)

View of Beaumont Hamel. (Authors' collection)

Meanwhile, staff officers and patrols were sent out at short intervals to report on the state of the ground to monitor the situation. Even on the night of the 10th there was still debate about whether or not the ground was sufficiently dry for the attack to go forward, even though there had been no rain for two days and a cold spell was slowly freezing the ground. On 11th November, zero hour was fixed for 5:45am on the 13th. The die was cast. The men would go forwards one and a half hours before sunrise.

Commanding one of the Naval battalions on Gough's front was a 40-year-old lieutenant colonel named Frederick Saunders. In command of Anson Battalion, he had spent a career in the Royal Marine Light Infantry before being given command of Anson and was awarded a DSO for his service in South Africa.

In such torrid conditions, Frederick's men struggled to prepare for their first big offensive in France. He lost a number of them on 8th November owing to a particularly vicious gas attack and the survivors were ordered to rest for forty-eight hours to recover from its effects. Some of the men were left to man the lines, while others came back to exercise at close order drill or form parties to carry up water and stores to assembly positions ready for the attack. On the 11th, Frederick collected all of his company commanders and explained the forthcoming operations to them at a conference. Then, at 8:30pm, all the junior officers were called in and they went through it again. The Royal Naval Division was doing its best to leave nothing to chance when it went forward on the Western Front for the first time.

By 12th November the preliminary bombardment had begun. It was emphasised to Gough that Haig did not want him going ahead in unfavourable conditions, but the decision was left to his subordinate and he was resolved now to either go ahead or the 13th or remove and rest as many troops as possible in the line and suspend offensive operations for the year. It was becoming cruel, having the men prepare to attack and then cancelling orders:

Up to the end of the first week of November, brigade commanders were generally of the opinion that conditions were too unfavourable for the attack to succeed. Then they became in favour of 'attack or cancellation' as repeated postponements were not fair to the troops.

As Haig arrived to satisfy himself that the time was right to attack, tanks were being withdrawn because the ground was too wet for them. Frederick was overseeing his battalion's departure from Englebelmer. The men were as relieved as they were nervous:

With the attack constantly postponed but never cancelled, all ranks had passed through a time of great tension, so that it was a relief to know the hour was actually at hand.

For the Anson's commander though, zero hour would never come. As Frederick made his way up towards Beaumont Hamel, the enemy began shelling a communication trench known as Gabion Avenue. High explosive and gas shells rained down, and, as the lieutenant colonel struggled through the mud, he was hit by a shell. Nearly twenty more men became casualties in the trench as they tried to progress up towards the front line.

Zero hour was fast approaching. Frederick Saunders' men filed into their assembly trenches, another officer picking up the mantle and taking command. Lieutenant Colonel Saunders left behind a widow, Muriel, and was laid to rest at Hamel Military Cemetery, plot II.E.9.

13TH NOVEMBER
#KW/272 Leading Seaman Fred Hattersley

NELSON BATTALION, ROYAL NAVAL VOLUNTEER RESERVE

TWENTY-THREE-YEAR-OLD FRED HATTERSLEY WAS WAITING to attack with the Nelson Battalion. Born between Sheffield and Huddersfield, before going to war Fred was a trammer at the Old Silkstone Colliery at Dodworth, near Barnsley. His father and two brothers were miners there and even his younger brother, Ernest, was working at the colliery by the age of 13 as a screen boy. Fred had originally enlisted in the King's Own Yorkshire Light Infantry in September 1914 with another brother, Charles, eight years his senior. Six days later both transferred to the Royal Naval Volunteer Reserve and were originally in the Benbow Battalion until reshuffling took place at Crystal Palace after the Antwerp debacle. Both brothers then found themselves in the Nelson by the end of the year. Charles was presently stationed at a depot in Blandford, Dorset, so at 5:30pm on 12th November Fred moved out without his brother towards his battalion's assembly positions.

Come zero hour the following morning, south of the Ancre, Gough's men would be pushing out from the area around Schwaben Redoubt towards Grandcourt in the distance. The main attack would be north of the river and would include the Royal Naval Division, attacking the original German defences that had been assaulted in vain on 1st July. Since then there had been months of active trench warfare in the area and plenty of time for the Germans to bolster their defences. The likes of Fred Hattersley and his naval comrades would be attacking parallel to the river. The Hood and Hawke battalions would advance first and take the first objective. The Drake and Nelson would then follow to leapfrog over them to head for the next, which was labelled as a green line on their maps. Then the initial attackers would jump over them to go forward again, and so forth.

The anticipation, mingled with fear as 5:45am approached, was almost unbearable:

No one can look back on the anxiety of that night without emotion. It was not only the culmination of weeks of agonising preparation, it was a gambler's throw.

This was the last big push of the Somme campaign. Planning was intricate, deliberate. The Nelson Battalion, numbering less than 500 men, had gone over its orders again and again. Officers had held conferences and explained every detail so that every single one of their men knew exactly what was expected of him. But war doesn't go to plan.

To begin with, as zero hour approached, the battlefield was shrouded in wet fog. Fred could not see further than 30 yards. Assembled on a forward slope, along taped lines, the signal to attack came when the ferocity of the British artillery bombardment suddenly increased. The men of the Hawke Battalion ahead vanished like spectres into the fog. The Nelson were supposed to wait until their counterparts had advanced 150 yards and then follow, but they now had no way of knowing when that was. After a rough interval they began to advance. Fred may have had some inkling as to how far the Hawke had progressed when the sound of German machine guns came from within the mist. The enemy barrage was negligible but as the leading battalion had got within sight of their objective, the Germans had opened a storm of rapid fire from in between their front two lines. At that point the last of Fred's unit were crossing the British front line into no-man's-land.

In front of them the Hawke Battalion was being ripped to shreds, nearly 400 of the officers and men becoming casualties early in the attack and many of them in falling on a German strong point in their path. Behind them the Nelson came under the same murderous fire. Blinded by thick fog and now smoke, Fred could hear the fierce British artillery barrage and the rattle of the machine guns. Somehow he and his comrades managed to get through the confused fight going on ahead, but they had lost pace with the protective artillery barrage creeping forward in front of them. The first two waves managed, after hand-to-hand fighting at the point of a bayonet, to get on. This savage fighting, 'virtually without any assistance from the artillery', had decimated their weakened companies. The rear Nelson waves met even more resistance, subjected to heavy enfilading machine-gun fire and accumulating crippling casualties. They lost cohesion among themselves and direction, and, except for small detached parties, ceased to exist as a fighting force.

Fred Hattersley's battalion had been annihilated in the first two lines of German trenches before they could get anywhere near their later objectives. The combination of the mist, the lack of officers who got forward and a not wholly effective artillery barrage had doomed the men of the Royal Naval Division to failure. And things continued to get worse for the Nelson Battalion. Its commanders crossed the original front line about forty-five minutes after zero hour, attempting to come up and make sense of the rabble that now clustered about the battlefield after the breakdown of the attack. The Germans opened fire at close range and decimated the surviving men, killing the Nelson's commander and his adjutant.

Those who survived cleared out any dugouts they could find with little opposition and the battalion advance continued to their second objective, where it ground to a halt. The Royal Naval Division had got forward, but its position was tenuous to say the least and it was low in numbers. Neither had it come anywhere near fulfilling all of the tasks put in front of it for the day. By 9:15am the attack was postponed.

Information began to filter in to Gough's headquarters. The general was reasonably pleased with the outcome of the day's fighting. In the eyes of those orchestrating the attack, it seemed reasonable enough to attempt to finish off what had been started, on a front of more than 3,000 yards. Gough wanted Redan Ridge, Grandcourt and Beaucourt before his men settled down for winter. Orders were promptly issued to renew the offensive on 14th November.

Less than half of the Nelson men would be present to take part. Almost 300 of them and their officers had been slaughtered on the north banks of the Ancre, including 23-year-old Fred Hattersley. His body, if recovered, was never identified and he is commemorated on the Thiepval Memorial, Pier & Face 1a.

14TH NOVEMBER
Captain Henry Begg

2/1ST HIGHLAND FIELD AMBULANCE,
ROYAL ARMY MEDICAL CORPS

Captain Henry Begg. (University of Aberdeen)

TO THE NORTH-EAST OF THE Naval Division, a formation of Scottish Territorials had succeeded in capturing Beaumont Hamel on 13th November. The 51st Highland Division 'probably included more deerstalkers, gillies, and gamekeepers – and no doubt more poachers – than any other division in the army'. These men were used to a life outdoors, and took well to being snipers and scouts. 'Many men, too, had in civilian life been shepherds, farmhands, or forestry workers, and so were used to long hours of arduous work in the open air.' The division recruited most of its soldiers from north of the Highland line: Caithness, the Inner and Outer Hebrides, Banff and the like. Although their catchment area was huge, the population was not and most of the communities drawn from were small, creating a family feel to the outfit. One historian claimed that 'Scotland as a whole ... had the highest mortality relative to its population of any part of the Empire, and certainly no region was harder hit than the Highlands'.

Working with one of the division's field ambulances to try to keep as many men alive as possible was a doctor from Druminnor in Aberdeenshire. Thirty-five-year-old Henry Begg had graduated from the University of Aberdeen in 1906 and moved to London. Here, prior to the war, he was in practice in Kentish Town, was a clinical assistant at the Great Northern Hospital on Holloway Road and also at the Mount

Vernon Chest Hospital in Northwood. Henry joined his division early and had done well in July, when his devotion to duty caught the eye of Haig himself.

Henry was well thought of by everyone. The men called him 'Sir Henry' and 'his heroic courage whenever danger was present was known to the whole division. Any lustre this unit may have for good work under fire is largely due to his personal work and example.' Despite his reputation though, Henry didn't say much. 'Quiet and unassuming, always cheerful,' he was a strict disciplinarian too, when it came to taking his men out to hunt for the wounded on the battlefield. 'When men were falling everywhere and the shellfire fiercest, there was Captain Begg, a tower of strength all around ... He was, I think, without doubt the best leader of stretcher bearers in the division.'

Since the advent of November, the field ambulance had been operating out of Auchonvillers, to the west of Beaumont Hamel, but Henry and his bearers were becoming well acquainted with an advanced dressing station on Redan Ridge known as Tenderloin, which was frequently under fire from the German artillery. As the Highland troops went forward in pursuit of Beaumont Hamel on 13th November, Henry waited to the rear. At 7am the wounded began to trickle in, and then became a steady stream. Evacuation from the field went on relentlessly all day, and the enemy was in no mind to give the British any quarter behind the front lines. Twice a command post belonging to the field ambulance was shelled, and all the men had to be cleared from a courtyard lest they be wounded a second time, or worse. From noon, German prisoners began appearing too, and 150 that were unscathed were turned around by Henry's unit and sent back to the battlefield bearing stretchers: 'They worked willingly and well.' The field ambulance had got off remarkably lightly in terms of their own casualties too, and the officers and men busied themselves checking reports, answering calls for fresh bearers and carrying up stores.

Like the Royal Naval Division, the Highlanders would attack again the following day and at 10pm their objectives were confirmed. Henry would be supporting his infantry as they assaulted Munich Trench, beyond Beaumont Hamel, which they had failed to take as part of their objectives on the opening day of the offensive, and behind that Frankfurt Trench, which should have been their final objective high on Redan Ridge.

Henry and his men worked all night. Fighting had died away, but the stream of wounded Scotsmen and others who had strayed into

Stretcher-bearers on the Somme move off to bring in the wounded. (Authors' collection)

their path and needed evacuating seemed endless. The British artillery shattered any form of peace throughout the darkened hours by keeping up their fire on the enemy's positions. At about 3am a rumour emerged that there were 300 wounded men lying at Y Ravine, which was to the south-west of Beaumont Hamel. Thankfully, when an officer rounded up some men from the Midlands to come up with stretchers alongside him, this turned out to be a huge exaggeration, and all those in need of assistance were steadily being moved down the line.

At 6am the British gunners began relentlessly pounding Munich Trench and twenty minutes later the Highland Division's infantry went forward. The fog began to dissipate as the morning went on. Early on another rumour arrived that there was a significant body of wounded men up at Tenderloin, the forward dressing station up on the ridge.

Henry collected a party of his stretcher-bearers and together they made their way up. They found nothing to do and, instead of carrying the wounded, they carried water up towards the front lines. Anywhere on the ridge, which was pocked by endless shell holes, was an unsavoury place to linger for too long. The men were sniped at freely, and the enemy's artillery barrage rarely ceased. Stretcher-bearers only did short stints in the area because of the conditions as it was apt to fray their nerves if they spent too long up there. Just before noon, Henry was making his way along a trench near the dressing station with his sergeant of bearers when a shell exploded nearby. The concussion killed the 35 year old instantly. 'His loss is a very serious blow to us, for we shall never get a braver or more willing officer,' wrote one of his comrades. Henry Begg was laid to rest at Louvencourt Military Cemetery, plot I.E.5.

15TH NOVEMBER
#4378 Private Stanley Callaghan

18TH AUSTRALIAN INFANTRY FORCE

WHILE GOUGH'S MEN WERE ATTACKING, Rawlinson's were playing a supporting role to the south. They did their best in terms of artillery, but it was becoming impossible to supply guns with ammunition to keep the overused and sodden weapons firing. The Australian contingent was still operating to the right of the Butte de Warlencourt and Le Sars, facing Bapaume, and with them was one man who had already lost his younger brother on the Somme. Horace Callaghan was finally confirmed dead in the middle of September after vanishing at Pozières on 23rd July, but his elder sibling Stanley had only joined the 18th Australian Infantry on the battlefield at the end of that month. Twenty-two years old and nicknamed 'Bomber', he was a miner before enlisting in October 1915 at a large training centre for Australian troops in Sydney. Having made his way to Europe, Stan left England for France on 10th August 1916.

On 15th November, as operations continued on Gough's front, the Australians and the Royal Fusiliers tried to bomb the Germans out of a nearby trench, but the mud was so great a handicap that the troops soon became exhausted. Stanley's battalion was out of the line. Thus far his countrymen's return to the Somme had been horrific: 'howling gales, pouring rain, endless mud, waist deep in places.' The communication trenches were barely in use any more, they were so full of water. It was safer for the men to make their way along in the open. The situation became even worse when the mud started drying. It 'tugged like glue at the boot soles, so that the mere journey to the line left men and even pack animals utterly exhausted'. Any journey bxy night was even more perilous. 'In the dark, those who stepped away from the road fell and again and again into shell-holes; many animals became fast in the mud and had to be shot, and men were continually pulled out, often leaving their boots and sometimes their trousers.' As Stanley became accustomed to life on the Western Front, three men of another battalion had to be dug out of their jumping off trench, and a company commander in a band of pioneers had to be dragged out of another by a mule. A few weeks later a rescue party broke the back of an officer of the 2nd Australian Division whom they were trying to haul from the mud. After each fight, the carriage of wounded across this area had to be performed almost entirely by stretcher-bearers. There was no respite from railways, and wagons or motor ambulances could not get anywhere close.

Stanley was doing forty-eight-hour stints in the lines, arriving already exhausted, sitting in the foul trenches and then being relieved again.

Private Stanley Callaghan (*far right*) poses with friends. (Private collection)

'At first the men tried to shelter themselves from rain by cutting niches in the trench walls, but this practice was forbidden, several soldiers having been smothered through the slipping in of the ... earthen roof, and the trenches broken down.' Stanley and his companions could not stand still for too long either, because they started sinking in it:

> No fires were allowed in the front line, and at this stage no food or drink could arrive there hot - except occasionally tea, which was carried in petrol tins and reeked so strongly of gasoline that men declared after drinking it they dared not light a cigarette.

By 15th November Stanley Callaghan's brigade had been relieved from the lines, but his battalion was still furnishing working parties in the trenches. On that day, 170 men of the 18th Battalion were selected to go up and work. As the men moved backwards and forwards, fetching, carrying, cleaning and digging, Stanley was killed by a shell. He had survived just forty-two days with his battalion and became the second of James and Mary Callaghan's boys to fall. Stan was laid to rest at Longueval Road Cemetery, plot G.17.

The eldest Callaghan brother who went to war, Les, was also killed on the Somme. As the war drew to a close in 1918, the Australians broke the German line at Mont St-Quentin in what Rawlinson apparently regarded as the finest move of the war. Les, married with children, received a gunshot wound to the head and died on 4th September. Thirty-one years old, he was laid to rest at St Sever Cemetery Extension, Rouen, plot Q.V.F.14.

In 1918, having lost three of her sons, Mary Callaghan was invited to unveil the war memorial in their hometown of Lithgow, New South Wales. An official present remarked that 'it was appropriate that the ... ceremony should be performed by Mrs Callaghan, who in losing her three sons ... had made the greatest gift of all. It was the mothers of the gallant Australians who had fallen fighting [for those at home] who made the greatest sacrifice in this tragic war.'

To all intents and purposes the offensive battle on Rawlinson's sector had come to an end. There would be no conquering of the Le Transloy Ridge in 1916. The Battle of the Somme had been a torrid introduction to offensives on the Western Front for the Australians, who were about to go into winter quarters. Since their arrival on the field in battle in July, the Australian forces had suffered some 23,000 casualties.

Mary Callaghan writes letters to her boys at the front, watched by their sister. (Private collection)

16TH NOVEMBER
2nd Lieutenant Daniel Johannes Cecil Morkel

8TH EAST LANCASHIRE REGIMENT

TWENTY-SIX YEARS OLD AND FROM Somerset West in the Western Cape, Daniel Morkel had had to go to great lengths to get to the Western Front. A farmer's son and a civil servant, from December 1914 to August 1915 he was in Orange Free State and German South-West Africa acting as a signaller for a mounted brigade of the Union Defence Force. At the culmination of that campaign in July 1915, Daniel wanted to see further active service and so he gathered together some references and sailed for England. When he arrived at the War Office on Whitehall with a friend from home, also looking for a commission, Daniel was carrying recommendations from an official at the South African High Commission. Even General Lukin, who had commanded the South Africans at Delville Wood in July, was willing to support his application. 'His family is well known and respected in South Africa,' explained the former. 'He has taken an active part in sport generally: rugby, cricket, tennis, golf, yachting.' In particular, he was a good oarsman and secretary of one of the leading clubs in Table Bay. His manager in the civil service, the Master of the Supreme Court in Cape Town, spoke up for Daniel. 'Strong and keen to serve', he was an ideal candidate for a commission. After a few weeks of waiting at his sister's home in Earls Court and visiting another in Oxford, Daniel was an officer in the East Lancashire Regiment.

Just after Henry Begg was killed on 14th November, as the Highland Division tried to seize Munich and then Frankfurt Trenches on Redan Ridge to the north of Beaumont Hamel, General Gough arrived in the area. Ready to hear what plans his corps commanders had made to resume the offensive and seize such positions, they were confident of having possession of both Munich and Frankfurt that afternoon. The V Corps commander then wanted Puiseux Trench, which ran north to south beyond, but a good deal further on. If he

was successful at pushing his men this far, Gough would have a view over Miraumont. If the rest of his force, to the south of the river, could secure Grandcourt then the British Army would be in a commanding position ready for 1917.

Neither of the trenches in question fell on 14th November. The troops who had made the initial attack on the Ancre were by now exhausted. Both the Highland Division and the Royal Naval Division were taken out of the line. Among the battalions coming to relieve them was Daniel Morkel's 8th East Lancashires. Their arrival was rushed and within a few hours of arriving at Mailly-Maillet to the rear, Daniel's battalion had been sent to join another division temporarily, pointed up a muddy trench north-east of Beaumont Hamel and sent off to fight. It set off at 1:30am, so any rest was out of the question. After struggling through communication trenches, Daniel and his men finally arrived at their starting position at 7:45am in thick fog. They would be attacking this terrain, brand new to them, just forty minutes later.

After a brief preliminary bombardment that targeted their objectives determinedly, Daniel heaved himself out into no-man's-land and led his platoon due east towards Munich Trench. He and his men advanced a considerable distance, some 200 yards, in such thick fog that the enemy failed to spot them any sooner. Some troops were losing direction with no visibility and as soon as the Germans spied khaki-clad figures labouring towards them they jumped on to their machine guns and began spraying them with bullets. The forward wave of the East Lancashires got to within 50 yards of Munich Trench before the British artillery barrage finally commenced. It proved to be hitting short of the mark and this, the fog and the uncut wire barring the way all conspired to rule out any chance Daniel Morkel had of getting into Munich Trench on 16th November. By 10am the impetus had completely gone out of the battalion's forward movement. The survivors found themselves pushed right back on to the ridge. Neither Munich nor Frankfurt Trench had been taken, despite the wealth of men thrown at them. There were simply not the troops available to attempt it again. The Battle of the Somme would close with both in German hands. A few Germans were captured elsewhere along the line, but casualties were severe, especially among the East Lancashire's officers. Ten had been killed, including 26-year-old Daniel Morkel. He was laid to rest at Munich Trench British Cemetery, plot B.4.

Munich Trench British Cemetery. (Andrew Holmes)

17TH NOVEMBER

#3605 Private John Valentine Heasman

1/1ST HONOURABLE ARTILLERY COMPANY

Private John Heasman. (Private collection)

ASTRIDE THE RIVER ANCRE THERE was still the monumental task of clearing the battlefield of the wounded. Casualty clearing stations had been working tirelessly to save those shot, maimed or otherwise incapacitated by the fighting on both banks of the river.

John Heasman had enlisted as a teenager. From Westcliff-on-Sea, his father worked for a transatlantic cable-laying company. John had gone straight from Felsted School into the army, enlisting in May 1915, and embarked for his first stint abroad at Southampton on 21st July 1916. After serving initially with an entrenching battalion, which helped to acclimatise new arrivals to the front, John joined the 1/1st Honourable Artillery Company on 17th October. John was incredibly proud to be part of it. The HAC was an illustrious unit; incorporated by Henry VIII by Royal Charter in 1537, it could trace its history back to the Normans and the only military outfit in the world that was older was the Vatican's Swiss Guard. The 'artillery' aspect of the name referred more, in this case, to long-redundant weapons such as longbows that hurled arrows as opposed to guns and shells. As well as seven batteries of guns, the HAC would raise three battalions of infantry during the Great War, and it was to one of these that John belonged. In a slightly confusing state of affairs, his served with the Royal Naval Division.

Like Fred Hattersley and the Nelson men, the 1st Battalion went over in the second group of attackers on 13th November along with a contingent of Royal Fusiliers. The advance went in four waves, starting at 6:30am in thick mist. Keeping direction was extremely difficult, but it may have helped their cause. John and his comrades had almost reached the German reserve line before they were spotted and ultimately held up by enemy snipers and bombers on both flanks. These men had evidently been in dugouts that had not been mopped up by the battalion ahead, and the fog made it very difficult to locate them. But by sending bombing parties out to test the water and then eventually locating and advancing on them, the offenders were either killed or taken prisoner.

It was a grim day for John's battalion. It suffered high casualties when attempting to cut through German wire, as well as in clearing out enemy dugouts in which the Kaiser's men were still hidden. Even without the fog, the trench system it was trying to enter was complex and confused the men as they tried to establish their positions and objectives. Nevertheless, the HAC pushed on, reaching the day's second objective. It began to frantically dig for cover in two groups spread out 100 yards apart. Survivors of the Hood Battalion were by this time digging in about 200 yards ahead of them and on their flank John's battalion managed to established communications with the Cambridgeshire Regiment across the river. Their left flank, however, was forced to wait until another company of the HAC battalion came up to fill the gap. The Naval Division men were still well short of their crucial objective, the village of Beaucourt ahead. Sniping soon began from the ridge in front of it and during the afternoon the HAC men were shelled heavily as they tried to work. A further attack followed in the afternoon; the men were ordered out at about 3:30pm to support the Hood Battalion in front as it went forward. An hour and a half later these attempts had also failed and, as darkness began to fall, John's battalion was ordered to fall back to its previous line and carry on its consolidation work. Shelling became so heavy that they left as few men in the line as possible, the others sheltering under a nearby bank.

At 5am on the 14th, the HAC men were ordered to push forward an hour later, pick up the survivors of the Hood before the yellow line, the third objective that still lay ahead of them, and then advance on to the Red line, the last task that had been allotted at the outset of the battle together. At 6am the survivors of John's battalion went forward to meet their fellow Naval Division men. 'Shell holes and trenches of the Hoods afforded cover while we waited for the barrage to lift.' At the appointed time they all advanced in tandem. 'The barrage put a curtain of shells over you, that was the theory and you advanced. Of course, you are bound to get casualties from your own shells, you were bound to get quite a lot of casualties when you were on a big show like that.'

Astonishingly, considering the advance was, in fact, a mash of different Hoods, Drakes, Nelsons and HAC men, they surged through Beaucourt under the command of an indomitable young naval officer named Bernard Freyberg, who simply did not know when to give up and on this day was awarded the Victoria Cross for his trouble. The final objective, the red line, was taken. 'It was astounding to me that on the second day we did take Beaucourt, because we were very thin on the ground in that attack ... I think luckily for us, their reinforcements hadn't been in the Somme before and they panicked. Otherwise we shouldn't have got through,' pontificated one survivor. 'We had a most gruelling time second day. When we got beyond the village [to dig in] there were no trenches, we went into shell holes as deep as we could get. But they gave us the almighty pasting that day with really big stuff ... it was very grey day and you could see things coming towards you before they hit, it was a most unnerving experience.' John Heasman's battalion picked up more casualties at the last. 'They came in salvoes of four over. That was only one part of the shelling. Of course, there were the ordinary field guns and that sort of thing, but I particularly remember those big guns, and seeing the little black balls getting bigger and bigger until they came in the most almighty roar around you.'

The 1st Honourable Artillery Company was relieved in the early hours of 15th November, but out on the battlefield were scores of wounded and dying Royal Naval Division men who needed attention. All the going backwards and forwards that had occurred in the previous two days meant it had been incredibly hard to keep tabs on their numbers and it could be almost impossible to establish what had happened to an individual. What is clear is that John Heasman, with a gunshot wound to the abdomen, lay on the battlefield for quite some time. Nobody was able to record if he had been wounded on 13th or 14th November. He was admitted to a casualty clearing station on the latter but all of its efforts to save John were in vain and he died on 17th November as the attack north of the Ancre began being brought to a halt.

In February 1917 his father was still awaiting these details as he had heard nothing from the HAC and had received nothing but the official notification of his 20-year-old son's death from the War Office, which only arrived after a kind letter from the matron of the clearing station. 'I have rather expected to have had some acknowledgement of his services and his death from the regiment he had the honour, and my son felt so proud to belong.' Despite his justification for feeling as if his son had been overlooked, John's father apologised for bothering the HAC. John Heasman was laid to rest at Contay British Cemetery, plot VIII.B.26.

18TH NOVEMBER
Captain Reginald Underhill

4TH MIDDLESEX REGIMENT

Captain Reginald Underhill. (Private collection)

HOWEVER MUCH DOGGED TENACITY GOUGH possessed, along with a belief that his men could still push on before winter, Haig had had enough. He ordered an end to operations for 1916. Despite this though, Gough pleaded for, and was given permission to have, one last shot at the enemy before a line was drawn under the Battle of the Somme.

The men earmarked for this questionable attempt would have to go forward in simply atrocious conditions. Among them was a 29 year old who had been born in Tipton Green, near West Bromwich. Reginald Underhill's father took his wife and six children to Vancouver in 1894, where the family nearly doubled in size once on Canadian soil. A bookkeeper and then an assurance real estate agent, Reginald and his younger brother Charles had rushed to enlist in the 7th Canadian Infantry in August 1914, and were with the first contingent of their countrymen to arrive in Europe in October. The brothers had sought and been given commissions on arrival in England. Reginald was well qualified, having offered ten years with the Duke of Connaught's Own Royal Canadians as a volunteer NCO. He had subsequently been sent to the Middlesex Regiment and separated from his brother. In March 1916, at the age of 22, Charles was killed in Belgium while serving with the 12th West Yorkshires. Eight months later, his brother was preparing to attack right on the banks of the Ancre.

Reginald and his men had already been in the trenches for days. The weather was bitterly cold with the mornings frosty, and the first flecks of snow had even begun to drift down at night. On the 17th, as Reginald waited to attack, it was heavier. Morning came and it had deteriorated into a blinding, wet sleet that was driven into their faces as they moved forward to their jumping off positions ready to play their supporting role when the advance began at 11am. 'The elements played their final part. A thaw set in changing the battlefield once again into a sea of mud, and mixed rain and snowstorms shrouded the movements of the infantry.' Reginald and his men could barely move. The mud in some places as they tried to advance was knee deep. The commanding officer of the battalion set to advance in front of them went forward after his men were supposed to have set off and found them in the midst of the sleet and rain, cowering in shell holes and trying to avoid the fire of their own artillery. Plans were quickly revised. The Middlesex men would come up, Reginald included, and, after a fresh artillery barrage, both battalions would go forward together towards Puiseux Trench.

Having come through Beaucourt, Reginald organised his troops and they found themselves involved sooner than planned. Before the revised time for attack, a number of Somerset bombers managed to get into Puiseux Trench south of the road to Miraumont. Reginald's company was sent up to help them seize it down to the Ancre and consolidate the position. Three of its officers were killed, throwing the company into disarray. Reginald Underhill was among them. The following day it transpired that, south of the river, the assault on Grandcourt had failed. It left the Middlesex men in Puiseux Trench in an untenable position. After all their suffering, they had to give up their hold on it and withdraw to conform with the rest of the line, demolishing the trench as they left. Reginald's body, if recovered, was never identified and he is commemorated on the Thiepval Memorial, Pier & Face 12d/13b.

EPILOGUE

Although Gough's men had got into Beaumont Hamel and Beaucourt on the north side of the Ancre, the German defence of Redan Ridge prevented any wholesale breakthrough in the final days of the battle. As the campaign on the Somme petered out in mid-November it was not surprising that the last scrappy, hurriedly planned and limited attacks in awful weather achieved next to nothing. Tanks could not be used in the conditions, movement was hampered and guns were becoming more and more ineffective. On 18th November Haig headed a conference where he laid down the policy now for the coming winter months. If his men were attacked, they would stand their ground, and they would try to maintain some semblance of pressure on the enemy to prevent him regrouping after a three-and-a-half-month ordeal. In the longer term, plans had already been started for a new offensive in the spring. The Battle of the Somme was over.

23RD NOVEMBER

Lieutenant George Neale Higginson

16TH LANCASHIRE FUSILIERS

JUST BECAUSE A LINE WAS officially drawn under the Battle of the Somme in November 1916, it did not mean that the gruesome loss and relentless cost in manpower was at an end. Troops continued to fight and die in pursuit of the upper hand on the battlefield and many of their endeavours, not attributable to a particular campaign, have been forgotten.

On 18th November, the final day of the battle, the 97th Infantry Brigade were charged with capturing portions of the German front and support lines on Redan Ridge. At 6:10am the British barrage commenced and the men advanced across no-man's-land in driving sleet, headed for enemy positions. Despite some of the soldiers reaching the German lines they were unable to hold it with any sort of numbers and by dusk all remaining soldiers had been pushed back by the enemy, or so it was thought.

Headstone of George Higginson and another member of the rescue party from the Lancashire Fusiliers, killed on 23rd November, at Waggon Road Cemetery. (Andrew Holmes)

As war was declared against Germany, George Higginson, a 28-year-old teacher from Tenbury in Worcestershire, applied for a commission. At the time there were more applicants than openings and many men impatiently enlisted in the interim. George did so as a private into the 19th Royal Fusiliers at Westminster in September 1914, offering two years' previous experience in the 2nd Warwick Volunteer Regiment. Until his commission came through in December 1914, George underwent training at a camp in Woodcote Park, Epsom.

In December 1914 George was commissioned into the 12th Battalion of the Lancashire Fusiliers as a second lieutenant. The battalion remained in Britain undergoing further training until eventually landing in France in September 1915. Less than two months later, George was injured by an explosion during grenade instruction at Bayonvillers on the Somme. During the instruction a grenade detonated accidentally, killing one soldier and wounding George and another officer. The injuries to George's right arm were so severe that he was evacuated home for treatment. A medical board hearing at the 1st Southern General Hospital, Birmingham, on 17th November 1915, noted that George's arm had healed sufficiently for active service but he was still suffering from deafness. After leaving the hospital, George was transferred into a different battalion of his regiment. From their arrival in France in November 1915, the 16th Lancashire Fusiliers spent most of their time in the Somme region, apart from a brief spell between August and November 1916.

Following their attack on 18th November, on Redan Ridge, unknown to the British, a party of 120 men from the 97th Brigade (a mixture of men from the 11th Borders, 16th Highland Light Infantry and 2nd King's Own Yorkshire Light Infantry) still held a portion of Frankfurt Trench and remained there in isolation, with the enemy completely unaware of their presence. Their presence did not go unnoticed for long, and on 20th November the Germans launched their first attack, which was beaten off by the beleaguered troops. The following day an NCO and one of the men from the trapped party broke back through the German lines and alerted the British to their predicament. An attempt later that night to bring back the marooned men failed as the rescuers were unable to breach the German front line. By this time, the isolated soldiers had run out of food and rations and so some of the stranded men volunteered and were sent back out over the enemy front line and into no-man's-land to take supplies from the dead lying strewn about them.

Lieutenant George Higginson (*fourth from left*) in training with the Royal Fusiliers at Epsom in 1914. (Private collection)

On 22nd November, a pilot from 15th Squadron flew over the trapped soldiers and signalled 'C.I. Tonight', which was quite possibly an instruction telling them to 'Come In Tonight'. His plane was seen by the stricken men who waved flags at him, but the pilot was unsure whether they had seen or read his signal. He also noted that the trench where the men were holding out was practically destroyed. Later that morning two other men from the trapped group managed to make it back to British lines and confirmed that the remaining soldiers would make an attempt to break out later that evening. Their attempt never materialised, despite men from their brigade being positioned 200 yards from the German lines to assist their dash for freedom. A second German attack was repulsed on the 23rd, although by now the situation for the stranded troops was becoming perilous. Over half of them were wounded and the lack of supplies was becoming desperate.

Whilst all this was happening, on 19th November George Higginson and the 16th Lancashire Fusiliers moved into the British lines opposite the German trenches where their imperiled colleagues were isolated. After the failure to break out from the German lines, it was decided that another rescue attempt should be mounted.

At 2:40am on 23rd November, orders were issued that 240 men from the 16th Lancashire Fusiliers and sixty men from the 2nd Royal Inniskilling Fusiliers would attempt to assist the soldiers trapped in Frankfurt Trench. The men were to form up in four waves. The Royal Insikilling Fusiliers would protect the right flank, whilst two waves of the Lancashire Fusiliers were to reach the Munich Trench and hold it, allowing a third, commanded by George, to push on through the Frankfurt Trench and rescue the stricken British soldiers.

Zero hour was 3:30pm. George Higginson and his Lancashire Fusiliers, along with the 2nd Royal Inniskilling Fusiliers, advanced under the cover of an intense artillery barrage. Initial progress was encouraging. Munich Trench, the German front line, was reached and occupied without too much opposition. Once inside, the attacking troops bunched up in places with the result that the trench was not occupied continuously. These gaps enabled the Germans to emerge from their dugouts to launch counter attacks against the British. Fierce fighting at close quarters took place. 'About 20 of the enemy, including one Officer were bayonetted.' Despite the ensuing maelstrom, George and some men from the second wave of the Lancashire Fusiliers that had gone out ahead of him managed to cross the Munich Trench and head towards Frankfurt in search of their trapped comrades.

Intense German machine-gun fire and the fact that a second wave of the 16th Lancashire Fusiliers appeared to get caught up in their own barrage ensured no further progress was made. Reports suggested that George and some of his men made it 150 yards beyond Munich Trench. Shortly afterwards George was seen to fall. German machine-gun fire drove the rest of the soldiers back. In the retirement, casualties were heavy. This brave attempt to rescue the isolated troops had failed and caused a further 231 casualties in the process. On 29th November, George Higginson's widowed mother received a telegram from the War Office informing her that he was missing, believed killed.

Immediately after the attack, the army received information that pointed to George Higginson being wounded and wrote to his mother passing on this information. The authorities then began making enquiries in an attempt to clarify what had happened. Statements were taken from seven soldiers who attacked alongside George and the contradictory nature of some of these statements revealed how difficult it was to accurately recall events that took place under extreme conditions. A Private Gordon said that he and Lieutenant Higginson were both near the German third line when George was hit. Sergeant Ablett said that the officer was shot some point between the first and second German lines. Private Kane had a slightly different recollection, saying that George was hit by a British shell. Private Thorne concurred with Ablett saying that Higginson had been hit by a bullet in the chest between the German first and second lines. Sergeant Ferber said that he had been informed by a stretcher-bearer that George was killed by shellfire shortly after going over the top. Private Conrad, who by this time was a prisoner of war, managed to confirm via the Red Cross that he had seen George badly hit in the attack. Finally, a Sergeant Holt said that Higginson was between the German first and second lines when he was shot by a machine gun. When Holt went to his assistance he found that George was already dead and so he dragged him into a shell hole and covered him with a waterproof sheet.

The majority of the army enquiries appeared to corroborate the information that they had received shortly after the attack: that George Higginson was shot and killed in the attack on 23rd November somewhere between Munich and Frankfurt Trenches. On 20th March 1917, the War Office wrote again to George's mother, sending their deep regrets, but informing her that they had received a report 'that Lieutenant G.N. Higginson 16th Lancashire Fusiliers, who was previously reported "Missing, believed killed", is now reported to have been killed in action on November 23rd, 1916.' George's body was recovered in March 1917 and he was laid to rest in Waggon Road Cemetery, C.3. The men stranded in the German trench were never rescued and managed to hold out for another couple of days. By the time that they came to surrender after another severe enemy attack, only fifteen unwounded soldiers were able to stagger out of Frankfurt Trench and hand themselves over to the Germans.

POSTSCRIPT

A century ago, the combined casualties of Britain and her dominions, France and Germany during the conflict on the Somme topped a million men killed, wounded, taken prisoner or missing, which ordinarily meant that the man in question was gone. Despite everything that Haig and his generals could fashion in an attempt to settle the war on the Western Front, the Germans doggedly held their ground. Setting aside the wounded, who sometimes faced a lifetime of pain and hardship owing to their part in the battle, we had to choose just 141 of them in an attempt to breathe life and colour back into sepia-toned portraits and black-and-white photographs in order to help people remember the loss suffered in all corners of the globe. We purposely avoided a book full of celebrities in honour of those hundreds of thousands of ordinary men and women who fought in or contributed to a battle that played its part in shaping the history of the twentieth century.

Even those who survived it all have left us now, but the name 'Somme' resonates still throughout Britain and her former territories, and rightly so. A watchword for a type of savagery that modern warfare means we will never see the likes of again, as the centenary approaches we hope that this collection of stories will remind the reader of the human face beyond the terror, the pain and the suffering inflicted by the Battle of the Somme and perhaps take a moment to remember all of those who fought in it.

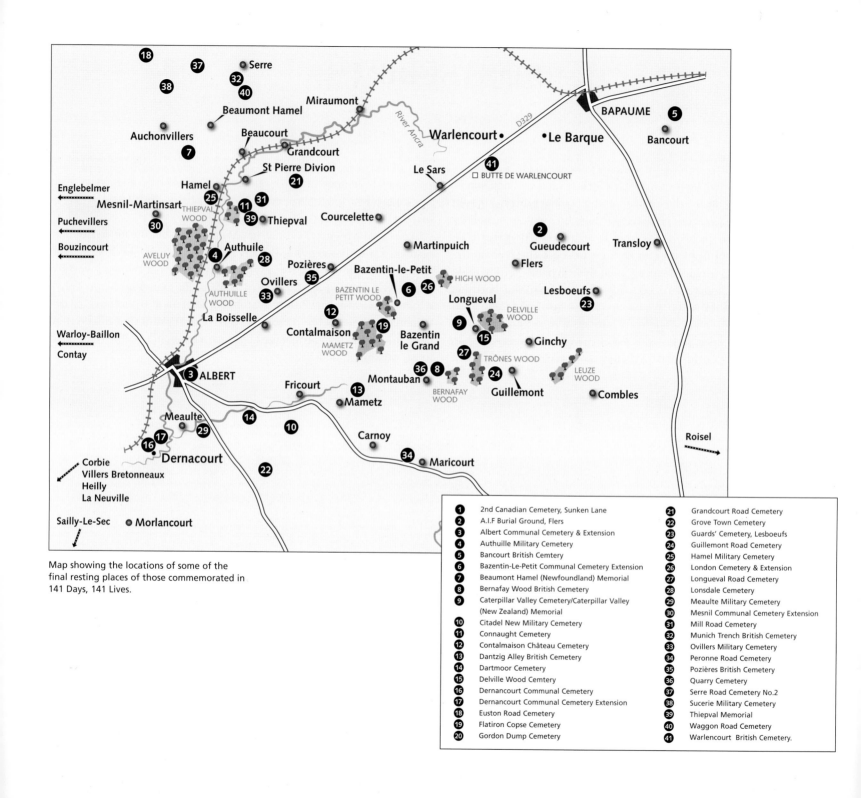

Map showing the locations of some of the
final resting places of those commemorated in
141 Days, 141 Lives.

①	2nd Canadian Cemetery, Sunken Lane	㉑	Grandcourt Road Cemetery
②	A.I.F Burial Ground, Flers	㉒	Grove Town Cemetery
③	Albert Communal Cemetery & Extension	㉓	Guards' Cemetery, Lesboeufs
④	Authuille Military Cemetery	㉔	Guillemont Road Cemetery
⑤	Bancourt British Cemtery	㉕	Hamel Military Cemetery
⑥	Bazentin-Le-Petit Communal Cemetery Extension	㉖	London Cemetery & Extension
⑦	Beaumont Hamel (Newfoundland) Memorial	㉗	Longueval Road Cemetery
⑧	Bernafay Wood British Cemetery	㉘	Lonsdale Cemetery
⑨	Caterpillar Valley Cemetery/Caterpillar Valley (New Zealand) Memorial	㉙	Meaulte Military Cemetery
		㉚	Mesnil Communal Cemetery Extension
⑩	Citadel New Military Cemetery	㉛	Mill Road Cemetery
⑪	Connaught Cemetery	㉜	Munich Trench British Cemetery
⑫	Contalmaison Château Cemetery	㉝	Ovillers Military Cemetery
⑬	Dantzig Alley British Cemetery	㉞	Peronne Road Cemetery
⑭	Dartmoor Cemetery	㉟	Pozières British Cemetery
⑮	Delville Wood Cemtery	㊱	Quarry Cemetery
⑯	Dernancourt Communal Cemetery	㊲	Serre Road Cemetery No.2
⑰	Dernancourt Communal Cemetery Extension	㊳	Sucerie Military Cemetery
⑱	Euston Road Cemetery	㊴	Thiepval Memorial
⑲	Flatiron Copse Cemetery	㊵	Waggon Road Cemetery
⑳	Gordon Dump Cemetery	㊶	Warlencourt British Cemetery.

BIBLIOGRAPHY

Personal archives relating to

Billy Disbrey

Oswald Webb

Henry and Tom Hardwidge

Ernst Hahn

Horace and Stanley Callaghan

Reginald Hobbs

Harold Smithers

William Morris

Edward Cazalet

The following series at The National Archives:

WO95

WO339, 363 and 374

ADM

AIR 1

Also:

French War Diaries

RAF Museum, Hendon

Newspapers and Periodicals

Aberdeen Journal

Birmingham Daily Post

Chelmsford Chronicle

Daily Mirror

Derby Daily Telegraph

Derry Journal

Dundee Courier

Essex Newsman

Gloucester Journal

Hull Daily Mail

The King's Royal Rifle Corps Chronicle (1916)

Liverpool Daily Post

Perthshire Advertiser

Sunderland Daily Echo & Shipping Gazette

Books

Anon, *The Fifth Battalion: The Cameronians (Scottish Rifles) 1914–1919*. Jackson, Son & Co, Glasgow, 1936.

Atkinson, C.T., *The Devonshire Regiment 1914–1918*. Simpkin, Marshall, Hamilton, Kent & Co. Ltd, London, 1926.

The Queen's Own Royal West Kent Regiment 1914–1919. Simpkin, Marshal, Hamilton, Kent & Co. Ltd, London, 1924.

The Seventh Division 1914–1918. John Murray, London, 1927.

Bax/Boraston, *The Eighth Division 1914–1918*, Medici Society, 1926.

Burrows, John William, *The Essex Regiment, 9th, 10th, 11th, 12th, 13th & 15th Battalions*. John H. Burrows & Sons Ltd, Southend-on-Sea, 1935.

Clayton, P.B., *Tales of Talbot House, Everyman's Club in Poperinghe & Ypres 1915–1918*. Chatto & Windus, London, 1919.

Coop, The Rev. J.O., *The Story of the 55th (West Lancashire) Division*. Liverpool Daily Post Printers, Liverpool, 1919.

Crookenden, Arthur, *The History of the Cheshire Regiment in the Great War*. W.H. Evans, Chester, 1939.

Cuttell, Barry, *148 Days on the Somme, 2nd July to 26th November 1916*. GMS Enterprises, Peterborough, 2000.

Ewing, John, *The History of the 9th (Scottish) Division 1914–1919*. John Murray, London, 1921.

Falls, Cyril, *The Gordon Highlanders in the First World War 1914–1919*. Aberdeen University Press, Aberdeen, 1958.

Gillon, Capt Stair, *The Story of the 29th Division, A Record of Gallant Deeds*. Thomas Nelson & Sons Ltd. London, 1925.

Gliddon, Gerald, *The Battle of the Somme: A Topographical History*. Sutton Publishing, Stroud, 1994.

Gould, L. McLeod, *From B.C. to Baisieux; being the narrative history of the 102nd Canadian Infantry*. Thos. R Cusack Presses, Victoria, B.C. 1919.

Grant, Capt D. P., *The 1/4th (Hallamshire) Battalion. York & Lancaster Regiment 1914–1919*. The Arden Press, London, 1926.

Grieve, Capt W. Grant and Bernard Newman, *Tunnellers: The Story of the Tunnelling Companies Royal Engineers During the World War* Herbert Jenkins, 1936.

Hart, Peter, *The Somme*. Cassell Military Paperbacks, London, 2005.

Somme Success: The Royal Flying Corps & the Battle of the Somme, 1916. Leo Cooper, Barnsley, 2001.

Kincaid-Smith, Lt Col M., *The 25th Division in France & Flanders*. Harrison & Sons, London, 1920.

Lyons, J.B., *The Enigma of Tom Kettle*, The Glendale Press, Dublin, 1983.

Maurice, Maj.-Gen. Sir F., *The 16th Foot: A History of the Bedfordshire & Hertfordshire Regiment*. Constable & Company, London, 1931.

Miles, Capt Wilfred, *Military Operations France and Belgium*, 1916 Vol. 2. Macmillan & Co., London, 1938.

Moody, Col R.S.H., *Historical Records of The Buffs East Kent Regiment 1914–1919*. The Medici Society, London, 1922.

Nichols, Capt G.H.F., *The 18th Division in the Great War*. William Blackwood & Sons, London, 1922.

Pagan, Bdr-Gen. A.W., *Infantry: An Account of the 1st Gloucestershire Regiment During the War 1914–1918*. Gale & Polden, Aldershot, 1951.

Petre, F. Loraine, *The History of the Norfolk Regiment Vol. II*. Jarrold & Sons Ltd. Norwich, 1924.

Renshaw, Michael, *Battleground Europe: Redan Ridge*. Pen & Sword, 2004.

Sandilands, Lt Col H.R., *The 23rd Division*. William Blackwood & Sons, London, 1925.

Swales, Roy, *Nelson at War 1914–1918*. Pen & Sword, Barnsley.

Various, *Canada in the Great World War: The Turn of the Tide*, Vol. IV, United Publishers of Canada Ltd.

Weston, Peter, *Redan Ridge: The Last Stand*. Self Published, 2012.

Wood, Maj. W. de B., *The History of the King's Shropshire Light Infantry in the Great War 1914–1918*. The Medici Society Ltd, 1925.

Wylly, Col H.C., *History of The Queen's Royal Regiment*, Vol. VII. Gale & Polden, Aldershot.

Wyrall, Everard, *The Die-Hards in the Great War, 1914–1916*, Vol. I. Harrison & Sons Ltd. London, 1926.

The Fiftieth Division 1914–1919, P. Lund, Humphries & Co., 1939.

The Gloucestershire Regiment in the War 1914–1918. Methuen & Co. Ltd, London, 1931.

The History of the Somerset Light Infantry 1914–1919. Methuen & Co. Ltd, London, 1927.

The Nineteenth Division 1914–1918. E. Arnold & Co., London, 1932.

INDEX

The History Press

The destination for history
www.thehistorypress.co.uk